ROY H. WAGNER

Roy H. Wagner

*A Cinematographer's Life
Beyond the Shadows*

Roy H. Wagner, ASC, *and*
Wayne Byrne

Foreword by M. David Mullen, ASC
Afterword by Todd Fisher

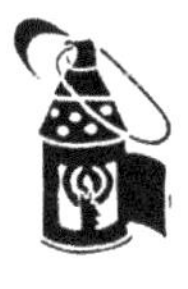

McFarland & Company, Inc., Publishers
Jefferson, North Carolina

Unless otherwise noted, photographs are from the collection of Roy H. Wagner

Library of Congress Cataloging-in-Publication Data

Names: Wagner, Roy H., author. | Byrne, Wayne, 1983– author. |
Mullen, M. David, writer of foreword. | Fisher, Todd, 1958– writer of afterword.
Title: Roy H. Wagner : a cinematographer's life beyond the shadows / Roy H. Wagner,
and Wayne Byrne ; foreword by M. David Mullen ; afterword by Todd Fisher.
Description: Jefferson, North Carolina : McFarland & Company, Inc., Publishers, 2025 |
Includes index.
Identifiers: LCCN 2025001479 | ISBN 9781476693798 (paperback : acid free paper) ∞
ISBN 9781476654843 (ebook)
Subjects: LCSH: Wagner, Roy H. | Cinematographers—United States—Biography.
Classification: LCC TR849.W34 A34 2025 | DDC 777.092 [B]—dc23/eng/20250307
LC record available at https://lccn.loc.gov/2025001479

ISBN (print) 978-1-4766-9379-8
ISBN (ebook) 978-1-4766-5484-3

Front cover image: Roy H. Wagner,
courtesy of photographer Tor Rolf Johansen.

———

Printed in the United States of America

*McFarland & Company, Inc., Publishers
Box 611, Jefferson, North Carolina 28640
www.mcfarlandpub.com*

To my wife Jill. You were the gateway to my success.
Without you, this book wouldn't exist. Thank you, I love you.

For Katherine, Michael, and Phillip Wagner.
And Scarlett.
And to all those who patiently believed in me.
—Roy H. Wagner

Table of Contents

Foreword
by M. David Mullen, ASC

My first exposure to Roy's work was in 1987, the year before I went to film school. That year I became an avid watcher of *Beauty and the Beast* on CBS. In particular, the pilot episode stood out for its visual quality, comparable to any high-end feature film. In the mid–1980s, this level of work was still uncommon in television cinematography; Roy was part of a handful of artists at that time who were elevating TV series work to something usually seen in a movie theater.

A few years after that, I started running into Roy at the ASC Open House and at industry trade shows—he never seemed to tire of my endless questions! Through discussion, we discovered a shared passion for classic Hollywood cinematography, the difference being that he got to know a number of these studio cinematographers that I had only read about. This only increased the number of questions I would pepper Roy with ... and still do today.

In 2003, I was honored when Roy decided to write a letter of recommendation for my membership in the ASC.

Even as a film student, I could spot certain traits in Roy's work that made him stand out. The word that always comes to my mind is "bold"—his use of contrast, shadow, and strong light sources gives his images dimensionality and drama, and his use of optical diffusion, when called for, evokes some of the glamour of classic cinema. I see techniques that Roy had picked up from his mentors and heroes but transformed into something personal, timeless, and wholly original. He is brave (braver than me!) and I hope everyone who reads this book will be inspired to be more fearless in their own work.

M. David Mullen, ASC, studied filmmaking and cinematography at the California Institute of the Arts (CalArts), where he received his master's degree. Since then, he has photographed almost forty independent feature films, plus several television series and pilots. He was nominated for the IFP Independent Spirit Award for Best Cinematography for Twin Falls Idaho *and again for* Northfork, *both films by Michael and Mark Polish. He won three Emmys and two ASC Awards for his work on the Amazon Prime series* The Marvelous Mrs. Maisel. *He also updated the classic textbook* Cinematography *with original author Kris Malkiewicz and was the co-editor of the 11th edition of the* American Cinematographer Manual.

Enchanted by the Light

An Introduction by Wayne Byrne

"It took years of my mother and father bringing me to the movies to convince me to turn around in my seat and watch what was being projected onto the big screen before me. I eventually did turn around, and it was in those smoke-filled theaters that my little mind tried to figure out the magic that created those giant illusions. At that moment I became enchanted by the light."
—Roy H. Wagner, ASC, FRPS

"Enchanted by the light" ... that is a beautiful phrase, and one that, when I heard Roy say it, I instantly knew what he meant, and I knew that our collaborative effort on this book would be engendered by our mutual love of screen art and storytelling. I was four years old when I first experienced the magical movement of light within the darkened auditorium of a movie theater. It was early 1988 and I ascended the red-tiled steps of the Dara Cinema in Naas, County Kildare. For those unfamiliar with the setting, this is small-town Ireland, still unaffected by the bland, anonymous multiplexes to come, and still charmed by the bluster of Hollywood blockbusters visiting our modest mono-screen movie houses. I settled into my seat flanked by my father and brother before I experienced the most thrilling sensory experience of my life. The lights went down and the heavy, elegant red curtains hanging closed were drawn back to reveal a blank silver screen until the booming electronic music sounded and a shimmering metallic logo appeared to herald the Cannon Films production that was about to unfold. Then, an image. *Masters of the Universe* began to unspool with a grand establishing shot of Eternia, scored by an initially ominous but then thunderously heroic theme by Bill Conti underneath a narration of immense gravitas detailing the epic battle of good and evil that I was about to witness; I was mesmerized, nay, hypnotized. What was this magical thing?

And just as I was transfixed by this audio-visual overload before me, I noticed a stream of light above my head, projecting forth from a small rectangular window at the back of the room. With that, my five-year-old brain discovered the artform that would consume my life. If I couldn't articulate it then, I felt it: "I love Cinema!" Since discovering this medium, I've always wanted to know about the people who decide what ends up on the screen, and how they determine what it is that we see. I started to take note of the names that appeared in the opening credits and what it is that they contributed to the picture, and one credit has always interested me: the Director of Photography.

They are the bridge between the art and the craft of film, and throughout my career as a film historian, they are the ones I am always thrilled to interview, because they offer insights on both the technical elements of filmmaking and the visual aesthetic of storytelling. My fascination runs so deep that I co-wrote a book with the great Nick McLean, whose work as a camera operator throughout the New Hollywood (*Close Encounters of the Third Kind, Sharky's Machine, The Deer Hunter*) and career as a cinematographer (*City Heat, The Goonies, Stick*, etc.) from the 1980s onwards was like a form of film school to me as a budding young film enthusiast. There was another name that I took note of very early on, because around the same time that my life was changed upon entry to the Dara Cinema I saw two things which boasted the same name under the "Director of Photography" credit. It was that of Roy H. Wagner, whose name appeared on *A Nightmare on Elm Street 3: Dream Warriors*, and the television series *Beauty and the Beast*.

I was never a Disney kid. While my schoolmates and neighborhood peers were enjoying *The Fox and the Hound* and the like, I was discovering horror movies. The other kids had Mickey Mouse; I had Freddy Krueger. My dad, Patrick, would record movies off the TV for me, and his selection amazes me now when I think about it, films that would be deemed "inappropriate" for a mind as young as mine was back then, but I also realize that it was essential to my discovery of and immersion in my passion; it was my film education. *Lethal Weapon, Halloween III: Season of the Witch, Die Hard, Death Wish II*—all regular viewings of my youth. But my dad would also encourage me to watch the films that comprised his own humble video library: *Fort Apache, The Quiet Man, My Darling Clementine*; and so, I was exposed very early on to the films of John Ford. Without sounding hyperbolic, these films and my parents' support of my interest saved me and gave my life direction. I hated sports, and I hated school. To this day, the memories of sitting in a classroom feel like a nightmare revisited. I love teaching, but boy, I hated being a student. So, when my friends were out kicking a round object around a field, or doing their homework, I was watching *First Blood* for the twentieth time.

I met Roy when I was conducting research for my book, *Welcome to Elm Street: Inside the Film and Television Nightmares*. Our meeting occurred in a professional context, but for me, it meant something much more. I was meeting a hero, someone who crafted images that are indelibly etched within the most cherished memories of my youth. Something about Roy's work on *A Nightmare on Elm Street 3: Dream Warriors* was different from the first two films, which were brilliantly shot by Jacques Haitkin, and whose style was appropriate for their respective directors: Wes Craven and Jack Sholder. Craven's film was surreal, contrasting searingly bright daytime exteriors and hazy suburban landscapes with dark industrial dreamscapes and dim back alleys of the subconscious. Sholder's film brought more color to the mise-en-scène, introducing garish reds and greens that would later become a visual signature of the Elm Street franchise. But when I first rented *A Nightmare on Elm Street 3: Dream Warriors*, I took note of the visual style. There was a tonal consistency which gave the film an unnerving quality; even outside in daylight, during the funeral scenes or around the exterior of the hospital, Roy's style is so rich. These days, an entire horror film would simply be bathed in a depressing blue tint to try to impart some idea of tone and atmosphere, regardless of the context of a scene; but Roy played with light like no other; watching his work in that film you feel the warm glow of mid-western Ohio (which is really the warm glow of sunny Los Angeles) juxtaposed with the cold clinical environs of Westin Hills psychiatric hospital, and the red fiery hell of Freddy's nightmare domain.

Indeed, it might not be too far of a stretch to say that it is because of his work on *Dream Warriors* that I ended up writing my Elm Street book, got to meet Roy, and have ended up here writing this very introduction. *Dream Warriors* was the film that inspired my passion for that franchise, the film I continually returned to throughout the decades and as I fell in and out of love with various other sequels in the series. Getting to know Roy since then, I have found a fellow film historian, someone who believes, like me, that the history of the art and industry of film needs to be preserved. Our canvas to do so is this book. Together, Roy and I will take you through his experiences across fifty years as a film professional and through various important times in the respective mediums of film and television. We will also detail what the craft of cinematography entails, drawing upon Roy's role as a mentee of some of Hollywood's master directors of photography and how he paid that knowledge forward to those he worked with throughout his career. What has always fascinated me about Roy is his willingness to adapt his style to each individual narrative, and even though there may be elements of him in every frame he films, he would perhaps balk at ever being considered an *auteur* as he has no interest in drawing attention to his own recurring techniques for the sake of signature. Roy is a child of both Old Hollywood and New Hollywood. He was mentored by the masters of Old and practiced his trade in the New, so his style, if one dares to set parameters of such, remains elusively subtle as his work ethic is that of the studio craftsman. He knows he is an artist, one of distinctly high caliber, but the humility and workmanlike fortitude of the old men dictate his spirit.

Roy himself will detail more eloquently than I can what was involved in making his work standout. Even within the confines of the 4.3 image of a 1980s 12" television, he made the earliest episodes of *Beauty and the Beast* feel like you were watching a theatrical film rather than a weekly episodic series. I didn't have the critical faculties or knowledge of craft back when these works first appeared, but when I revisit them these days, I can see the light. It is Roy's genius with illumination that makes these works so memorable, so deeply engrained in my brain that I now know why I was drawn to them, and to him.

To those of us for whom cinema is our first love, there is an indescribable feeling when we think back to those moments of sitting in the dark and gazing upwards at the dancing light emanating from a narrow window at the back of a movie theater. That light, visible to the naked eye but also elusive, untouchable … intangible. Nay, magical.

Sikeston, Stories,
and the Silver Screen

"I never read and saw words; I read and saw pictures."

Born to Gusta Irene and Roy Wagner II in the winter of 1947, Roy Henry Wagner III grew up in the Midwestern town of Sikeston, a modest settlement of 20,000 people in Southeast Missouri. It is a place that may seem inconsequential in a landscape comprised of many such communities, but it was in this rural countryside that he found and fostered a love of storytelling. It is here that he discovered the magic of the local theater which projected the fantastic spectacles crafted on Hollywood soundstages, the very ones on which he would eventually work and craft his own cinematic illusions. It was with awe and fascination that young Roy would gaze up at the light beaming from the booth at the back, casting images straight out of the Hollywood dream factories. For Roy, the intangible stream of light was just as intriguing as the melodramas that it projected before him. It wasn't anything new for the ineffable grandiosity of such a milieu to capture his attention and spark his imagination, as before he had the controlled environs of theater auditoria he had the natural ambience of Sikeston. Roy was brought up on the ploughlands and porches of his relatives, where he would bask in the golden hour twilight after a day's labor on the land, and just as day turned to night his mind's eye began to accumulate the stimuli provided by the terrific atmosphere of the evening shade.

"All my family smoked," he remembers, "and as the light in the sky would transition to darker and darker, all you could see was the light of the burning tobacco coming from their cigarettes which would illuminate their faces. It was so mystical. They would sit around telling their stories, and of course in those days ghost stories were prevalent. We don't seem to tell those kinds of tales anymore, not like we used to, but many ghost stories were told and I always remember being really interested in them. And there was something that happened more than one time that I've never forgotten about. It used to happen specifically at my uncle's farm, which was out in the middle of nowhere. There was this old thing that they called a rural route, which was really another highway, but it had two lanes made of asphalt. This particular route was a mile away from my uncle's house and how you reached his property was you turned off that rural route and on to a dirt road. They had a bend in that road and the last hundred yards would go towards the house. And it was always interesting because we would sit around talking in the twilight after working all day and my relatives would always say that they knew everybody who was driving a passing car; they would say, 'There goes such and such a person,' because they knew their cars—'Oh, that's so-and-so, he has a new car.' And occasionally, there would be somebody that they didn't know and then that would become a mystery and get them wondering. And of course, it wasn't as big a mystery to them as it was to me being this little boy, but it sounded very spooky. And then when the car would turn onto their dirt road, which would not happen very often, that would enhance that mystery and become more and more like a Hitchcock film. And if the sun was still in the sky, you would see the dust coming up from the road, so it was a very visual experience for me, and I can still remember it to this day. And then, of course as the car got closer, they would, at a certain point, discover who it was. I've always sort of attributed that to my work in cinema—not so much going to the movies as much as that sense of vastness and nothingness that surrounded me; when things like that would happen they took on this enhanced, heightened reality to them that would make them even more mysterious to this little boy."

When Roy first discovered films on the big screen, he found that this medium relates back to that early fascination: the marriage of imagery and symbolism with storytelling. With film, he found an artform that perfectly encapsulated all those creatively influential curiosities. "I've thought about this a lot," Roy ponders, "I never read and saw words; I read and saw pictures. And I'm not quite sure when that started or if it was just something that was inherently in me, but when I read things, I don't intellectually process them as thoughts and ideas, I process them as images. I'm very deeply into subtext, but it's been the case that if I have to intellectualize something I have to think back on it instead of at that moment in time understanding what it is, and I think that is because I seem to have a direct connection to what the words mean visually. If there's some sort of literary meaning in the words then I really have to think about it. I'm not sure if that

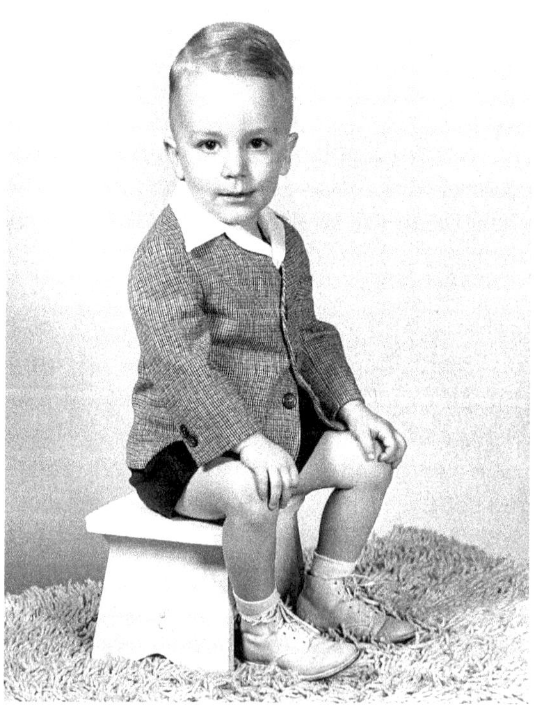

A well-groomed Roy H. Wagner, late 1940s/ early 1950s.

makes me less intelligent or more intelligent, or how unusual that is. I don't really know. I just know it's been my process."

It was only a matter of time before the illusions of American cinema began to captivate Roy's imagination and interest in the people behind the camera. "Going to the movies was a big deal when I was young; it's not like going to the movies today where it's such a common social activity. Back then you just didn't go to the movies all the time, and when you did you would often go by yourself. I would manifest myself as one of the heroes as I made my way home, daydreaming my way back to my house. The other thing that I didn't realize then, but I know now, is that I was not as inclined towards technologies as much as I was to the people. I was much more interested in the people, and I think that came from being taught as a young boy to respect my elders; I really wanted to know who these people were and why they were what they were, and why they were so important to what they did. So, I started studying biographies. I did that more than I could study technology because there were no books on technology at that time."

Artistic endeavors didn't play a big role in the lives of the Wagner family. Working hard, providing, and making sure one's future was financially secure was more important than anything as elusive and nebulous as filmmaking. Roy's mother, Gusta Irene, was a straightforward, down-to-earth person; a farm girl

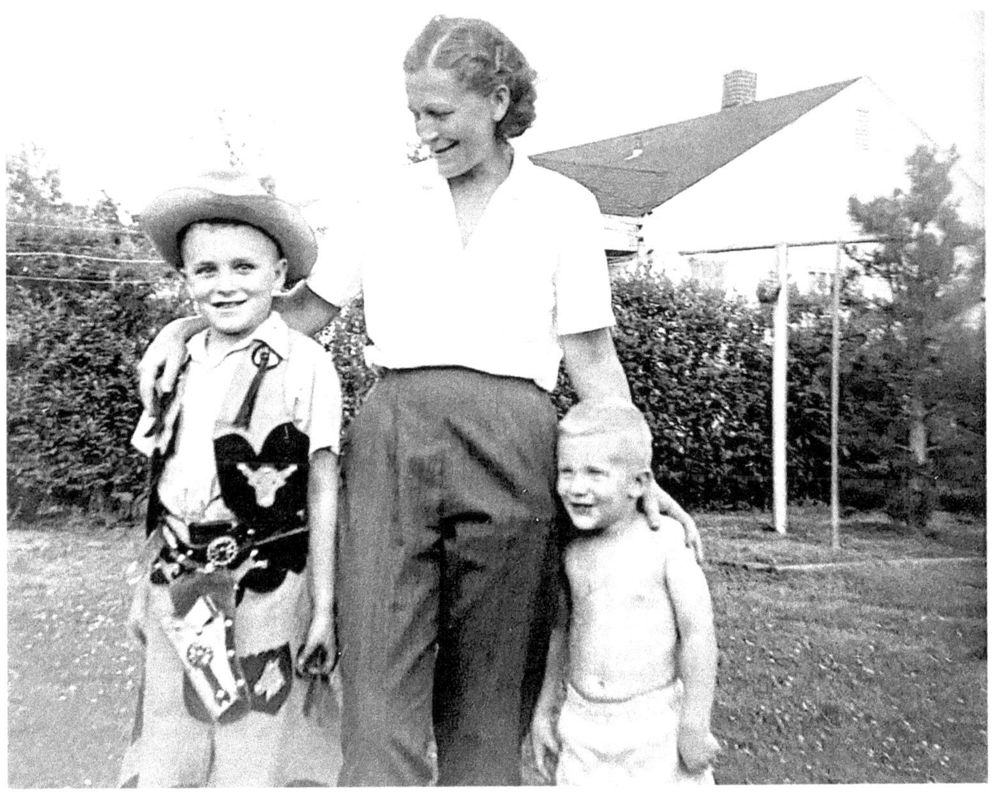

Roy and his little brother John with their mother, Gusta Irene Lough Wagner.

who harbored no ambitions what-soever other than to be a good mother and a good wife. His father was a hard-grafting territory manager for the BF Goodrich tire company. A practical man with a keen interest in sports, and something of a disregard for the artistic industries.

"I don't think either of my parents could figure me out at all," Roy says. "Both of them wanted me to be a journalist because I was a really good writer. All the way through high school and college I was a performer; I was an actor and a singer in the local theatre and summer stock, and then I did a lot of legitimate theatre and concert performances with my musical group called The Shiloh Singers. The group was comprised of three of us; we were like Peter, Paul and Mary, and we had an offer

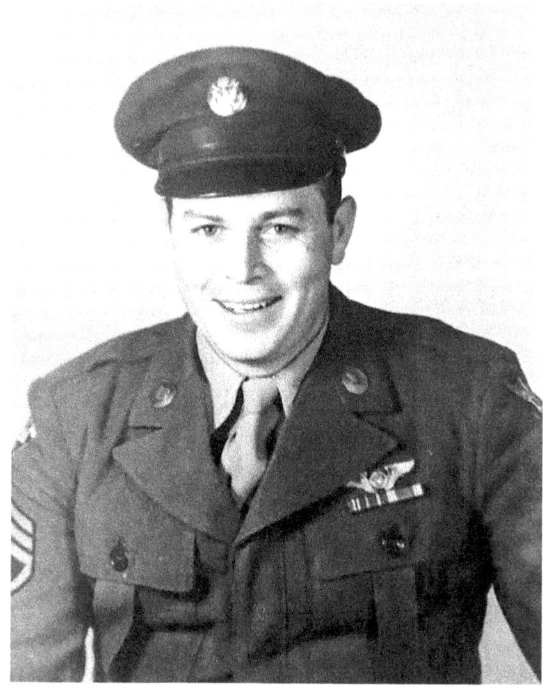

Roy Wagner II during World War II. He was stationed in Iceland during his service in the Army Air Corps.

of a contract from RCA Victor to record folk music after Floyd Cramer and Chet Atkins had gotten in touch with us. And I loved it, I loved being in front of people and performing, though I didn't love it as much as movies. But my dad was a jock, he was a very sports minded person and he thought that everybody in motion pictures and the entertainment business was a homosexual; he was afraid that would be my penchant, which it wasn't. I love artistic people and many of them are gay, so I've been around gay people all my life, but that wasn't my way, but it certainly was a fear of his. What he was right about was this being a very ephemeral business where you're never sure if you've made it or not, nor are you ever really sure if you're successful or not successful. So, I think from that point of view, he wanted to make sure that I had something that I could be grounded in. But I was just too much of a daydreamer, and too arrogant. And I also considered my parents to be beneath me, which was horrible to say. But I felt the people that I admired greatly were those who were making films. And even until the day my father died, I felt more connected with cinematographers than I did with my father, even though my father did nothing wrong, did nothing to try to hurt me at all."

Despite aiming for a career which is founded on the inherent chaos of the marriage of artistic temperament and corporate bureaucracy, in contrast to the orderly straight world of his father's profession, Roy took away some key life lessons from the way in which his father conducted himself within the comparatively staid world of tire sales. Roy recalls some words of advice that inform the

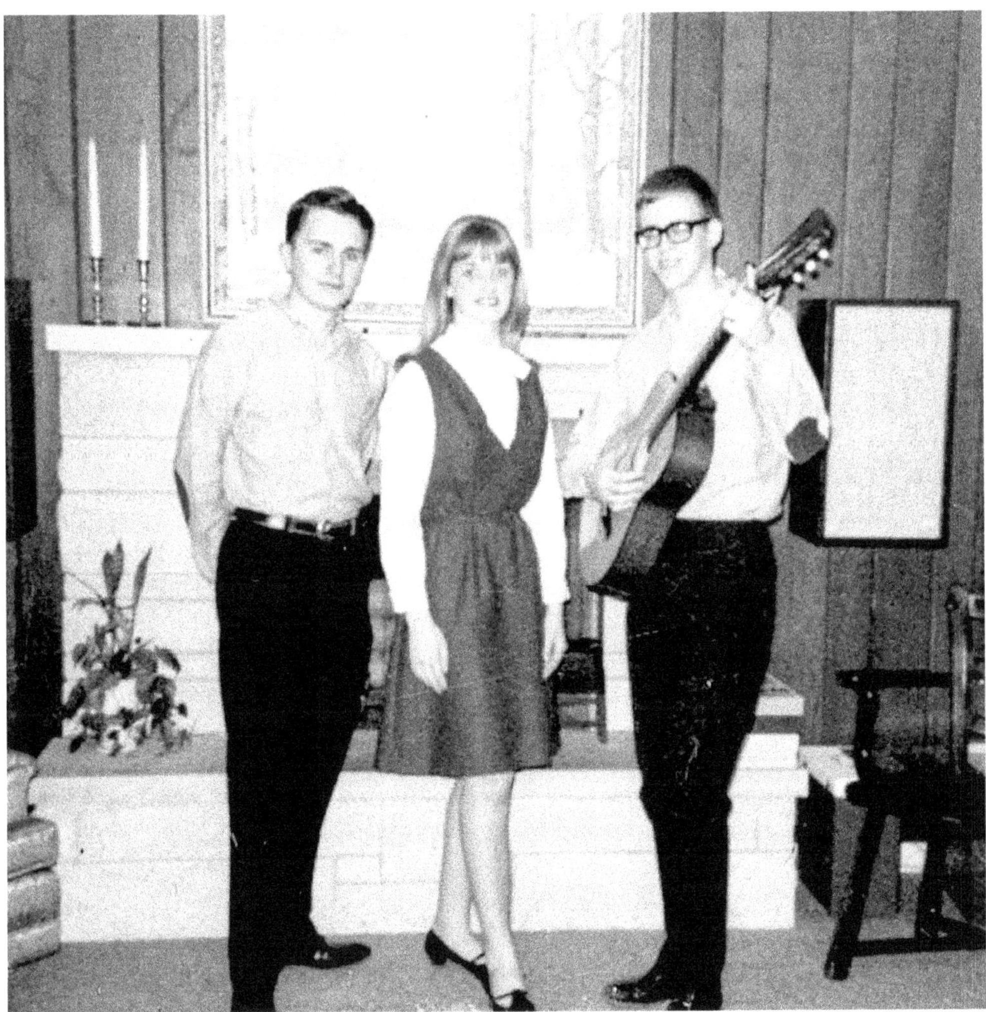

The Shiloh Singers, circa 1960s. From left: Roy, Jane Dixon, Paul Carpenter.

kind of man that his father was, words that he would apply throughout his career to his relationships with directors and other artistic collaborators:

"When my father was at BF Goodrich he didn't sell to customers, his clients were dealers, and he was very good at his job; he became their most successful salesman. In the summertime I was forced to accompany him around to all his dealers in the territory that he covered, and I hated doing that because it was so boring to me. I just wanted to be a daydreamer; I wanted to read; I wanted to go to the movies. And I remember thinking that if he sold for BF Goodrich then they must be selling them the best tires in the world; I told him this one day and he said, 'Oh, no, they're not.' I replied, 'I don't understand,' and he informed me, 'It's not about the product. It's about relationships. It's about who you are in relation to who you're selling to.' That became critically important to me. It was never about the movie being the best movie—it was about the people being the best people. I had a great connection to that idea, and you can see it with someone like

Peter O'Fallon. Peter never really made it. I mean, he's successful, but he should have been much more successful than he was; because of himself and his own demons, he didn't become the great director he should have been, and you could say the same about me. I ended up repeating certain patterns of my father's career in my own life and work. Because he was so good at his job, he would be moved from one territory to the next. So, I also had this life of moving, finding friends, developing relationships, and then four or five years later moving on to another place, which I've heard people say is pretty harmful. But what it forced me to do was to find my own way and to learn how to become friends with other people. And it didn't hurt me a bit; it was actually very good for me."

Despite his parents' best efforts to persuade him towards a more secure profession, Roy would follow his dream and enter the film business with the guidance of some of the finest filmmakers in the business, "the old men," as he refers to them. One of these eminent elders was Harry Stradling (whose lauded work includes *Easter Parade*, 1948; *A Streetcar Named Desire*, 1951; *Johnny Guitar*, 1954; *My Fair Lady*, 1964). He was one of several cinematographers that received a phone call from a young film fan who took note of the names of the cinematographers who impressed him enough to look them up in the phonebook and introduce himself. Regular correspondence over the years led to his eventually meeting these men, and Roy soon found himself in Hollywood and under the mentorship of the masters. However, Roy wasn't the only Wagner to head for Hollywood, as he was soon followed by his younger brother John, who would work with his older sibling as a grip or camera assistant on a variety of films and television shows such as *Dolemite, Houston Knights, Quantum Leap, Another Stakeout, Nick of Time*, and more. John's detour west was perhaps even more surprising to their father than Roy's, as John had displayed more traits of the Wagner patriarch and seemed destined to follow suit into a life of labor and athletics. But it wasn't to be:

"John and I grew up together and we were the closest of friends. He put up with all my wanting to be in the movie business. He was there for all of it, but bringing John into the movie business and working together did not make our relationship stronger. He was a completely different person than I am. If you look at pictures of us together you would never dream that he and I were brothers. He was a very big man, standing at 6'4", and he was a jock. John was very much my father's son, and I've tried to think about that, and I've wondered if that really bothered me. I don't think it did, but I knew early on that he was much more my father's son than I was. John was six years younger than me, and he just kind of followed my lead whatever I was doing. After my father passed away, John kind of got lost and became a biker and a tough guy; the thing is, he really was not a tough guy, but that was his MO because he was a big guy and had to protect himself. I found a lot of work for John, so he ended up on a lot of the same shows as I did in the camera department, but he didn't really have a life outside of me, and that is unfortunate because he was his own person. I think in many ways us working together hurt our relationship because I so wanted him to have the same focus I had. And he never did. I was hard on him. And I was hard on myself ... very hard. Which made me hard on other people."

For Roy, it wasn't an early nor immediate transition from the starry nights of rural Indiana to the heady lights of Hollywood. In 1967 he was drafted into the military but was let off on a hardship discharge when his father died suddenly at the age of fifty. Within two months of that tragedy, he suffered the loss of his hero and mentor Harry Stradling. With a mother and brother to look after, Roy's aspirations for a career in Hollywood seemed unlikely to manifest, but upon hearing that his father had previously compromised his ambitions to be a professional sportsman, Roy was resolutely not going to follow suit.

"Towards the end of my mother's life, she told me that my father had given up his dream. I learned that he wanted to be

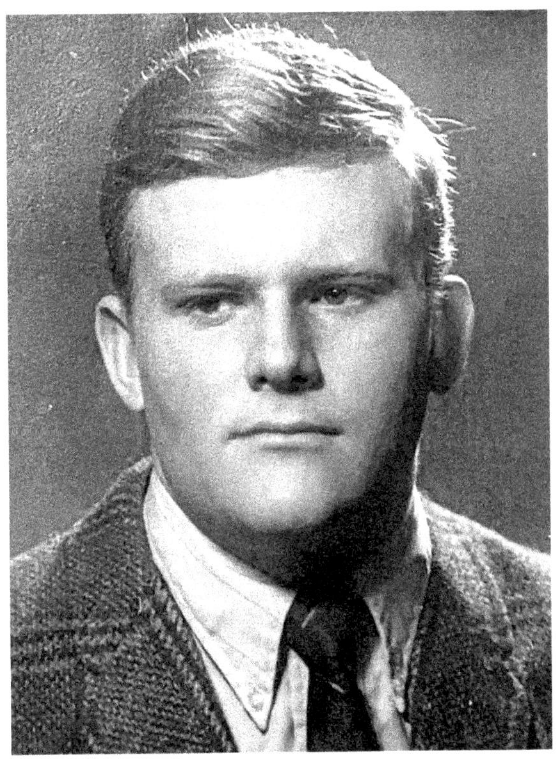

Portrait of young John Wagner.

a professional baseball player, but he was told by the doctor upon receiving the results of his blood tests when he and my mother were getting married that if he didn't stop playing baseball then he will die by the time he is fifty. He loved sports and he loved baseball. He was playing for the St. Louis Cardinals in the minor league. So, he took the doctor's advice and gave up playing baseball, but despite doing what he was told, he still died when he was fifty years old. So why did he have to give up his dream? There had to be something in him to press me to never give up on my dream and yet I never heard him say that. He really didn't want me to be in the motion picture industry. But there was something about the fact that my father gave up on his dream that forced me to never give up. And even now at the age of 76 I'm still not giving up. I didn't come from Hollywood, and I didn't have family in the business, so the fact that that I was a complete outsider made it a great deal harder for me, and it made me fight harder."

With Harry Stradling gone, so too were Roy's connections in Hollywood. He now had to start again, pounding pavement, and knocking on doors to re-establish himself in an industry so often closed off to those not from there or born into it, as he recalls:

"No matter what businesses you get into you don't just jump into doing what you want to do; you have to do a bunch of other things to get there, and that's what happened to me. When I got out of the Air Force, all those opportunities that I thought were going to happen didn't happen because Harry Stradling died.

All my connections were through Harry. And so there I was, out in the middle of nowhere, a small-town hick kid in the middle of Hollywood, and I just suddenly fell into the midst of chaos with two of the closest and most important people in my life—my father, and my mentor—both gone within two months of each other. I was on the streets of Hollywood without any kind of protective mat underneath me and starting over. I worked as a projectionist in virtually every theater in Los Angeles. I had some friends that helped me get into their theaters, but I was not in the union, I was a permit worker, so I was allowed to work for a certain amount of time without getting into the union. That was incredibly helpful, because it was a night job, which meant I could continue to look for movie work during the daytime. But in the late 1960s and early '70s, Hollywood was literally a closed shop, there was no work if you weren't in the union, so I took my resume, parked the car, and walked from one end of Sunset to the other knocking on the doors of all the independent production companies. I would do the same thing on every street in Hollywood that had a production company. I was not successful, but sometimes you must do things that generate energy in order to make things happen, and although my efforts did not result in getting me a job doing what I wanted to do, it did get me introduced to people who were crucial in my journey."

Among those important early connections was Franklin Levy who was working at MGM Studios. Levy ran a production company along with the multiple Tony Award–winning theatrical producer Robert Fryer. Driving his beat-up Nova

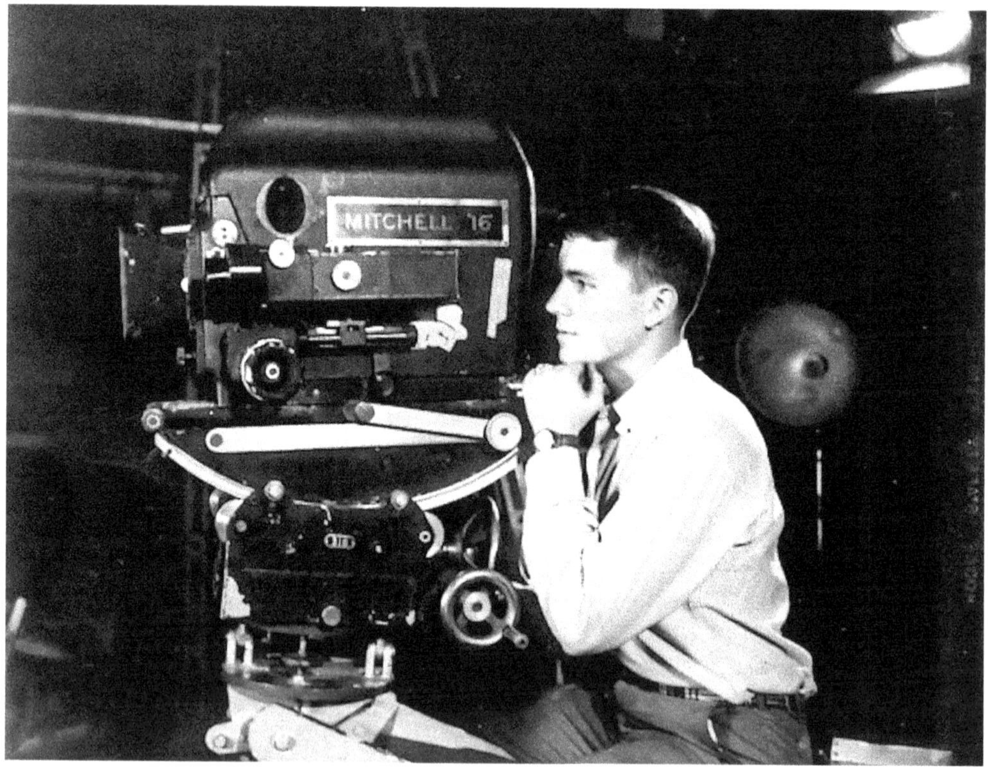

In love with the motion picture camera, 1965.

to the MGM lot daily, Roy was enjoying the opportunity to be part of that Old Hollywood world, and it was here he would mingle among Levy's production outfit which included powerful people like literary agent and movie producer Mike Wise, as well as famed playwright and screenwriter Tennessee Williams.

"A lot of writers and production people began to say, 'We're doing these little things, why don't you help us with that,' and I did. One the things I worked on with them was this tiny three-reel movie called *Hype* that Bobby Fryer financed. And it was probably the best thing I've ever done, frankly. The director, Trace Johnston, was extraordinary, but the only other project that we did together was a film that he wrote called *The Family Three* which starred the Hudson Brothers. It was a series of shorts that was supposed to be like the Three Stooges, with a lot of physical comedy, a spoof of movies like *The Exorcist* and *The Great White Hope* and things like that. The Hudson Brothers really wanted to send up the styles of those movies, but we didn't do it like a bright comedy, they were all dark and brooding. Our version of *The Exorcist* was darker than *The Exorcist*. It was funny but didn't go anywhere for the Hudson Brothers, although it did lead to somewhere for me, because I met more and more people. Trace didn't have the patience or the endurance to survive all the bullshit of Hollywood, so he just gave up on Hollywood afterwards. But he was a USC film student and through that I met Richard Franklin, who became a huge influence on my life with *Beauty and the Beast*. At that time, I was mentoring a young man who was studying film at UCLA named Chad Hoffman and I brought him onto that set to give him his first experience on a movie. He was Dustin Hoffman's nephew and years later he became the head of programming for ABC, but at that time I got him started in the business. And another person that I got started was Andy Cohen, who was an assistant film editor. And through helping him, he helped me get on to other shows; I worked with his brother up in San Francisco shooting industrials, which were not artistically rewarding, but they were financially rewarding. I was meeting people throughout that whole period, but I couldn't see that at the time, I could only see that I was not doing big movies. I had been around Harry Stradling and around all these big people, so I thought I was just going to jump right into that, and it didn't happen at all. I couldn't get into the union. It took me thirteen years to get into the union, which is totally absurd, and that gave me a love-hate relationship with unions that I have to this day. I think that if my mentors had not died, I would have had a better way in, but it didn't happen that way. It was a struggle. I ended up doing a lot of industrials and shorts. The one thing I didn't ever do was porno. A lot of guys did pornos because that was a way to get into the industry. If I had been given an option to do it, I probably would have done it, but I was never given that choice. I did get a lot of work on the Blaxploitation films; I worked on the likes of *Dolemite* and *Blacula* as an assistant cameraman, as well as a bunch of other ones. Working on those films affirmed to me Harry's whole philosophy of moving fast, being efficient, and saving money; if you do that, you will work forever. Another thing about those shows was that we would have union guys coming in and working on them while they were not working on union productions, so I was making connections in these kinds of places that I probably wouldn't have been able to make in any other way. And you were also meeting other people that were like you who were similarly struggling. My first wife and I struggled incredibly through that period. There was a lot of emotion. I often thought, 'I'm not going to make it. I don't know how I can survive.' It was tough. But I have always jokingly said that rather than crawling up the ladder of success, I've been crawling backwards to success. I thought that the only way was up, but often up was down. Something would divert you somewhere you weren't expecting to go, something you did not expect to happen, but where it took you was a much better place than where you thought you were going to go."

Ninjas and Nightmares

"The key to being successful in this business is listening to people."

Roy's first screen credit as cinematographer wouldn't appear until 1985 with the releases of the martial arts pictures *Pray for Death* and *Nine Deaths of the Ninja*. But prior to those he provided uncredited photography on a curious low-budget production commonly known today as *Meatcleaver Massacre* though originally released theatrically (mainly drive-ins) in 1977 as *Hollywood Meatcleaver Massacre*, a title conceived to cash in on the infamy of Tobe Hooper's controversial, and popular, *The Texas Chainsaw Massacre*. The film's authorship has long been ill-defined, having had multiple directors work on it through various complicated production stages including erstwhile NBC editor Keith Burns; the king of low-budget cult movies, Ed Wood; and, on the final product, an elusive Evan Lee. The latter name was in fact a DGA pseudonymous credit placed on the film due to none of the actual directors having shot enough material to warrant an official directorial recognition by the Guild. The film was shot sporadically when funding would dictate over the course of three years, beginning production in 1974 and eventually released three years later. Several cuts exist, most notorious of which is the widely circulated and perhaps ultimate version that includes the appearance of horror icon Christopher Lee. However, the reason for his appearance is not due to standard modes of casting—rather, his footage, which is inexplicably out of context from the rest of the narrative, was purchased from another failed production in which he appeared; this was then edited into the film which was then re-released under its accepted title of *Meatcleaver Massacre*.

The film is a revenge slasher with occult themes, in which Cultural Mythology Professor Cantrell (James Habif) wreaks vengeance upon the scumbag college students who murdered his wife and children; he does so by invoking the 3rd-century BCE Gaelic demon Morak to haunt, taunt, and ultimately destroy them in a most gruesome manner. The price of summoning Morak for such sweet revenge is that Professor Cantrell's soul will become the property of the demon "until the fires of time are quenched."

While directors changed as production stopped and started as funding came and went, Roy was there from the beginning, tenaciously shooting with his 35mm Mitchell and a dream of union membership. His involvement with the film was thanks to his acquaintance with the film's co-writer (and occasional director when others were absent) Ray Atherton. Roy recalls: "I was a film collector and that was my link to these people. Roddy McDowall was a film collector, and Rock Hudson was a film collector, so I was beginning to meet people in that league. Another fellow that I met through this world was Ray Atherton. He was this guy from Chicago who wanted to make a movie. So, he came up with this idea which became *Meatcleaver Massacre* and that's how I ended up working on that. We shot it in four days."

A persistent myth surrounds Ed Wood's involvement in the film, as due to the nebulous nature of the film's on-again/off-again production, some of the cast and crew were not always there when certain directors would stand in or take over. But one man can vouch for Wood's presence on set and behind the camera: "Ed was there!" Roy states. "It was originally directed by Keith Burns, but after about a quarter of the first day he quit and then Ed Wood took over. He had been on the set because he was someone's friend and was there with a still camera doing some stuff, but he ended up principally directing the movie. Ed was very ebullient. He believed he was making a great movie and he convinced all of us that we were making a great movie, but really it was just a piece of junk. It was the last film that he made."

Not that Ed Wood would have been instantly recognizable anyway. In 1977, Wood was not a well-known figure outside of cult film circles. Pictures such as *Glen or Glenda* (1953), *Bride of the Monster* (1955), and *Plan 9 from Outer Space* (1956) were long the reserve of underground cinema patrons and B-movie enthusiasts. That is, until Tim Burton's affectionate biographical masterpiece *Ed Wood* was released in 1994, thus bringing his bizarrely entertaining works and disreputable career to mainstream consciousness. Even Roy had not been aware of Wood's status as the King of the Bs until his A-list colleague reminded him....

"It was Johnny Depp who came to me and brought it up," Roy affirms, "he said, 'Do you know who you worked with on that film?' I said, 'Yeah, this guy named Ed Wood.' And he went, 'Do you realize who Ed Wood was?!' All I knew of Ed was that he was a sweet guy who really loved movies—that is the key thing that I remember about him. You could mention any movie and he knew everything about it. I don't know if it was that he didn't have talent or just that he didn't have opportunity, but I think it was probably both. As a director, Ed didn't tell me to do anything; he was just there, almost like a cheerleader. He kind of allowed you to do whatever you wanted to do. He genuinely believed that he really was making great art out of these B movies. That legend is true, but it was also scary because it meant that you too could be thinking you're pretty special but maybe you're not much better than Ed Wood."

Ultimately, Roy's name remains off the final film, something he is rather happy about. "Initially, I was devastated. I thought, 'Oh my gosh, this was to be my first feature film cinematography credit, but my name isn't on it!' But then I saw it and it looked like shit. I wouldn't talk about that film for years; I was too embarrassed. I never mentioned it for a long time, until finally Ed Wood became this big deal. The whole thing is a mess; the producer didn't have the money to finish it and later he had another director shoot some pickups that I didn't

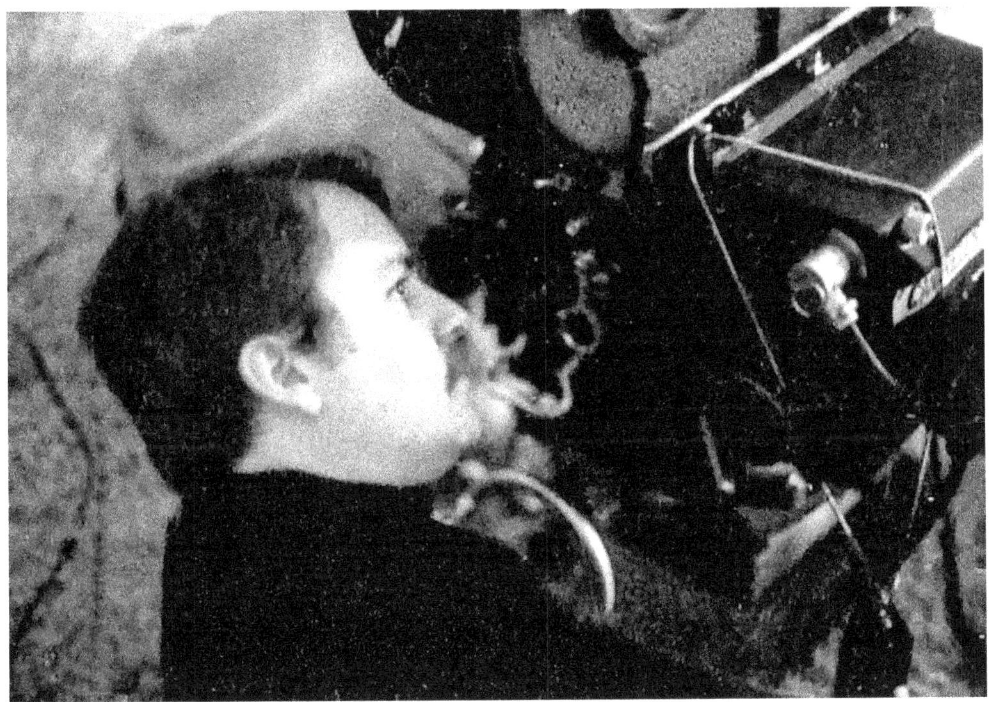

Roy shooting *Hollywood Meatcleaver Massacre,* aka *Meatcleaver Massacre,* with his Mitchell BNC in the mid–'70s.

photograph; they ended up including a lengthy introduction with Christopher Lee and he didn't even know he was doing it for this. He was pretty upset about it because it is a horrible film. But the reason I didn't get credit is because I didn't get paid. It wasn't that Ray Atherton didn't want to pay me; it was the distributor who didn't want to pay me. And they didn't even pay for the release of the camera negative. It was the workprint what was printed for the release, and it looked like shit. Not that I did such a great job on it anyway, because I didn't know much of anything and frankly, we didn't have any time to discuss anything. It was just survival and trying to get all this work done in four days. It was guerrilla filmmaking. I was operating as well as being the cameraman. We had four lights, a Mitchell BNC with a zoom lens, and an Arriflex IIB. We stole those shots in the trippy surrealist mausoleum scene. We went into the Hollywood Forever Cemetery, which is right behind Paramount, and we shot it handheld and with no lights using a wide-angle lens. A 9.8-millimeter lens. My camera assistant was Jim Bagdonas. He was a friend of Ray Atherton's, and I gave him his first job on this film. Since then, Jim has become a very successful director of photography. He went on to do TV shows like *Hunter, Chicago Hope, Boston Legal,* and *Modern Family,* but I got him started on *Meatcleaver Massacre.*"

Roy's first true opportunity as a cinematographer occurred in the early eighties when he ventured into a series of ninja films starring Japanese martial artist Sho Kosugi, including *Enter the Ninja* (1981), *Pray for Death,* and *Nine Deaths of the Ninja* (both 1985). *Enter the Ninja* was particularly influential in ushering in something of a new wave of low-budget martial arts films which were primarily produced by schlock studio Cannon Films throughout the 1980s. Cannon was run by an Israeli duo, Menahem Golan and Yoram Globus, who very much functioned as the brash alternative Hollywood moguls throughout this decade. They operated on the principle of "make it fast and cheap" and by tapping into the genre film market for which there was an obvious appetite. They made lucrative deals with stars whose names still had some marquee value (Charles Bronson, Chuck Norris) and used them prolifically. Occasionally they would use the income from their easily marketed genre films to fund prestige (nay, vanity) projects for esteemed filmmakers of international acclaim such as Franco Zeffirelli, Jean-Luc Godard, John Cassavetes, Andrei Konchalovsky, John Frankenheimer, and Norman Mailer. Perhaps their most flawed business move was attempting to give Hollywood a run for its money with large-scale productions that ultimately sank the studio (*Masters of the Universe* and *Superman 4: The Quest for Peace*, both 1987). But the studio's bread and butter were the low-budget martial arts films that amassed a cult following regardless of perceived quality, and Roy was right there to see how they operated, though not for long...

"I left *Enter the Ninja* after working one day with Menahem Golan when he took over as the director. I hated everything about him. I started on the film because an old friend of mine, Emmett Alston, was the original director. Emmett and I were in the Air Force together; he was my captain. He started out as a cinematographer and had gone to film school with George Lucas. Emmett had photographed George's original THX short film, *1:42.8*. He loved the Philippines, and he kept trying to make a movie that he could film over there and he finally convinced Cannon Films to finance it. And before I knew it, I was going to the Philippines to do *Enter the Ninja*. But I didn't do much on it because Emmett got fired, and when he got fired I quit. Menahem Golan came on as the director, and when that happened the movie changed a lot because as soon as he arrived he threw money at it. When we started the film we had no money because the guy who was originally cast as the lead, Mike Stone, was unknown. But that all changed when Menahem took over—for one thing, they replaced Mike with Franco Nero. Emmett stayed on to do the second unit, but I left. I couldn't stand it; Menahem was just not a good guy at all; he was just really crass and cruel."

The cinematographer ultimately credited on *Enter the Ninja* is David Gurfinkel, a fellow Israeli and go-to DP for Cannon Films, especially when the studio's mogul Menahem Golan was on directing duties and needed an ally usually after annoying his original choice. A later example of this occurred when Golan hired the acclaimed cinematographer Nick McLean (*Staying Alive*, *City Heat*, *The Goonies*) for the absurd 1986 Sylvester Stallone arm wrestling melodrama *Over the Top*, but the Cannon style of filmmaking caused McLean some concern over their penny-pinching practices and cavalier attitude to professional filmmaking processes, and so he duly walked halfway through production, much to the chagrin of Stallone, and leaving Golan to call Gurfinkel to replace him.

"David was a very rude guy," Roy states, "he might have been very nice to some people, but they stayed within their own group. I should have persevered and shot the second unit for Emmett, but I didn't. I was unaccustomed to working with someone like David who was just unkind. So, I left. But Sho Kosugi liked what I did on *Enter the Ninja*, and he brought me to do his next movie, *Nine Deaths of the Ninja*, with Emmett directing again in the Philippines. Emmett desperately wanted to go back to the Philippines and make another movie. But I had no interest in those films whatsoever. I hated the ninja genre. I loved the Hong Kong chop socky movies; they are fantastic. But they were more legitimate, more real, whereas the ninja films are not. So, slowly but surely, I wasn't going where I wanted to go, I was going where I was yanked to go. I couldn't really say no, so I was the cinematographer on several of those films. *Nine Deaths of the Ninja* was hilarious. I mean, we

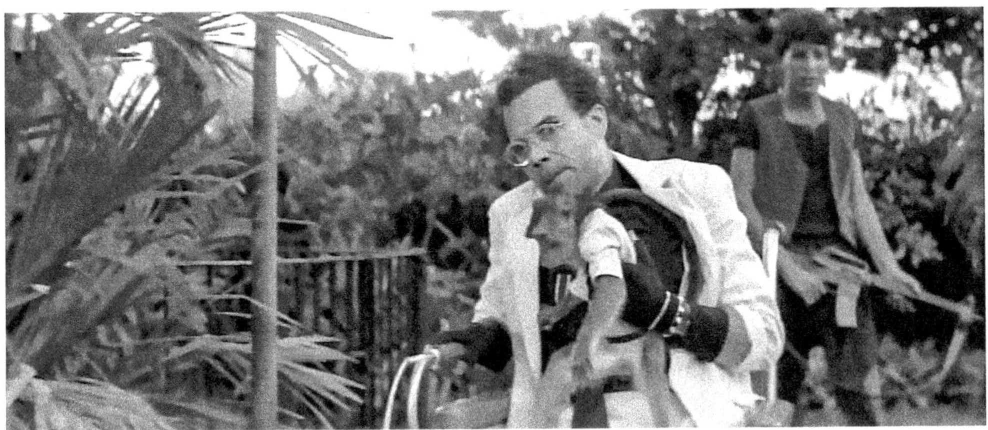

Blackie Dammett as terrorist Alby the Cruel in *Nine Deaths of the Ninja*, 1985.

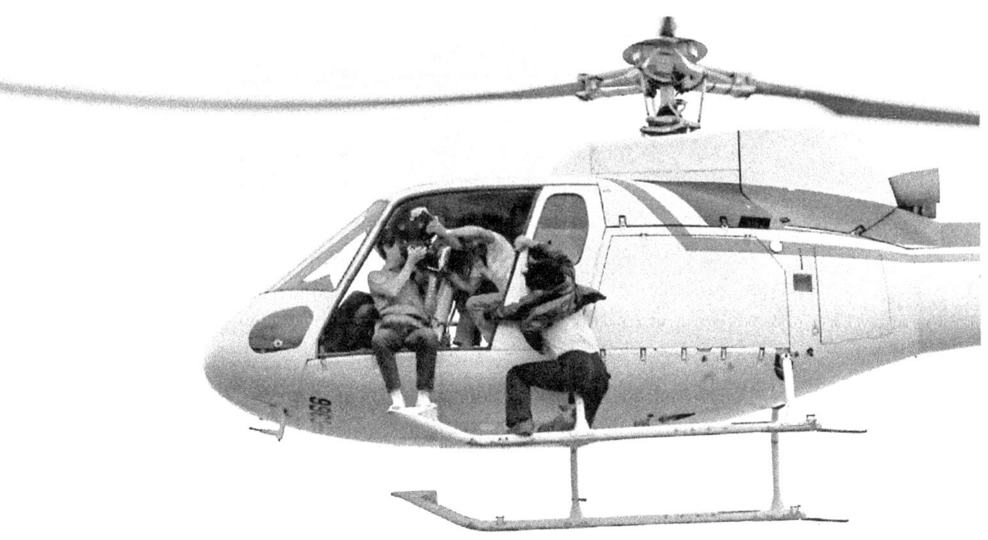

(From left) Roy, camera operator Eddie Buenaflor, and Sho Kosugi hanging around the helicopter filming *Nine Deaths of the Ninja*.

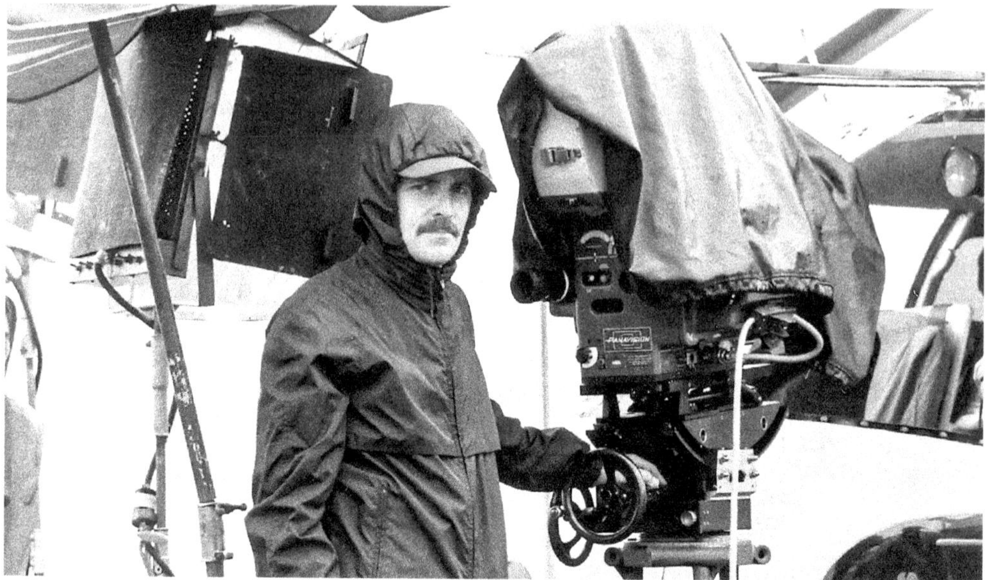

Roy alongside his Panavision PSR #150, preparing to battle the imminent elements as a typhoon approaches. Manila Bay, Thursday, June 21, 1984.

had Blackie Dammett and Regina Richardson in there, and they were all crazier than hell. Blackie was something of a character in real life, as was Regina."

The best of the three ninja films that Roy shot is easily *Pray for Death*. Produced by independent production company Trans World Entertainment, the film represents an increase in production values over the previous films, and the aesthetic polish is largely thanks to Roy's slick cinematography and director Gordon Hessler's assured hand on the action sequences. Essentially a showcase for Sho Kosugi, the film is a revenge thriller about a retired ninja named Akira Saito who moves from Japan to Los Angeles to leave behind his ninja life and raise his two sons along with his beloved wife. The family plan to open a Japanese restaurant but they become unwittingly embroiled in a scheme involving corrupt cops, the mob, and stolen jewelry.

"*Pray for Death* was the most elaborate of the ninja films I've done. We shot it in Texas and it was a much bigger film than the rest of them: bigger budget, bigger production. We shot anamorphic in Houston, Texas. Fortunately, the director Gordon Hessler had been a partner to Alfred Hitchcock on the *Alfred Hitchcock Presents* television show, so he was a very accomplished filmmaker. Gordon knew exactly what he wanted but when it came to photographic composition, he didn't care, he would just look at the frame and say, 'Yeah, let's go ahead,' or he would say 'No' if he didn't like it. I am very proud of what I did on *Pray for Death*; there are things in there like that scene with Parley Baer when he takes Sho and his wife to that old, abandoned part of the house. If I remember correctly, it's one shot and then we came in for close-up and it was really dark and brown and grungy. I really like that."

However, things weren't entirely copacetic on the set, as Roy was almost

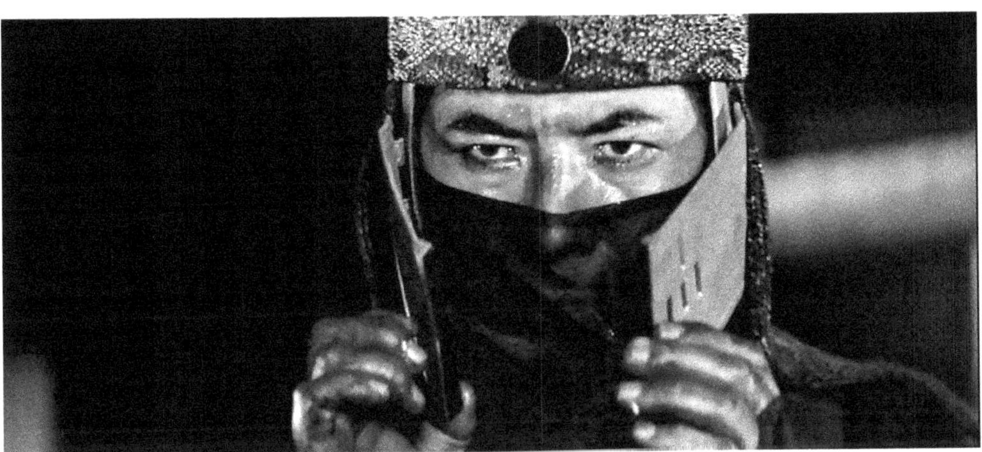

Japanese businessman and former ninja Akira Saito (played by Sho Kosugi) is forced to return to his old fighting ways as he battles an L.A. crime boss who threatens his family and his restaurant in *Pray for Death*, 1985.

fired, and he suffered due to a sometimes-strained relationship with the film's leading man. "I did three or four movies with Sho, and I found him very cordial but also very inscrutable. If you did your work and if you did everything the way he wanted you to do it, everything was fine. If you refused to do anything, then everything was not fine. I didn't like the way he operated, and it was mostly due to stunt safety. There was a Hong Kong style of safety on a set, which was just balls out, everybody trying to survive for themself. Then there was a Philippines version of that safety, which was, 'Whatever you asked me to do, I'll try to do it.' We worked with Jackie Chan on the movie in the Philippines, and it wasn't his movie, he was doing it as a stunt person where he did a stunt fall off a waterfall for $50. I'm sure he calculated it all, but it was a different kind of approach to stunt work in the United States with professional stunt people."

Roy continues, "What I did not respect about Sho was how flagrant he could be about stunt safety; he had a son who had a blood disease and if he got hurt in a fall or anything it could kill him. Sho just had no sense of that whatsoever. One night we went into a location which the crew did not like because they had serious safety concerns; in that situation I'm behind the camera, so I'm not really in any great jeopardy unless I'm filming a stunt where the car is coming towards me or something like that. But because the crew felt they were in jeopardy, I stood up for them. I was afraid for the crew, and Sho did not like that. When it came to safety, I just couldn't have it on my conscience if I felt the crew was going to get hurt. So, I would just say no, and that was not the thing to do, ever. But I still refused to work because the crew was in an unsafe predicament. And that night they attempted to fire me, but they couldn't find anybody to replace me, so I continued and finished that film, but I came very close to being fired. Sho could be such a bully; he tried to bully everybody around. We had a really good producer on that too, but he was also afraid of Sho. Ultimately, I didn't like him, so *Pray for Death* was the last film I did with him."

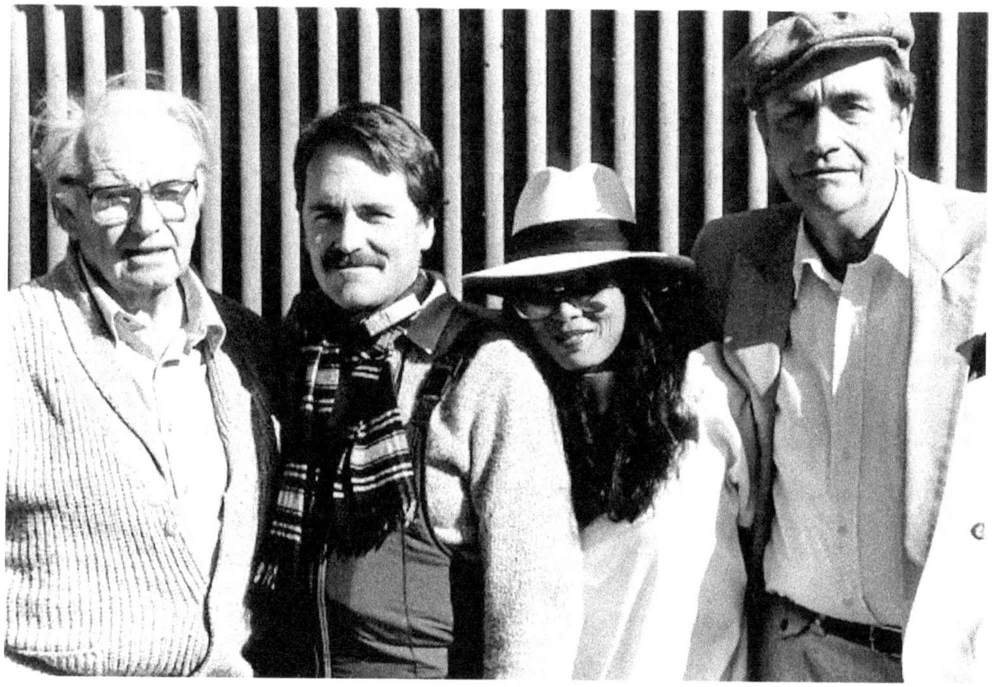

Behind the scenes on *Pray for Death*. From left: Parley Baer, Roy H. Wagner, Donna Kei Benz, James Booth. Houston, Texas, 1984.

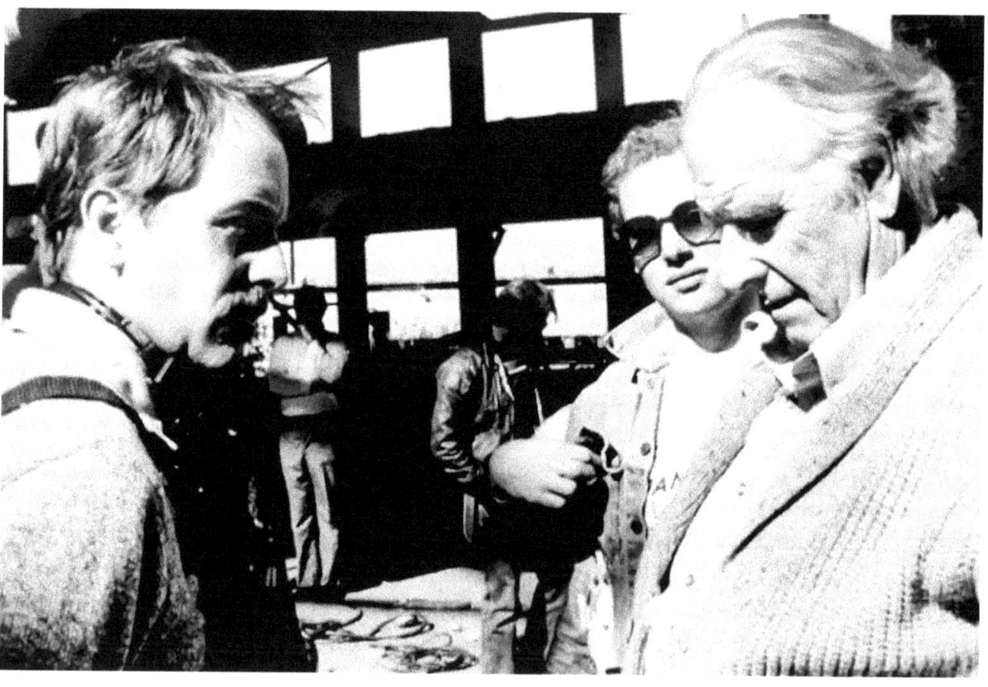

Roy (left) preparing for the car explosion stunt on location in Houston, Texas, on *Pray for Death* with assistant camera Randy Shanofsky (center) and actor Parley Baer.

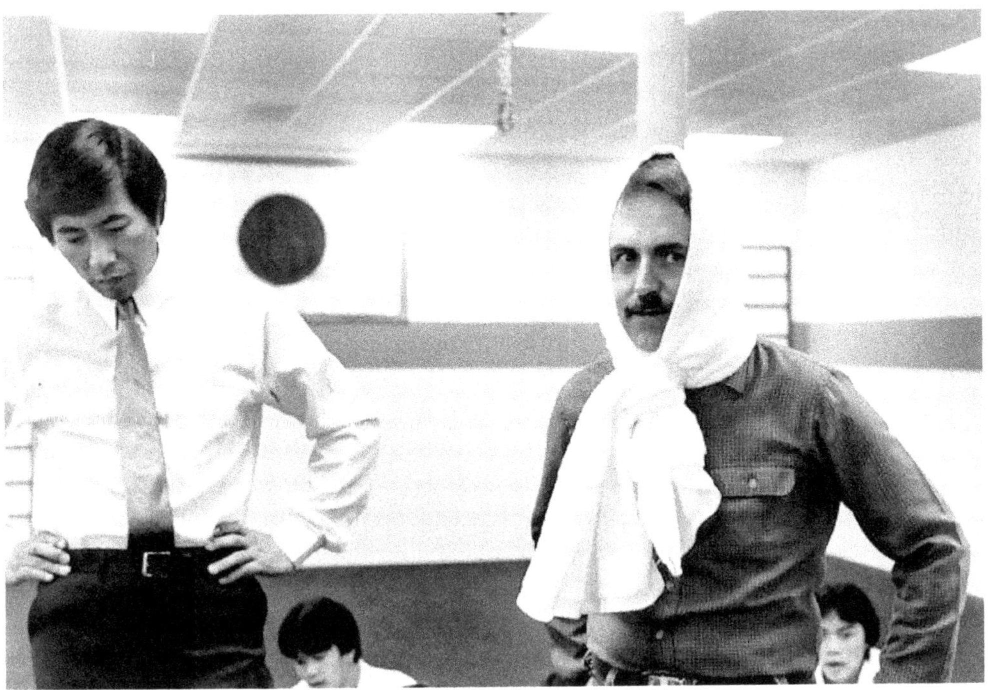

Roy (right) looking ready to shoot some action scenes with Sho Kosugi on the set of *Pray for Death*.

• • •

Over the ensuing couple of years, Roy moved from the world of low-budget martial arts movies to the more surreal realms of low-budget fantasy and horror, including Kevin Tenney's *Witchboard*, Bill Froehlich's *Return to Horror High*, and Chuck Russell's *A Nightmare on Elm Street 3: Dream Warriors*. Interestingly, each of those films were the feature debuts of their respective directors, and in some cases, Roy was replacing other cinematographers who apparently lacked the skill, speed, and precision that would become his calling card in the industry. But that reputation was hard-earned, as these tough productions saw Roy enduring some of the most challenging filmmaking moments of his career. If Roy has a keen eye for the dark side of cinema, then it relates back to his childhood in which he felt his first experience of the spiritual, as he recalls:

"I don't like horror films as much as I like ghost stories. I grew up along the Mississippi River and I've seen ghosts and experienced the metaphysical thing of having orbs of light come into my room in the middle of the night and being terrified by it. Those kinds of supernatural events have fascinated me; it feels like an interesting puzzle to me. It's all to do with our psyche and how we perceive things; you and I could experience the same event but perceive it entirely differently from one another. It is the same with film, we might watch the same film and take away two completely different interpretations of it. Within the context of their stories, all films, characters, and situations must have rules. If the filmmaker violates those rules, it must be for a metaphysical point, or the film falls apart. A horror film is one that places vulnerable characters into a situation that is outside of their ability to resolve. Often their horror is their inability to cope with situations that have repressed them. I find that horror and comedy are interesting genres as they are virtually the same in the setup, as they often play in threes: the comedian will tell you a joke, then he'll set you up for the next joke which doesn't play as well as the first joke (he lets you off the hook so to speak), and then it's the third joke that really gets you. Horror is much the same: you get scared, and you get a laugh out of it; you've gone over the rollercoaster first hill, thinking 'That's not so bad. I'm safe now.' The next scare is minimal, making you believe you can control your emotions and then they hit you hard with a real fright. That third shock is the greatest. The setup is the most critical part of a great horror film. Characters must be well defined within the context of what the author wishes for us to know. Initially the audience should feel that the characters are well rounded—someone the audience can identify with. Often these characters have a previous conflict that has caused the moment that we find them in. One trick often used is to take the weakest character and make them the hero. For example, the strongest character, the most physically fit and most capable of any situation, might be isolated or removed, forcing the weakest character to find a resolution. It's often important to establish a sense of safety. I love films like *The Innocents*, with Deborah Kerr, and *The Uninvited*, with Ray Milland. The place, the setting of these films, may be more important than the characters. Indeed, the place may be one of the characters. In one instance the place can also feel like it's a living thing. For example: *The Others*, in which the quality or lack of light in the house is an important plot point. When you get to do a horror film, or a ghost story, you are dealing with the meticulous tools of filmmaking, and not only that but the meticulous tools of discovery of your own life and your own perceptions. I love that kind of filmmaking. Doing dramatic pieces and more thoughtful pieces are interesting but they're not always fun, not like this, because when you are making horror films you are using all the tools to take the audience on a particular journey and then cheat them. And I love that."

Roy also considers displacement an important factor in the psychological aspects of crafting an effective horror film. As such, environment is key, and placing characters in unnatural circumstances plays into the sense of discombobulation that the audience is expected to feel along with the character. In *A Nightmare on Elm Street 3: Dream Warriors*, the teen characters are all out of their comfort zone. They are ignored and cast aside by their families into an institution that does little to help their vulnerable states of mind, run by staff who similarly fail to listen to their concerns. They are literally trapped, under lock and key, with only their dreams for escape; but that realm is also unsafe as their subconscious is home to their greatest fear: Freddy Krueger.

"The entire film works on the premise of 'whatever you do, don't fall asleep,'" Roy says, "and that is the genius set up—the conflict of being unable to fall sleep, but we all must fall asleep. We can't resist it. In the film we place a character into a situation without their permission. The character Kristen thinks she's safe but suddenly finds herself in the Elm Street house. I always say it's critically important to set up the chaos that will come. And don't forget the power of symbols: Light and Shadow. It's not what you see—it's what you don't see that's most important. Do not be afraid of the dark. What we don't reveal is often more important, it forces the viewer to fill in the blanks. The audience's imagination is the most powerful tool for any filmmaker. In many cases they can create a greater horror than any of our intellectually thought-out concepts. Trust the audience. *A Nightmare on Elm Street* functioned initially because the 'monster' Freddy was unidentifiable. The audience was unsure of what he was capable of. The less that he was seen and the more that others could talk about him, the stronger the structure of the film. If you look at the original Howard Hawks version of *The Thing from Another World*, the entire film is spent with the characters expositing about the monster. By the time we see the monster the one in our mind is much greater than any monster we would literally see. So, you do not show the monster until absolutely necessary. Do not rely upon special effects or make-up to create the monster. The more the audience sees, the less threatening that monster will be. Spend your time developing the situation. Establish the place, the character and their specific character flaws and strengths, and then place them into the situation. The audience is more interested in how they deal with the situation. Once the threat is revealed, the movie is over."

With his acute knowledge of how the horror genre functions, and with an eye for the surreal and the fantastical, director Kevin Tenney did well to promote Roy from camera operator to cinematographer on *Witchboard*, the first of three consecutive horror films that Roy would shoot in the mid–'80s, and which remain among his most innovative and unique works. *Witchboard* details the demonic takeover of college student Linda Brewster (Tawny Kitaen) who is seduced by the occult powers of the Ouija board that her friend Brandon Sinclair (Stephen

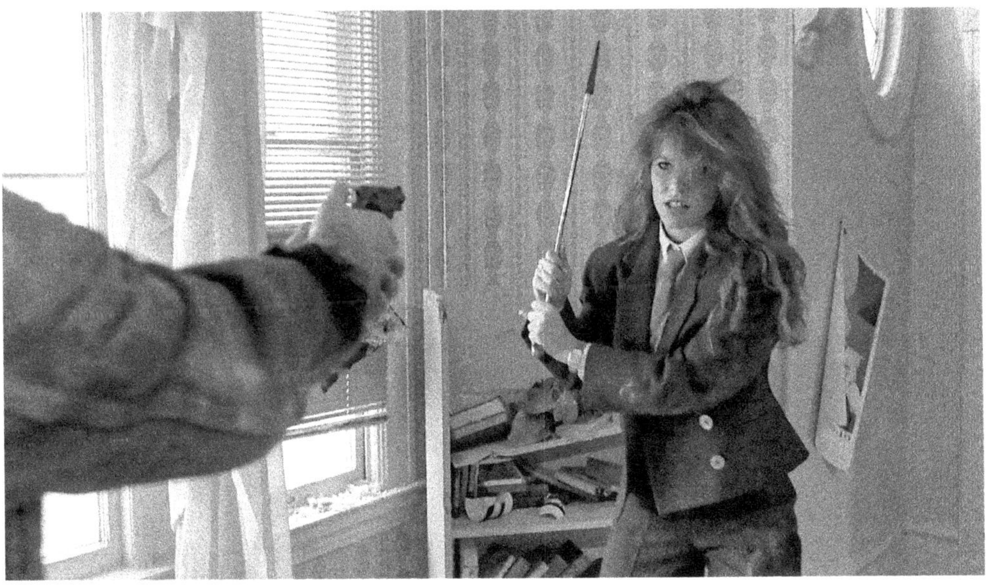

Tawny Kitaen plays the possessed Linda in *Witchboard*, 1986.

Nichols) unwisely uses as a party piece to summon the spirit of a child named David by whom he has been psychically contacted. Linda's boyfriend Jim Morar (Todd Allen) insults and angers David, leading to a series of cursed events including the death of friends and the progressive possession of Linda.

USC film school dropout Tenney enjoyed good times directing his first feature film, despite an inauspicious first week of production, when it soon became clear that the original cinematographer hired by the director was in way over his head. After three days of filming, the producers realized they had an issue that needed resolving. Enter: Roy.

"It was my first movie, so I was happy to just be there," Tenney admits. "It meant I didn't have to get a real job. I mean, that was a real job, but not really. I'd hired a lot of friends from film school, and none of us had made a feature. We had done a lot of 16-millimeter thirty-minute shorts, but this was our first feature and most of them rose to the challenge. But there's always one who can't, and this guy happened to be the nicest person there is. The stuff that he lit at USC was good but when he was under that much pressure with a bigger crew, I guess he just wasn't ready."

This became evident to Tenney on one particularly tough night during which the grips had to build a stage on the exterior grounds of the main location house. The camera crew could not reach the first-floor window of the house due to the incline of the hill on which the structure was built. Therefore, the grips purposely built a stage upon which the Chapman crane would be placed so the camera could reach the window of the house.

"That's the night that I decided we were firing our DP," Tenney admits, "because the police were there as it was a residential area and we had to be done by ten o'clock. But we were having trouble with the crane; it wasn't working. So, we're eating up time, and while we're in the middle of this and I'm standing there wondering if we're even going to get a shot, our DP comes over and he says, 'Where's *American Cinematographer*?' I said, 'Why?' and he goes, 'We've got this big crane doing this great shot. The magazine should be out here.' And I'm like, 'That's what you're fucking worried about? That there's no one here to take your picture?' I think I walked off set. We had our production offices in the basement of the building, so I went down there, and [producer] Geoffray was on the phone, but I said, 'I've got to talk to you—we've got to fire him. That's it. I'm done.' If his priority was to have *American Cinematographer* there to do a profile of him with the big crane, then that was it for me."

That was the moment that Kevin made an offer to Roy. "He was our camera operator and he, unlike the rest of us, had experience. So, we pulled him aside and said, 'Roy, I have got to get rid of this guy. Would you be willing to take over as DP?' And he said, 'Yeah, for more money.' So, my charm didn't work on him as well as gold."

Assuming the role of director of photography, Roy recalls the decision to replace the original DP was more complicated than a mere business move: "This was a hard decision for Kevin to make because this original cinematographer was a friend of his; they'd gone to school together. And I had gotten recommended to this guy because his crew were friends of mine; I had actually taught the key grip and the gaffer in film school at UCLA; they had said, 'you should come over here and help with this, because this guy is in way over his head.' The problem with being a director of photography is that they teach you in film school that you are the author, you are the visionary. And the truth is that as much as you want to contribute and have your own personal point of view, the real author is the director. And you must conform to what the director wants. What happened with that cinematographer was that he was doing it his way, the way he wanted to do it, even though Kevin had told him another way. But he assumed, because he was the director of photography, that Kevin would just fall, and that doesn't happen. It was pretty much a mess and Kevin just started melting down; when you have that much money thrown at you by a producer, a studio, or financier, you have the responsibility of accomplishing what they want you to do, and that can be difficult and scary if something or someone is prohibiting you from achieving that. I have met so many people who claimed that they wanted to be directors of photography, but they ended up becoming directors, because they realize that being the director of photography means it's not their voice; they are contributors, but it's not their voice. And it doesn't matter how many movies you've done, and how brand spanking new the director is, it's still their movie. It's complicated, it's very much like a marriage. I'm sure I've had cat fights with directors on the set and disagreed with them, but I don't recall ever having had such with Kevin—I just had a good time with him because he exudes this sense of fun. He wants to have a party because filmmaking is fun for him. And the truth is that if you do go and confront Kevin with something, you realize that he has a point of view and if he believed in what he is doing you couldn't argue him off that point of view; you can do that sometimes with directors, but not with Kevin, and I really admired that. *Witchboard* is his voice; it's nobody else's. But every day we were falling further and further behind, and it became clear that something had to be done about the cinematographer. It's always tough, especially when he's a nice person. However, one of my favorite expressions is, 'I've been killed by more nice people than I've ever been killed by assholes.'"

Tenney concurs: "It's always easier to tell someone who is an asshole to get the hell out of here, but when they're a nice guy you keep hoping that they'll get better. I don't think yelling at people gets the best work out of them. It doesn't create a happy set. But on the other hand, as Roy does say, you can't be niced to death. I didn't want to yell at our DP or at anyone. To this day, I don't believe in yelling at people. If they're having trouble doing their job, I will pull them aside and I say, 'You're not getting the job done. So, you either must figure out a way to do better work, or we're going to have to let you go.' And then in a couple of days, if they still can't get their act together, just pull him aside and I will, as my wife says, offer them the opportunity to go be successful somewhere else. You have got to move on."

With Roy firmly ensconced as the new director of photography, he had his work cut out to bring his own sense of style while not straying too far from the material that had already been shot for the sake of continuity. Tenney recalls the effort:

"We couldn't reshoot the party scene that the original DP shot; it was just too bright. But I thought we could at least go in with the lead actors and have Roy shoot close ups. So, he went in, and he had the two actors on the couch, he pulled the shade off the window, and hung it on a C stand to shoot through it. And I said to Roy, 'It doesn't look like that in the master,' and he just went, 'I know, but I can't bring myself to light the way he did.' So, I was worried about continuity, but I thought that people weren't going to notice because once we go from that master and we get into the close ups I didn't go back to the master. I said I would rather have them look good than be one hundred percent accurate to what the master was. There is a shot in the kitchen in which there was supposed to be coverage, and not only did the original DP over-light it but it took so long to light it that I had to restage it and shoot it in one shot. For this whole two-page dialogue scene I had the actors moving in and out of frame to make up for the fact that I wasn't moving the camera; so, the frame would keep changing even though the camera was locked. And in the color timing they were right at the edge with that. They have so many points that they can go either way to make it brighter or darker, and they had to go all the way down to the dark side just to get it to look normal. When we were filming the party scene, Todd is sitting there talking and he gets up to go to the kitchen, and the camera pans up and watches him walk down. So, I go off set and soon the DP calls that he's ready. We go in and sit Todd down. He looks great, he has been lit fairly well, but there's a big giant flag right there. I said, 'Well, he's getting up to walk.' And the guy says, 'You didn't say that.' I said, 'I'm pretty sure I did.' And he said, 'Well, if you're going to move them, you got to tell me.' I said, 'That's why we have blocking.' But you know what? It was my first film and I just assumed that anything that was going wrong was probably because of me fucking up. So, the guy went off to relight and went to sit next to the dolly where Roy is just there waiting to shoot. I said to Roy, 'I apologize, dude, I'm usually much better organized than this. I think maybe I've bitten off more than I can chew.' And Roy said, 'I can tell you're a good director. I've made a lot of films and you're the best director I've worked with to date.'"

Stepping into to help control an already fraught milieu with time ticking away after going three days behind schedule, and with reputations at stake, Roy had to summon what he learned at the feet of his Old Hollywood mentors to get the film back on track and bring it in on time and on budget under these difficult circumstances. In doing so, he recalled the wise words of Harry Stradling:

"Harry told me, 'If you want to have beautiful images then you better fit it in with the schedule that you've already gotten. Any time that you take for yourself is stolen time; you don't get a turn.' Harry said that because any time you take is stolen from the director and the actors. A lot of people on a film set think, 'It's my turn ... it's time for makeup, it's time for hair, it's time for dressing,' and all that. When you do that, that's your ego. So, if you want to be successful, if you want to survive, and you want to work all the time, then you have got to find a way of being invisible. And you have got to find a way of being so fast that nobody ever walks up to you looking at their watch, or that nobody ever walks up to you and says, 'Hey, we're behind, we have to get going here.' If the film looks good, it's not because you indulged your ego—it's because that's what you're supposed to do. You don't get to decide how long you're going to take to make it good, because it's not your film, it's somebody else's, it's somebody else's journey that you're on; you just happen to be there to support that journey. They may only have three days to make this movie and that's all the time you've got. And I think, frankly, that my success is not whether my images look good or not, it's really that I've been able to deliver what is wanted within the time frame that I'm given. To me, it is always an honor to be allowed to work with

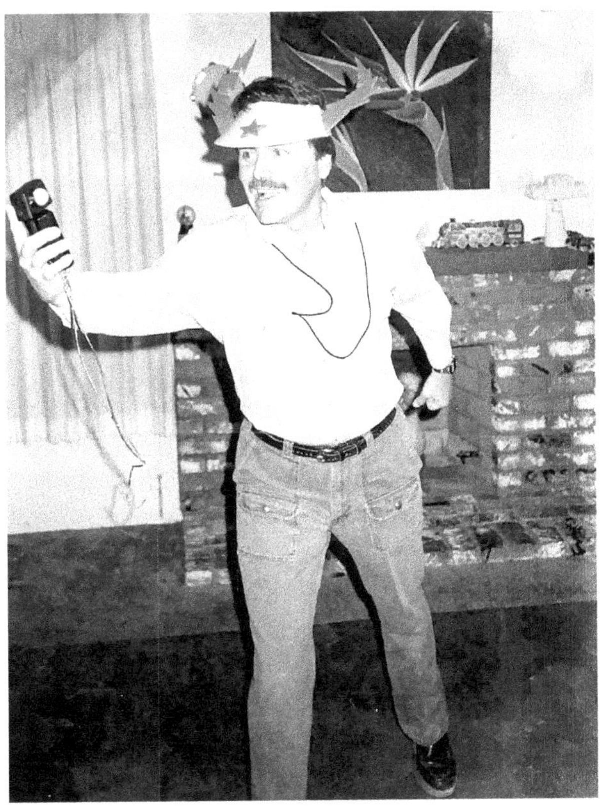

"Flash" Wagner on the set of *Witchboard*. The visor with lightning bolts was a gift from the crew in reference to his speed.

somebody who has a vision who then trusts you with that vision to make the movie. The old Hollywood cameramen worked fifty-two weeks a year, they were under contract, and when they weren't working, they were playing cards in the camera room. But often a studio executive would come in and say, 'Hey, you've got to go fill in for a guy on Stage 12, he's sick, or he's drunk, whatever, but you have got to come in and fill in.' And that's what you did. There was no ego back then with those guys. They were factory workers. The whole ego issue came about for all of us in the 1960s when we all thought we were movie stars. Fortunately, I was trained by a group that didn't think that way. And so that was why doing Kevin's movie for little money was fine with me. It wasn't about the money; it was about the experience of working with people that love to do what they do. It's a fun movie and I think the reason people like it so much is they can feel what we felt when we were making it."

"I'm just glad we could afford Roy," Tenney says, "though I'm not sure if we could afford him if we were making it today. Hiring 'Mr. Multiple Emmy Winner' would cost me a couple of billion! But Roy saved us. We were several days behind schedule. We never finished the day when we shot everything that was in the script, so we never finished the first week. Roy not only had to be fast enough to shoot the film as it was, but he had to always be fast enough to find a window to go back to shoot stuff we didn't get when we had the other cinematographer. I appreciated the fact that his stuff looked great in dailies, but he could move quickly and that was very important in that situation. It doesn't matter how good you are— if you're slow, then it doesn't count. But I am always willing to listen to ideas. On the first day of *Witchboard*, as I do on all my movies, I say I'm willing to entertain anybody's idea. If you have a great idea for a shot, bring it to me. Because if I use it, I'll end up getting credit for it anyway, so I don't care. I say, 'I'll listen to your idea, and if it's better than what I was going to do, I'll use it. But if I decide I don't want it, then that's it. I don't want you to stay in my ear.' There were a couple of times when people came up with ideas that I liked better than what I was doing, or they enhanced what I was doing. I went to film school with Larry Karaszewski and Scott Alexander, who have together written a lot of smaller budget studio films, and we were at a school reunion when I told them about having to shoot eight pages a day. I could see their jaws drop and I said, 'That's a normal day.' I've worked days where I've done sixty setups and shot twelve pages, whereas Larry and Scott probably shoot two or three pages a day. So, it comes down to you needing someone who can give you high quality work in a very minimal amount of time, and Roy had that kind of skill and efficiency."

Despite Roy delivering the film with speed and economy, he still managed to make the film look aesthetically unique and imbue the film with a style that is full of intricately designed and executed camera movements. One of the most

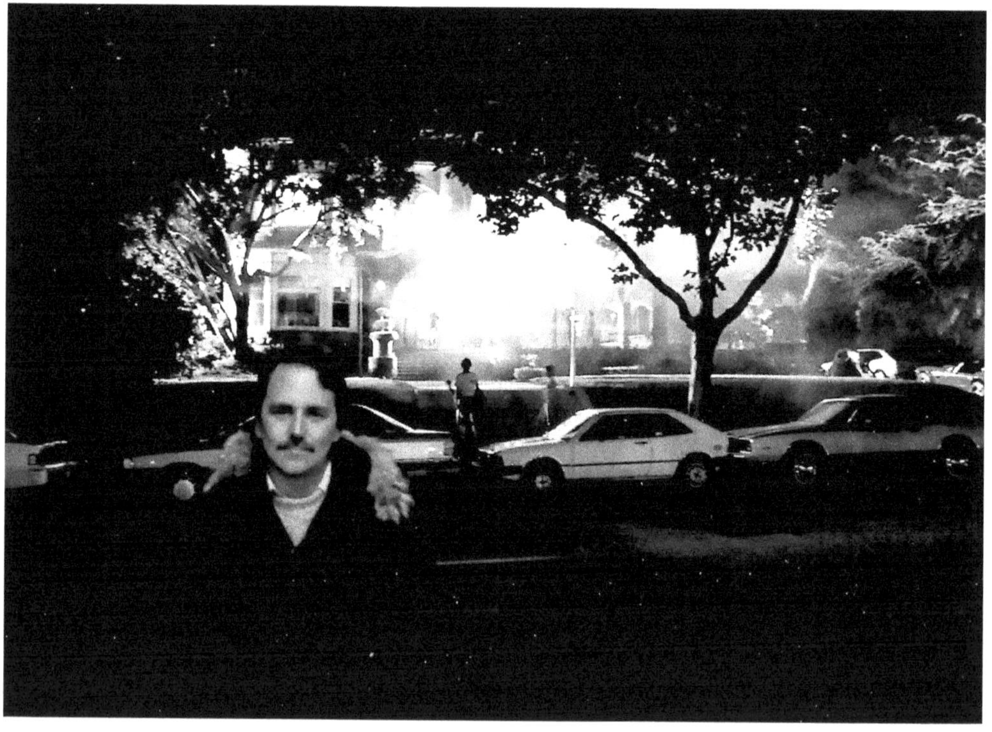

Roy in front of the main house location for *Witchboard*.

obvious of those aesthetic elements is the subjective shots from the demon's perspective, which were not always easy to achieve. One such notable camera movement occurs near the end of the film when Jim goes out the window and the camera follows him out for the descent of the fall. The tricky shot proved to be the only occasion on which a disagreement arose between Roy and his director. It was the last shot of the movie and was designed by key grip Pat Daly before Roy came onboard. Upon learning of the plan for the shot Roy raised a flag that while it was an interesting shot it would be technically difficult to achieve. But for Tenney, there would be no other way. The crew had to build a fake wall up on a scaffolding at the location, which was in a parking lot in Encino, Los Angeles. It took them all day to rig the setup, and by the time they were ready to shoot, the sun began to set.

"The problem with that shot was it took the effects people all day to build it," Roy recalls. "It's the same old story: you wait all day for the perfect shot, and it doesn't turn out as you planned. So, I'm not that pleased with it, but I did like the idea of it. As far as what I did, I don't think I did a very good job."

The demon point-of-view shots proved a further challenge for the lighting crew. For those subjective perspectives, Tenney wanted his cameraman to use a 9.8mm lens which made it difficult for lighting as the lens would capture much of the location as it stalked its way through. "Roy couldn't put his lights anywhere!" Tenney says, "They were fine for the objective shots, but as soon as we went to the spirit's perspective, we were going to see the room. We actually built a grid and put it on the ceiling, so we could hang the lights. We didn't want any light stands. I wanted to really be immersive when the ghost was moving, so that you would feel the scenery going by on the side. The séance table scene was that way too, so we obviously couldn't have any lights anywhere. So, we hung all the lights from the center. If you look at that shot, you can tell the lighting is completely different than the wide shot. But all our lights were big, they were not like what we use today. They were very big lights and they had to hit each one of the people properly. And it was tough to find a light that small that would hang without tearing down the ceiling. One of the ways we got away with the master and the dolly shot looking different is because they turn off the lights and then they turn them back on after the séance so we were able to say okay, they're going to start, so click, now it's lit differently; then as soon as that is over, she goes, 'Brandy, get the lights!' and he goes over and click, now we go back to the master which is lit differently, which is okay because we threw the lights. A lot of it looks like we just put four people at a table and went around them while they were talking. But because we had to light the guy who's sitting here, we must have a light on him. But then as the camera crew goes through, they're going to cast a shadow across him, so we had people with flags walking by that would flag off one light and then open it back up after we were passed so that you wouldn't see the shadow pass across someone's face. It was very coordinated, like, five or six people working in sync together to get that shot. It was only after I told Roy that I wanted to do this dolly shot that he said the room might not be big enough for the track. And it turned out we had to do something that no one notices—when they're going around the table, the couch is gone. Because we couldn't have done it any other way. We had to take every other piece of furniture out of the room to accommodate the dolly track. It was well worth it, but it was not easy. It wasn't something that Roy just pulled out of … you know…. We filmed that scene near the end of the shoot, by which time everyone was getting punchy. It's a single two-and-a-half minutes long shot, so if we get to two minutes and someone flubs a line then it's back to the start again. And they kept laughing and fucking up, so I had to yell at everyone because they've all got the giggles, and I said, 'Guys, we cannot get out of here till we get this and I don't know about the rest of the group, but I'm done. I want to go home.' So, I really lambaste them and then we start the shot. And we're about ninety seconds in and coming up to two minutes. I can tell I'm going to start laughing, I can feel it. I'm going to break it, but I'm fighting and fighting it. And just when I'm about to break, Todd laughs and I jump up and I go, 'Goddammit, Todd!' but secretly I was thinking, 'Thank God.' It was time. So, we got it the next day."

Roy recalls pulling off the tricky shot: "I was initially unhappy with that 360-degree séance scene because I had put too much light through the blinds. Pat Daly had built this scaffold outside the window because the other cinematographer wanted light through the window, so I just emulated that because it wasn't my movie in the first place, but it is too bright. It would be relatively simple to pull off that shot today, you would use a candle and a Steadicam. But we had no Steadicam. We had none of that stuff. That was all on a track with an Arri BL and Zeiss superspeed lenses. And we did it over and over again. Looking back on it, I'm very proud of the way we did it; I would not do it any differently today. Pat Daly was an exceptional key grip and he ended up doing Scorsese movies and was a key grip on *Forrest Gump*. His crew called themselves 'The Grips from Hell' after working on *Witchboard*, and they are still to this day the best grips in the world. They came with me to work on *A Nightmare on Elm Street 3*. And we had Shane Kelly as our gaffer; I'd known him since he was a film student. We had an extraordinary group of people that didn't know how to say 'no.'"

"I've always felt bad that Pat's career declined after working with me," Tenney says with characteristic sarcasm.

To complement the stellar crew was a cast that included model and up-and-coming actress Tawny Kitaen as possessed student Linda Brewster. Kitaen had made a name for herself after appearing on the cover of '80's hair metal band RATT's 1984 debut album for Atlantic Records, *Out of the Cellar*. She subsequently appeared in E.W. Swackhamer's television film *Malibu* (1983) before she attained more high-profile roles in *The Perils of Gwendoline in the Land of the Yik-Yak* and the early Tom Hanks comedy *Bachelor Party*, both 1984. Kitaen's career in film didn't take off as well as her starring role in *Witchboard* may have suggested she was destined for, though she did have a prolific career in television throughout the 1990s and later appeared as herself on multiple reality shows throughout the 2000s. She died in May 2021 at the age of 59.

"Tawny was just a sweetheart," Roy remembers, "but she had her little idiosyncrasies, one of which was bringing OJ Simpson on the set. I remember the nude scene with her in the shower where she wouldn't let anybody but Kevin and I in the shower with her."

"Yes," Tenney concurs, "and I had to borrow somebody's wedding ring because she would only have married men be around her while she was naked. I was wearing a ring which was not a wedding ring, but she made me put it on my ring finger. It was tough to shoot only because Tawny was uncomfortable with it. I've shot with other women who do nude things and they're perfectly okay with it, but Tawny wasn't comfortable. She did it, and she didn't bitch and moan about it, but she had certain demands she wanted met before she would take her clothes off. Most of this stuff was only shot from the waist up, but there is that one shot of her coming out of a shower, which was a locked-off slow motion camera for the breaking glass. She wanted a professional set."

"I made three horror films around this time and *Witchboard* is my favorite," Roy states. "*A Nightmare on Elm Street 3* is my least favorite. I hated that film. I hated the way it looked. I hate everything about it. But I came into both the movies the same way—I was hired after the fact. So, I kind of inherited the look of those movies. But *Witchboard* is by far my favorite of the films I did, and I think it has a lot to do with the party that Kevin created with this great cast. Kevin was fun every moment of every day. We were always playing horrible practical jokes and laughing. And there was no reason for any of it to be that much fun because it was hard work; that was a tough shoot. I've always loved working with people that enjoy what they're doing and know what they're doing. And the key for me with Kevin was he knew what he wanted, though he was not so staunch a person that you couldn't persuade him. When I look at it now, I don't think I did very much, and I don't think I did it very well. I certainly never consciously tried to make it look like a horror film. Only on certain scenes does it have a look that one would associate with horror imagery, such as the cemetery scene. That was one of only a handful of times that we really went for the horror look. I do think that looks really good. That cemetery scene was a big deal because our production manager got me the right crane, a huge Champion crane which is something like 150-foot, and we put a light on that. And that was the night that Bill Fraker and Conrad Hall came to visit me. It was a good night for them to come out. And they were sort of teasing me all through everything. But they both said, 'Wow, this really looks good.' So, I'm really proud of that."

"I wasn't even a big horror fan when I wrote *Witchboard*," Tenney admits, "I just knew that horror films were the best way for an unknown director to get a theatrical release. I was a huge Hitchcock fan and when we were first shopping for distributors this hack distributor who watched the film actually said, disparagingly, 'Holy cow, you call this a horror film? This is Hitchcock, for crying out loud!' He meant it as an insult, but I was like, 'You're damn right it's Hitchcockian!'"

◆ ◆ ◆

Following on from *Witchboard*, Roy continued further into the horror realm with *Return to Horror High*. This intricate meta horror-comedy is the directorial debut of Bill Froehlich, a successful television writer-producer whose prior credits include *Scarecrow and Mrs. King, Hart to Hart, Mike Hammer,* and *Mac-Gyver.* The 1987 film would be co-written by Froehlich along with Mark Lisson, Dana Escalante, and Greg H. Sims, the combination of which resulted in a distinctly original commentary on the slasher film. The story is set at Crippen High, an abandoned school where a series of horrific murders took place five years ago and which is now the setting for a film being produced which tells the tale of what happened when these halls of academia became a slaughterhouse. Unscrupulous producer Harry Sleerek (Alex Rocco) cuts corners to save a buck, casting one actor in several roles and insists on increasing sex and violence to make his movie more salacious and sellable. This leads to a rise in tensions while several cast and crew members are murdered. Or are they? Don't underestimate the cunning of an indie filmmaker to capitalize on a massacre to promote his movie.

Return to Horror High is notable in its style and storytelling, which unfolds in a non-linear manner that requires an attentive viewer to keep track of the proceedings. The film is a clever self-reflexive look at the slasher genre and plays with audience expectations and manipulates them to surprising and satisfying effect. Few films at this point had taken an introspective perspective on the genre, with the occasional exceptions such as Michael Ritchie's *Student Bodies* (1981) and Fred Walton's *April Fool's Day* (1986). It turned out Froehlich and his partners were ahead of the curve with the meta concept of commenting on horror cinema within the context of a horror film. They did so almost a decade before director Wes Craven truly brought the idea to the mainstream with the *Scream* franchise and turned it into a popular and profitable subgenre. But just what was Froehlich trying to say about the horror genre?

"I will try to be completely honest in recreating that sense of writing it," the

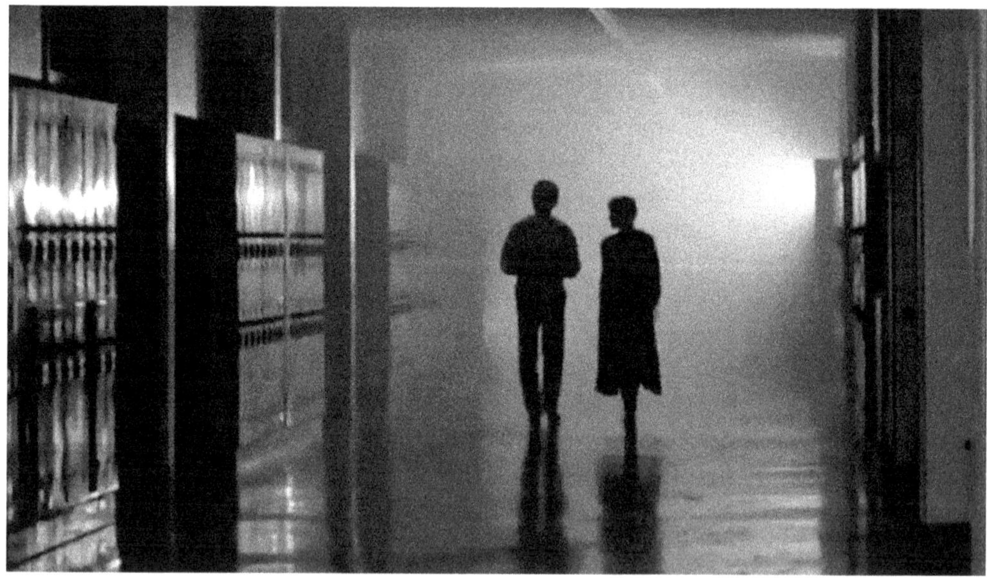

The stylish shadows of Roy's cinematography in *Return to Horror High,* 1987. From left: Brendan Hughes and Lori Lethin.

director says, and continues, "Greg Sims, who was our partner on this project and the executive producer, helped to pull it together. He helped put us in touch with New World Pictures, who financed it. Greg was a talent manager at the time, in addition to wanting to produce things, and he brought together a lot of the cast. But how it originally started is that Greg sent a horror script that he and his friend Dana Escalante had written which was a real kind of gritty, very bloody slasher film, very straight forward. He sent it to myself and my then partner who produced the film. And he said, 'Hey, would you guys like to do it with me?' We were doing a television series at the time, and we had done some television movies as writer-producers; I had never directed before except for stage productions at college and one little documentary, but I had not stepped into the Hollywood business of directing. So, this was an opportunity for me as I was looking for something to direct. But you had to have some proof of how and why a studio or financing company would allow you to direct, why they would give you the helm of a show or a film. So, I read the script that Dana wrote, and I didn't have any interest in this straight, really gross slasher film because there wasn't enough of a story and underlying meaning of anything in there. I knew this genre was very popular at the time, and I knew that this is a genre which if you kept within the budget to a certain extent then I would have a lot more leverage of being maybe allowed to direct it."

Froehlich convinced his writing and producing partner Mark Lisson of his desire to direct this story and to let him take a stab at the script; and being that the pair had other projects in the progress, Lisson turned his attention to those while Froehlich retreated to his Encino condo, where he set about laying down the blueprint for what would become *Return to Horror High*.

"I just started writing and I didn't stop," Froehlich admits, "it flowed out in just a few days. I wrote late into the night till I couldn't keep my eyes open, only then I would go to sleep. And then I'd wake up early in the morning, fired up to get back into it because the story was running around in my head. A lot of writers have experienced the fact that when you're in the zone, you feel like you're downloading something from the universe. It's just flowing through you and feels almost like you're taking dictation. I mean, the thoughts and ideas and dialogue and characters and the things that came to me… I laughed! I jumped! I was experiencing that movie as I was writing it. It just flowed out so quickly. But when it was done, I realized, wow, this is something that I think would be a lot of fun to make because it exists on a number of levels."

There was one particular scene in Escalante and Sims' initial script that stood out to Froehlich as the catalyst for making the film not only a funny and thrilling horror film, but one which uses self-reflexivity as a tool for the audience to engage further and more proactively rather than passively letting the film wash over them.

"There was something in Dana's and Greg's script that intrigued me, and it was a sequence that—even though I rewrote some of it—made me laugh. It was the sequence with the biology teacher, played in the movie by Vince Edwards, and the student that he is tormenting. And then the teacher ends up in the nightmare scenario of getting dissected by the evil being that is stalking the school. And there was something about it, as grotesque as it was, that made me laugh; it was kind of a perverted sense of justice and revenge. And so, while I was reading that, suddenly—and I kid you not—the entire idea for the film came to me in five minutes of reading that scene. And the whole thing that came to me was this thought of—because here I am wanting to make this movie—'what if there's a movie crew that is trying to make a movie of this horrific thing that happened in this high school, but the killer was never caught or killed, and while they're shooting this, they start disappearing?' That came to me in a flash, because I saw not only the humor in it, but I saw the opportunity to be able to say something, not only about filmmaking, which I loved, and the whole process of storytelling, but also to say something about the horror genre from an angle that had more humor, while also was respecting the nature of what it is that scares us. And it asks the question: 'why does it scare us?' And what does that say about us as human beings and how we affect each other along those lines? Somehow the feeling came to me that fear and humor crisscross each other many different times."

"The humor is evident in *Return to Horror High* straight away," Roy applauds, "from the opening credits when it says, 'Cast in alphabetical order and in pieces.' That sets the tone perfectly, right down to the final line of the end credits: 'The end, or is it?' I love that. I learned a great deal from Bill, and one of the things I learned from him was that comedy and horror are almost identical. The way that you set up the joke, the way you play it out, the way you play the response, and how the audience responds to it. That is very much the same whether it's comedy or horror. That is what I brought back from my revelations with Bill Froehlich. That was critically important to me on the rest of the films that I made; not only that, but timing, which is everything. And he saw the humor in the shadows, he saw the humor in camera movement, or when you did something and when you didn't do something. It was that sort of yin and yang that I really liked."

Froehlich concurs: "I think Roy and I discovered during the making of this film that humor and horror can be so inextricably mixed. It also has to do with the way we think as human beings; once you get somebody's thought moving in a certain direction—for instance, with the positioning of the camera, the movement of the camera, the lighting, the dialogue, what the actors are doing or not doing— then you can start leading human thought, because human thought has a tendency to move in certain directions if that is where it's being told to go. And then you can end up playing with people's perception of reality and illusion, because you get them to start thinking down a certain line. And in some cases, you can start building up fear. That is also an opportunity, then, to thrust something in, whether it's humorous or otherwise, that throws a whole different equation to it, that causes somebody to have to rethink where they're at. And that's why we do jump at moments in horror movies, because of expectation; the expectation is fulfilled in some scenes and then sometimes the expectation is not fulfilled. Then you relax, and then a little later you get them, and they can be surprised, whether humorously or from a scary standpoint. I think Hitchcock understood that clearly, and we watch Hitchcock movies all the time because people love to be scared. That is something which brings us a sense of really being alive, when you are shaken that way. But I also think humor does that because it reminds us of some of the other aspects of life."

Froehlich continues, "I really, really liked Richard Rush's film *The Stunt Man*, which starred Peter O'Toole, Barbara Hershey and Steve Railsback. It was about filmmaking, and it goes in and out of reality and illusion and it is about the sense of what filmmaking brings to you, and what the writer and the director were trying to say about society, about how we deal with certain things. And there's something about that film visually that really hit me at my younger age. And in thinking of that film, I realized that *Return to Horror High* would be an opportunity to have some fun and to say something that you might not normally get to say in the horror genre; to be able to say something about the nature of illusion, reality, life, how we look at things, and the effect that the horror genre can have on people. I thought this is clearly one of the things I want to do. In the right hands you can really move people in many ways. Even if you're making a low-budget horror film with humor, there are things you can get across beyond just pure entertainment. And I don't know if we were the only ones to do so, though I feel we were, but

we were certainly one of the most prominent ones at the time that really injected this much humor into a horror film. And I have subsequently learned that some of the *Scary Movie* and *Scream* franchises took some inspiration from *Return to Horror High*, which I always felt pretty cool about ... although they never sent us any checks."

With a concept as potentially uncommercial and with an aesthetic approach as distinctly original as that of *Return to Horror High*, it was as much a surprise to Froehlich and his colleagues when the independent production and distribution company New World Pictures, which was founded in 1970 by B-movie king Roger Corman and his brother Gene, expressed their eagerness to roll film on Froehlich's meta exercise.

"That was one of the

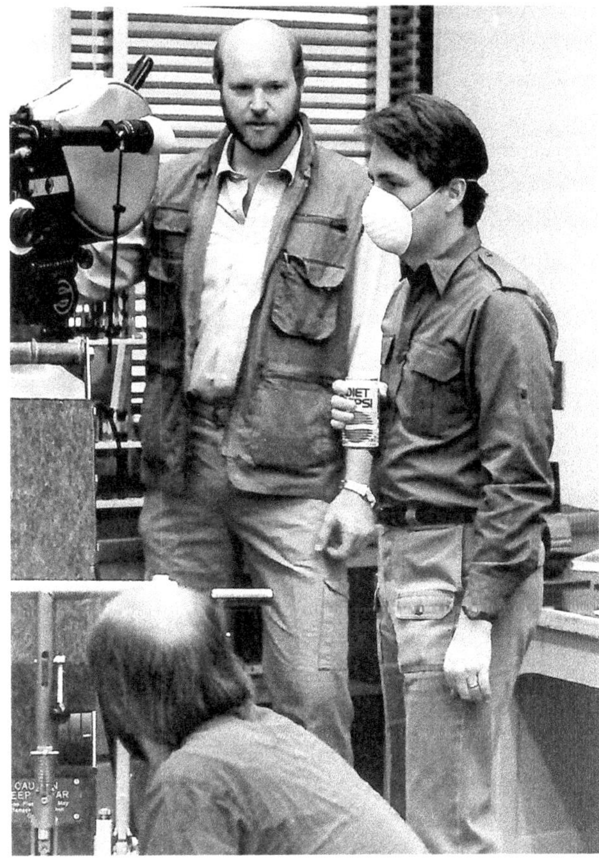

Director Bill Froehlich (standing, left) and Roy setting up a shot on the classroom set of *Return to Horror High* (courtesy Bill Froehlich collection).

surprising things to me when we were making the film that I was thrilled about," Froehlich enthuses. "My partner at the time, Mark, was thrilled about it, as was Greg. I'd had a very strange experience up to that point. I was involved in producing television series, I had done two television movies, I had co-produced an independent feature film with Katharine Hepburn, and I'd worked at MTM Enterprises [Mary Tyler Moore Enterprises] for a couple of years learning the television business. So, I got to see clearly and experience how things work when you are interacting with the studio levels and network levels and the kind of pressure that they put on you to change this, that or the other to come around to their way of thinking. And, Wayne, you are right, we were really doing something that really hadn't been done before and in this nature. When the script was sent to New World, I was bracing for them to say they want so much rewritten. I thought, 'They're not going to buy half of this!' and I was really shocked when they came back and said, 'We really like this. We want you guys to start production as fast as possible.' We were braced to be hauled over the coals and I remember the meeting distinctly because there we were: me, Greg, Mark, a couple of the New World executives, and Roger Burlage, who was the CEO of New World at the time, and they said, 'We really don't have any notes, we think this is intriguingly different. It's funny, it's scary.' And we talked about doing it on a budget that made sense to them financially. I think the other thing that helped us initially was that they had two big films that they were going ahead with; one was *Death Before Dishonor*, starring Fred Dryer, who was the star of the NBC series *Hunter*, and the other was *Wanted: Dead or Alive*, which starred Rutger Hauer. These were two big financial expenditures for New World at the time. So, Roger Burlage, the CEO, looked at me in that meeting and he said, 'Bill, we know you guys understand production because of what you've been doing on television and this feature that you have done; we know you have that background, but you have not directed anything before. So, why should I let you direct this film?' And he was very serious. He wanted to see what my attitude was. So, I looked him straight in the eye. And I gave two reasons. One: I said, 'Roger, I wrote this script, I really know it, I understand the story I want to tell and how I want to tell it, which I've explained to some of you guys in the meeting,' and I laid out some of the concepts of how I wanted to go about it. And then I looked him straight in the eye and I said with a perfectly straight face, 'Roger, if we keep this on budget,'—and our budget was around $800,000 at the time—'I could deliver you two hours of fogged film and you will still make money in the horror genre.' And I kept that straight face. He just looked at me and went, 'You're right. Okay, you guys start as soon as possible.' We walked out of that meeting on a cushion of air. And I was thinking, 'Holy shit, we just got the go ahead to make this movie!'"

Froehlich and his production team were plunged into pre-production on the Warner Bros. lot immediately, but the executives kept calling to see what progress they were making. However, being thrust into the forward momentum of a greenlight left little time to assess the script they were already committed to making. For Froehlich, this meant shooting scenes that ultimately never made the final cut, as he was still editing his story during the filming.

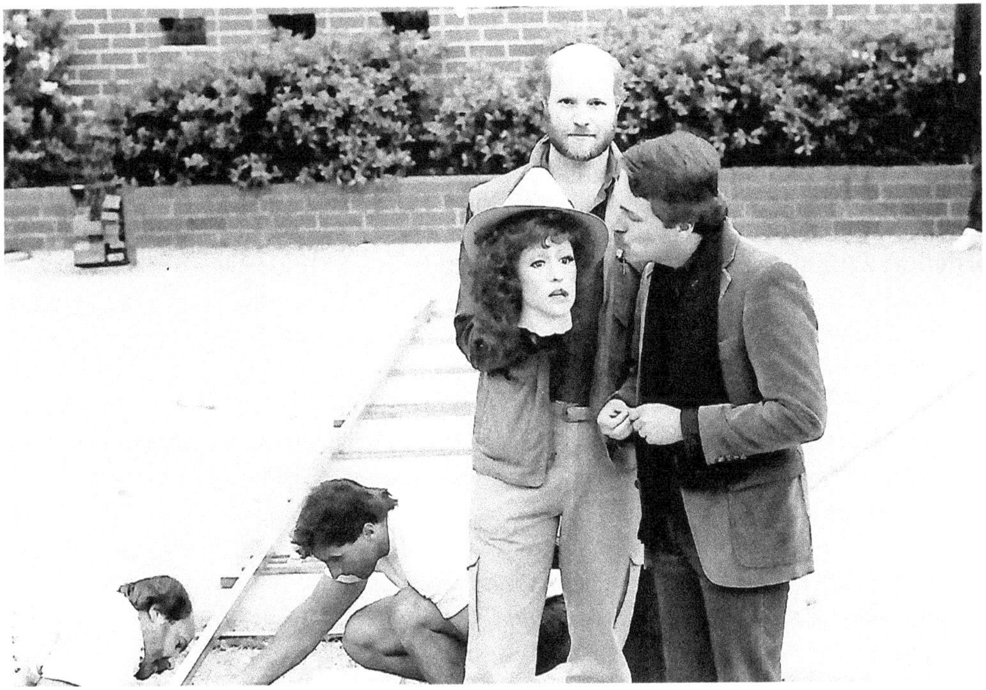

Bill (left) and Roy joke around while the crew lays down the dolly track for *Return to Horror High* (courtesy Bill Froehlich collection).

"That was an example of the kind of mistake that rookie directors can make. When you get the shock and surprise of being thrown into getting a green light immediately and they are pushing you to make it, you don't have a chance to really assess what you need to cut from the script. I was expecting that would happen in the rewrite process after the studio said, 'we don't like this, we don't like that, you have got to rewrite it,' but they didn't want anything changed or rewritten. But I still knew we were too long. Unfortunately, being thrown immediately into pre-production and being the director, I had to be the creative guide through that process as we were hiring people. So, I never really got a proper chance, nor did my partner Mark, to take a hard cold look at the script and cut stuff that needed to be taken out. And there were a couple of days of shooting an interesting scene that Roy would remember shooting which had some really cool visuals, but had I been experienced enough and tough enough I would have known to cut that, and we would have had more time to put into other scenes. So those are some of the things you learn by experience. You learn from your mistakes, and I didn't make that mistake again. In my career going forward, I always was able to make sure to take the time to get the script down to the essence of what I am trying to say. So, at this point all these years in the future, I apologize to Roy for making him shoot extra days that didn't end up in the film. We were doing the best we could, but that was a rookie mistake."

Not that Roy was aggrieved for having worked on those scenes that ultimately remained on the cutting room floor, for here he was given an opportunity to work with a director of style and substance, an artist who brought intellectual subtext and unique sensibilities, the kind of visionary with whom Roy had envisioned collaborating for a long time.

"I was raised in the Hollywood studio system," Roy says, "but I had not been able to break through into the union yet. I was desperately trying to find that movie that would help me become a union studio cameraman. I had a lot of experience and had been mentored by some of the finest cinematographers in Hollywood, so I didn't want to do slasher films, I didn't want to do sleazy bikini movies or things like that. But I met Bill at Warner Brothers, and he was just not typical for a low-budget horror director. He was intellectually inclined; he was very thoughtful and careful about what he said. And he was generous. He allowed you a great breadth of opportunities to do things. He stood behind you. And that was unusual for me at that place in my career. And it was a great regret of mine that we never got to continue to grow as partners, because Bill had all the layers that I had seen in the great directors that I had met before. He was just too kind in many ways for the industry. We got to do things together that would have probably taken me a few years to get to the place where I would be doing that. And that meant everything to me. When you find a filmmaker like Bill Froehlich, you want to connect and stay connected. And although we haven't gotten to work together again, we've stayed connected as friends throughout all these years, which has been a long time."

Being that this was the beginning of Froehlich's directing career, he quickly discovered that there are those who are essential collaborators in bring the director's vision to the screen, namely the 1st A.D., the production designer, the editor, and especially the cinematographer. One of the things that Froehlich looks back on fondly is the feeling of total collaboration with the crew and other filmmakers who contributed to *Return to Horror High*, but definitively so his partnership with his particularly creative cinematographer:

"Those people are all vitally important to the director, and Roy was my right arm in helping me tell this story. It was to my great delight that he was there and a willing collaborator. I have since learned that if the director and the cinematographer are not on the same page, and if they are not humming together, there's going to be all sorts of problems in the film. As this was my directing debut, I knew I needed a real creative partner in making this film. But I was also fully aware from a business standpoint that we were making what technically amounted to a low-budget film in the horror genre, and at that time the horror genre wasn't taken as seriously as it started to be taken in the coming years; it was always taken with a sense of interest and they saw box office possibilities, but horror films usually never got reviewed, they just came out. We got submissions from several cinematographers, and I got a sense of them when I looked at their reels but most of the time the sense that I felt was that they just wanted to do the job, collect the check, and then move on. But then I saw Roy's reel, but most importantly I was able to talk with him and then meet him, and I was like, 'Thank you, God!' because I knew I was a neophyte director, a beginner, and I wanted somebody who was not only going to be inspired by what I was hoping to do with this film, but who would also be a great support because I knew I needed support. And I needed somebody who was a hell of a lot better than me, because I think you do your best work when you hire the best people you can get. You hope that they are as talented as you think you are, but hopefully more talented so that you can rise on their shoulders and make the kind of story and film that you want. And that turned out to be the case with Mr. Roy H. Wagner, ASC. I learned a lot from working with him and from seeing how he did things. We had a lot of laughs. We also were under a lot of pressure, time pressure. And thank goodness for Roy with what he was able to deliver. It was so ridiculously fast. There were times where he would start to light the set and I'd want to step aside so I could go to the bathroom, and Roy, the rascal that he is, would sometimes finish the lighting before I could get my pants unzipped. Roy is fast but he is also technically brilliant. There were things that Roy did from the cinematography standpoint which helped solve certain challenges—we had very inconsistent light outside the windows of the location, and we couldn't control that. I wasn't David Lean, and we didn't have that kind of luxury where we could just wait for the weather to be cooperative or for the sun to be cooperative. So, I turned to Roy who became the commander of the sun."

"We never used actual daylight," Roy recalls, "We were on the second or third floor of this place, and we were shooting day-for-night so we had to build a scaffold outside in order to control the light. We had an HMI outside, and that's all control, that's not just what is coming in the window; it's what is coming in the window plus light behind it. That was all shot during the daytime."

Froehlich recalls, "In the scene with George Clooney walking down the hallway we had built this set up on the third floor and we made it so that we would have the focus be this vortex that he is being led into deeper and deeper. This is

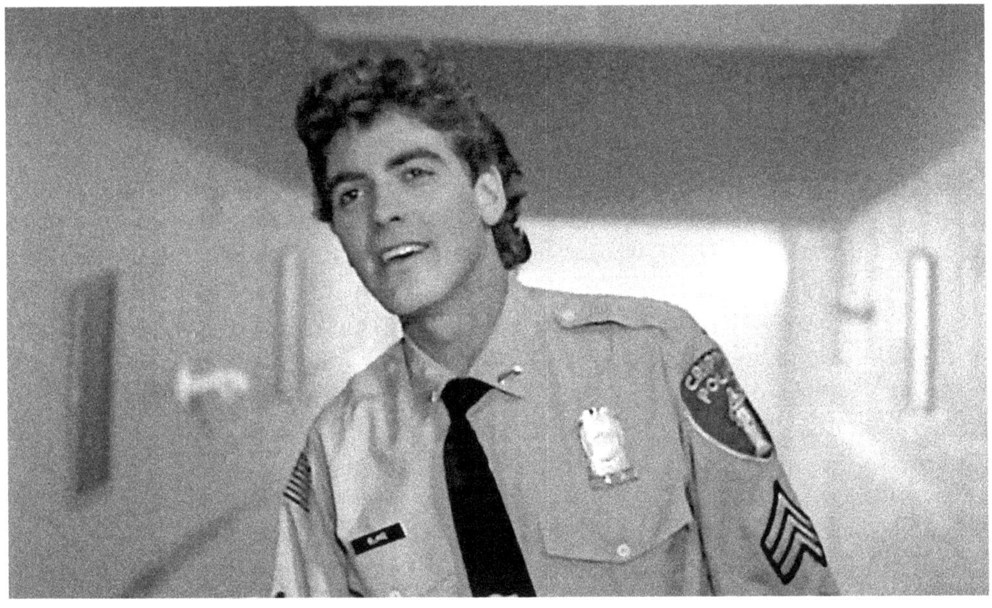

George Clooney plays the ill-fated Oliver in *Return to Horror High*.

another example of how well I thought that Roy and I worked together because he so thoroughly understood what I wanted to see. And then given the limited time and resources that we had, I thought he captured it so brilliantly. In many cases throughout the film Roy did things that made what I had originally envisioned even better."

Speaking of that scene with Clooney, Roy recalls, "I used wider lenses, a 14-millimeter lens, which was a complicated thing because that set didn't have a ceiling. And so, you can see over the top of the ceiling, but it was more important that we create that illusion of him going down this long vortex than it was that it had any reality to it. And having Clooney very close to us made everything else fall away very quickly. When I watch it these days I am surprised at how well it worked. The thing is, when you have a lot of money and a lot of time you can do everything better, but we were just working and doing more than we should have been doing. And it was up to us to be better. If we didn't work better, we would just be making another crappy little horror film. And so that is why I like to work fast, it is not to be cheap. It is up to you to figure out what chess pieces you need, where to move them, and do the most efficient thing. That has been the whole mantra of my career, and I find it makes you far more instinctual, instead of intellectual. You run the risk of getting stuff stuck in your head when you read the script, when you have time to think about how you are going to do things; in pre-production anything is possible, but when you are in the middle of production anything is not possible. When you are in production you have to stand there with the director and with the cast to observe what's going on around you and respond to what they're doing. You have to do this because oftentimes what they are doing is not what you previously discussed or what the script says. So, if you don't come to the set with all that baggage but do come armed with all the knowledge that you've carried with you from your studies and from your mentors, then you're way ahead of the intellectual. I have used that as a basis of much of what I have done, because it allows you to discover and be inspirational. I was just responding as the other partners were to the work that we had in front of us."

"That is a really important thing to understand," Froehlich concurs, "it helps if we are alert and connected to our instinct based on the electric energy of the moment when you're on the set. Roy and I had our time prior to production to have deep intellectual discussions about what I wanted to do and how he was going to bolster that. And those were fun and exciting discussions for me because they were so creative, and he was so into that part of the storytelling process and brought his own knowledge into that. But then obviously when you get to the set location and you are in production, a whole other dynamic starts coming in. You really must be alert, be aware of, and be connected to your intuition and your instinct in the moment, taking advantage of that kind of collective energy going on. And if you do that, you get out from under and away from your ego and get connected to the story that is beginning to unravel and flow in front of you. If you have done your homework well enough, you can retain the essence of the principles of what you want to tell in that story. You can take advantage of the fun accidents that happen that end up making things better than what you had planned.

And we had instances where a number of those things happened, where some of the stuff that we captured was better than some of the in-depth discussions that we had had. Because we did take advantage of a certain creative energy that was there at that moment. And we were open enough to it. I can remember a couple of times where having a filmmaking partner like Roy really helps you in this regard. And I always felt Roy and I were partnered in this venture creatively, because there were times that he talked me into taking advantage of that moment, where part of me was still locked into what I thought was a great vision that I had of how it should really be done. But because I was a first-time director, and my heart was really in doing the best that I wanted to do, I wasn't fully aware at the moment of that devil of production, the eating away of time; I wasn't paying enough attention to that and realized we have got to keep going here, we got to get the best that we can do or we're not going to get the whole film done. I remember the first day of shooting, we tried as best as possible with the schedule to start doing some easier stuff; and the first shot was really easy. And then I went, 'Cut. Print. Moving on!' I thought, 'Hey, this is fun. This is cool. This is great!' We went to the second setup, which was a shot that I really liked. Roy and I had discussed it; the camera was locked off. I mean, it was steady, it wasn't moving; we had the actors moving in and out of their close ups carrying some body parts and some makeup stuff. And there was interesting dialogue going on. But it required timing on the actors' part. I was really excited about the scene, but what happened, unfortunately, was that our female star Laurie, who is a fabulous actress, hadn't fully memorized all those lines. And that scene required everybody to be right on. And so, the scene was dying on its feet. And after several takes, it was clear that this wasn't going to happen in one shot. And I can remember everybody, including Roy, and all the crew kind of turning and looking at me as if to say, 'What are you going to do about this?' And that was my moment of thinking, 'Okay, this is where you have got to be the real director.' So, we very quickly had to break that scene apart to get the kind of coverage that would allow us to edit out the problems. Ultimately, that scene never made it into the film, because it never fully worked as good as I wanted it to. But we got through that. And that got me launched into being much more aware of being connected to one's instincts on the set and to what is happening in the moment."

"We had a great crew," Roy enthuses, "we had a really good production manager who never said no. Even though we all knew we had no money, he never said no to us. We had an assistant director who ended up becoming a star as far as production people go. And she was going through some real tribulations at that time. But she was wonderful."

"Barin Kumar was the production manager," Froehlich says, "and sadly he passed away rather young, but he was brilliant in what he did, and such a wonderful man. And Rachel Talalay was our first assistant director; a really bright woman who knew what she was doing, and she has gone on to have an amazingly strong career as she should have, because she was really good. But we had a lot of challenges on that film—there was a day or two where I kind of had to be my own first assistant director because she was dealing with some challenges outside of the film—but when she was on, she was great. And that was an interesting experience. But we did have a good crew; Greta Grigorian, our production designer, was pulling some amazing things out of the hat."

"We also had technology," Roy states, "we had lighting instruments that were way beyond our budget, but we had them. And we had cranes. There was not a thing that we could afford that somehow Kumar didn't find a way for us to get. He found a way for us to have those things and you could not have done it without those kinds of partnerships with people who go beyond what is on the page. We never encountered things like, 'Well, I can't do this because that doesn't exist,' or, 'I can get that but it's going to cost you this much money to have it.' They pulled upon their own personal experiences to get you what you needed. That happened a lot on this film. And it is just remarkable because those people went on and did very successfully with their lives."

Froehlich concurs: "Everybody down the line was genius because I think they all—well, this is me guessing what I felt then and I still feel now—felt like, 'Hey, we're trying to do something different here. This is not just a normal movie.' They wanted to be there. And that extends to the cast and the crew. We were really blessed with the actors that we got. They were all in on the fun, because they knew this was different than things they had been asked to do before, but the talent was there in spades. Lori Lethin had done some major television movies that she was the star of, and she was great. Brendan Hughes was a delight to work with. Scott Jacoby had done really good work. And it was a funny thing, Scott played the director in this and I kept watching him and realized that he was watching me intently during it all because he ended up taking some of my expressions, some of the things I would be doing when I was thinking through trying to get the shots in, and he would incorporate that into his performance. God bless really good actors; they are willing to throw themselves into the situation. And what I really want to see in an actor is an inherent truth. I want them to be believable, no matter what they are doing. And they were all so into their own sense of the reality of the moments that they were asked to participate in. I mean, Alex Rocco had been in *The Godfather* and *The Stunt Man* with Peter O'Toole. He was in major feature films and went on to co-star in television series and many other things. Andy Romano, who played Principal Kastleman, was in a variety of big TV shows since the sixties and he went on to be in a number of major feature films. All interesting, fabulous actors. And what I liked about these actors is they were all professional and all passionately involved in what they were doing. And I knew that the most important thing is to hire a good actor, because then there is a lot less directing of the actor than you need to do, because they will understand their part; they will be in on the game and really invested. So, I knew I needed to just give them some guidance, some things to think about in regard to where we were in each particular scene and to give them a sense of the tone."

Froehlich continues, "Alex Rocco and Andy Romano really grabbed onto that, because at one point Andy said to me, 'Why am I so interested in flies?' And I could see that he was struggling to make a final connection with his character in that scene. So, I just took him aside and I said, 'You know that there's

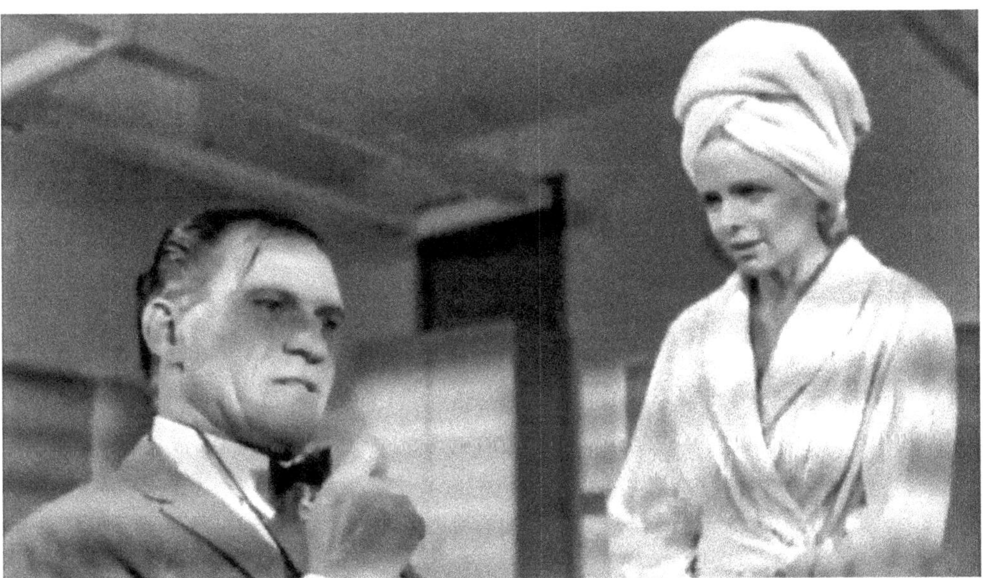

Andy Romano and Lori Lethin stylishly lit within Roy's framing in *Return to Horror High*.

this classroom at the end, and the corpse of your daughter is in that classroom that you've set up? Well, what's one thing that would be all over corpses that you wouldn't want to be desecrating your daughter's form? Flies. That's why you don't like them, you want to get rid of every one of them. They don't deserve to be near your daughter. And with that his eyes lit up. And he went, 'Got it!' And from that moment on, anytime you see him taking an opportunity to get a fly, his timing is just impeccable and it's natural. Those are the only type of things you need to give an actor like that, a sense of a deeper understanding of a moment of behavior as to why they're doing it and where it comes from."

"Andy's timing was amazing," Roy says, "he was absolutely brilliant. As was George Clooney! I didn't even know who George Clooney was. He was constantly asking me all these questions, and I'm thinking, 'Who is this guy? What's with all the questions?' I wish I'd been more open with him. But he was just an amazingly interested guy and that's how he was throughout the whole production. Everybody was in love with what they were doing. They were all in on the fun. Everybody. It was like a great class party. We all wanted to be there. I've only had that experience twice in my career. Truthfully, twice, and that was on *Witchboard* and *Return to Horror High*, where the whole ambiance of the crew and the cast was so strong and so connected that you would do anything to make the film better. It was just such a kind and generous experience."

"Encouragement is key," Froehlich affirms, "because when you are making a film self-doubt enters in the arena for all of us. There were times at night during the making of *Return to Horror High* that I would wake up in the middle of the night going, 'Oh my God, am I a complete fraud?' And then I would get to the set in the morning and see Roy standing there and I would think, 'Well, this is good.

I know Roy knows what the hell he is doing.' Of course, I did not know that maybe Roy was standing there also going, 'Oh my God, am I a fraud?' We bonded with each other and built a sense of chemistry off each other's creativity and sense of fun. Roy's sense of humor is vital to helping make production a good time and creatively loose and open. There are many examples, but I will tell you one: there were a couple of times where I would want the dolly raised so that the camera was up a little higher. So, I'd be standing there looking through the eye of the camera when Roy would come over to look in the camera to see what it was that I wanted to be set up, but he had to bring an apple box over to stand on because Roy's height is smaller than mine. And he would look through the eyepiece and would then look at me with a sense of feigned condescension and say, 'Okay, we're ready for you.' So, I would go back over to the camera and look down at the apple box and kick it aside with a sense of indignancy, like, 'I don't need this!' Then I would look through that camera and say, 'Okay, we're ready to go.' Well, at the time I was not wearing a hat, and let's just say it's like the joke that goes, 'God made a few perfect heads, the rest he covered with hair.'—this is what my look was like back then. So, we would start getting ready to shoot and Roy would go, 'Stop, stop, stop! Something's wrong here. The lighting is all fouled up.' And then he would turn to me and say, 'Bill, what are you doing? You're a moving bounce card on my set, you're ruining the runway, you've got to put a hat on.' So those moments would cut the tension on the set. And it reminded everybody that we are being as creative as possible, but we are also having fun here. And that is vital. That was one of the things I really enjoyed about working with this rascal named Roy Wagner, who is in my estimation a humble artist with a capital A on Artist. He is not a 'Look at me!' filmmaker. He does the great work that needs to be done and does it brilliantly. He was such an amazing, creative, collaborative artistic partner to have on this little venture of ours, this low-budget film that was a humorous spoof of horror films which also had a level of seriousness. There were times that I have desperately wanted to work with Roy again and one of the few regrets I've had in my career is that this has not worked out; there were some things that didn't go as planned and this is just the nature of the business and the nature of the ups and downs of life. There were some projects that I was trying to work through as features and other stuff in the business that just didn't ultimately get the go ahead, but I ended up being a co-showrunner or showrunner on quite a number of hit TV series and it never worked out that I was able to get Roy to come aboard to be the DP on those. His work on television has just been brilliant, and he deservedly won Emmys for *Beauty and the Beast* and *Quantum Leap*, work which is just astounding. If you look at Roy's work on those shows or on *CSI*, his delivery of that level of quality under those constraints is just mind blowing. And yet people who don't know all the ins and outs of filmmaking will look at those and go, 'Oh, this is really cool,' but not fully understand how Roy was able to deliver what he was able to deliver."

Horror films of the early-to-mid 1980s were not prone to receiving good reviews from critics, regardless of audiences flocking to them in droves. One only need look at Sean S. Cunningham's breakthrough sleeper hit of 1980, *Friday the*

13th, and the massively successful pop-cultural behemoth that it became as proof that horror films did not need critical approval to find their audience. And while Paramount embraced their low-budget/high return darling stepchild enough to market a franchise through seven sequels, New World Pictures underwent a change in management and those newly positioned in power failed to see the market potential of *Return to Horror High* and subsequently failed to release it with appropriate fanfare. As a result of executive disinterest, Froehlich's budding career as a director suffered. When New World Pictures had greenlit *Return to Horror High* they were up to their ears with *Wanted: Dead or Alive* and *Death Before Dishonor,* understandably so given that they put a lot of money into both pro-

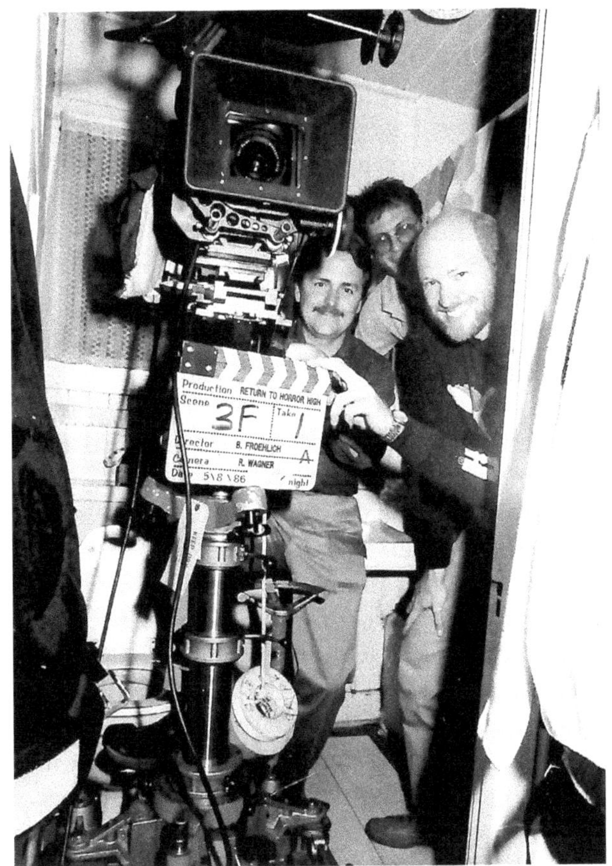

(From left) Roy, camera assistant Ed Giovanni, and Bill getting ready to roll on *Return to Horror High* (courtesy Bill Froehlich collection).

ductions. New World Pictures CEO Roger Burlage agreed that if Froehlich stayed on budget and within the first several days delivered dailies that were true to the film that they all agreed to make, the company would leave them alone to go make the film. The executives paid close attention to the first few days of dailies and liked what they saw, liked the way the production was being run, liked what Roy was doing as cinematographer, and liked what Froehlich was doing as director. So, Froehlich and his team were left alone to face the challenges and constraints of time and money. This suited Froehlich, and it suited New World as they were busy working through problems with the two big action films already in production. However, those good early feelings about *Return to Horror High* changed when Burlage left New World Pictures for greener pastures just before the film was going to be released. Robert Rehme joined New World Pictures after a successful run as president of AVCO Embassy Pictures and later held a high position at Universal Pictures. Taking over from Burlage as CEO of New World Pictures, something happened which is unfortunately not a rare instance in Hollywood—a new executive comes in and wipes the slate clean of what their predecessor has in development. Due to the amount of money already invested in *Wanted: Dead or Alive* and *Death Before Dishonor*, Rehme poured further financial resources into their distribution while deciding to pull back on the capital and effort needed for *Return to Horror High* to make a significant impact on the market. Instead of the original plan to amplify the film's dual comedy and horror aspects in the marketing and distribution campaign, the new order at New World decided to put the film out misleadingly as a straight horror film in the vein of other more generic slasher pictures.

Said Froehlich, "*Return to Horror High* was a film which when it came out should have propelled me, and Roy, and all those involved to much higher status quickly for the following reason: Roger Burlage was really great to us. So, it got to the end of production, and I took the edited movie to show Roger and the other executives, and it was a thrill because they loved it. They said, 'You have delivered exactly what we hoped you would deliver and the type of film that we wanted. This is something different.' And they put together a distribution campaign and marketing campaign that was based on the fact that this is a horror film with humor and wit and comedy and is unlike anything seen before; that is what they developed, it was a great campaign. We were going to have a pretty wide release because they realized that within this genre this movie would make some noise. And the other thing that happened when we started giving critics the opportunity to see it is that we got great reviews. Tom Shales from *The Washington Post*, who was a major critic, loved the film! We had positive reviews in *The Hollywood Reporter*, *Variety*, and several other newspapers—some of the blurbs in those reviews were like they had been written by my mom! We were astonished because horror films just didn't get reviewed at that time. But then Roger left, and Bob came in and had other ideas for the film. Now, I was surprised to see that the executives under him, and to their credit, had some courage and stood up to him and said, 'No, we've got a great campaign here.' I showed the whole film to Bob Rehme, and he didn't crack a smile at all. That is when I realized, 'Uh-oh, we might be in trouble here.' His executive said, 'This is funny, this is clever, this is inventive, it's going to do something in the horror genre; we've got to keep sticking to the campaign that we have.' But Bob forced them to change the nature of the campaign; he took a lot of their money away and cut back on the number of theaters and areas that it was going to roll out to. So, when the film opened in the regions it opened in and in the theaters that it was in, here's what happened: it was selling out! Every single show. Each night. Because people would come back to see it again. It was selling out almost every single theater, but New World had made a deal with the theaters that was only going to allow for the film to run for a much shorter time. But the theaters found a way to contact Greg Sims, my partner on the film and the executive producer, and they were begging Greg to beg New World to allow them to keep the film longer because at times the lines were going around the block and critics were liking the film. But Bob Rehme wouldn't give in, and I think he just didn't want to admit that he made a mistake. I don't think he was ever in the position where he wanted to admit that.

"*Return to Horror High* was well on its way to being a blockbuster for a horror genre film, and Roy and I would have immediately gone on to have different careers; there would have been offers coming to both of us, but that did not happen. The film was allowed to quickly run through its distribution. And then when it eventually arrived on video, it became their number-one video seller for quite a long time. So, this work that we did was appreciated, but it wasn't appreciated in a way that did for us business-wise what it should have done. We all had to learn how to roll with those punches and keep doing what we love to do and figure out ways to continue to work and survive in this crazy industry. I watched it again recently and thoroughly enjoyed it. It brought back a lot of great memories, and it reminded me of the long friendship that Roy and I have enjoyed since making this film. It also reminded me of what he was able to do under the great pressures of time and money that we were working under. Roy clearly elevated what we were doing to a level that I had hoped for. But if we had more money and more time there are things that we would have done a little differently and maybe with a little more depth of delivery. But we did a pretty good job. And to find out all these years later how many people have a cult appreciation for *Return to Horror High* feels very good."

"I think *Return to Horror High* is an undiscovered masterpiece," Roy applauds. "It's fun to watch, but I wish people got to see the movie we wanted to make. I don't think it has found its audience as it should have for a very long time. It's like everything else, it will come back in a revival, and it will surprise people. I've always admired my work on it far more than I did my work on *A Nightmare on Elm Street 3*. I think it's a much more interesting film with better characters. I'm always more interested in why something is what it is, what makes it the way it is, to find out the truth behind why something is successful or why it failed, and I guess that's the historian in me. And I think discussing *Return to Horror High* the way we have is a good example of that."

◆ ◆ ◆

Roy's next project was to prove his most high-profile work to that point, and one of his greatest challenges. *A Nightmare on Elm Street 3: Dream Warriors* was the second sequel to Wes Craven's hugely influential 1984 surrealist slasher film, *A Nightmare on Elm Street*. That film spawned a modern monster movie icon in Freddy Krueger, the razor-gloved dream demon haunting the surviving teens of the vigilante parents of Springwood, a suburban Ohio town in which child-killing Krueger stalked his prey until he was caught by police. With his being let off on a legal technicality, the town's parents decided to mete out their own form of justice and ended Krueger's mortal life by burning him alive.

The huge financial success of Craven's film meant that its producer Robert Shaye and his fledgling distribution company New Line Cinema wanted more of the same, and what audiences got was Jack Sholder's *A Nightmare on Elm Street 2: Freddy's Revenge*, an underrated horror film in and of itself though lacking the independent hunger and creative genius of Craven's original. Both films were brilliantly photographed by Jacques Haitkin, but his often bright and consistently colorful work on the sequel meant audiences saw too much of Freddy, at one point even bringing him out of the shadowy dream realm and onto a suburban backyard to bring menace to a barbecue. For the third film, New Line wanted to put Freddy back into the black and make him a mysterious and elusive entity once again.

Cameras began rolling on the third Elm Street film in 1986 with a cinematographer whose lack of speed would result in the production immediately running over budget and behind schedule. New Line duly panicked, and they needed to draft in some men of much experience. And so, Roy Wagner and assistant director Dennis Maguire got called for duty on the horror movie frontlines. These film veterans would enter the fray to battle dwindling time and money, an inexperienced first-time director, and a culture clash that would pit these inveterate studio-trained pros with the young art department and special effects crew who were making a name for themselves on what would turn out to be a commercial touchstone for New Line Cinema.

Roy remembers receiving a call from line producer Rachel Talalay, with whom he had worked previously on *Return to Horror High*. Her role on that production was as assistant director but having worked her way up the Elm Street ladder on the previous two films, she was now under pressure in a producing position. As Roy had shot several independent horror pictures and could bring everything in on time and on budget, he was an ideal candidate to assume the crucial role of cinematographer on this latest Elm Street film; this would be New Line's most expensive, and thus riskiest, film to date at an ultimate cost of $4.3 million, and those involved could not afford to hire anyone with anything less than skill and economy. Talalay duly arranged for a meeting between Roy and director Chuck Russell.

"I met Chuck at New Line's headquarters in Beverly Hills," Roy recalls, "and it went very well. So, I called Rachel afterwards and told her that Chuck and I had a great meeting and I expect my agent to call soon." That was when the film's makers made their first mistake... "I never got the call!" Roy states, "I found out from friends in the industry that another cinematographer got the job. And I was very bitter about that. Although not for long, because they soon came crawling back to me in a panic."

Roy was lunching with a friend at a restaurant on Sunset Boulevard when he began receiving persistent alerts on his beeper. Not recognizing the number, he ignored it. But then it was followed by a 911 which got his attention. Roy ran to the nearest phone booth and a voice on the other end asked with urgency: "When can you meet with Chuck?" It took a startled Roy a minute to realize that the voice was that of Rachel. "We're in trouble," she insisted, "we want you to take over on *Nightmare 3*. Can you come over to discuss it?" And with that Roy made the good career move to swallow his pride and agreed to the meeting that night at UCLA, where production was lagging and the recently hired original cinematographer was to be relieved of his duties. There the crew was busy working on another setup, while Rachel took Roy straight to Russell's trailer, where the director informed him that despite only being three days into production they were already behind schedule. "We'd like for you to take over tomorrow," Chuck urged. Cut to the next night and Roy is literally, and figuratively, chest-deep in the Hollywood trenches.

Roy's inaugural night of shooting would be the Ray Harryhausen–inspired Freddy gravesite scene in which John Saxon's disgraced former policeman Donald Thompson and Craig Wasson's psychiatrist Neil Gordon visit a labyrinthine vehicle wrecking yard in which the remains of Freddy Krueger are buried. The pair dig up the bones of the Springwood Slasher only for the skeletal spook to attack them both, all the while the previously written-off cars come to life in a cacophony of screeching metal, deafening horns, and blinding lights. The scene would give Roy an insight into the madness of production to come. Luckily for him, a kindred spirit, Dennis Maguire, also started work that night as assistant director. Maguire brought exactly what the production required: a no-nonsense Old Hollywood–style studio mentality to get the film back on track, and he should know how that is done having grown up on the sets of classic films with legendary directors such as Elia Kazan, Robert Wise, and Robert Rossen; his father was Charles Maguire, assistant director on the likes of *On the Waterfront*, *The Sand Pebbles*, and *Odds Against Tomorrow*, and with production credits on *The Friends of Eddie Coyle*, *The Parallax View*, *Shampoo*, and *Heaven Can Wait*. It was perhaps inevitable that Dennis would end up in the film business, doing so with a series of early credits as a second assistant director on Ted Kotcheff's *Uncommon Valor*, Herbert Ross's *Protocol*, and John G. Avildsen's *The Karate Kid Part II*.

Maguire was busy on location shooting Bill L. Norton's road comedy *Three for the Road* when he received a call from Rebecca Greeley, who was working on *A Nightmare on Elm Street 3* as assistant production manager.

"I knew Rebecca from a previous project," Maguire says, "and so she tracked me down in Arkansas when we were doing *Three for the Road*. We spoke on the phone, and she asked me if I could take part in a conference call the next night with some people from New Line: Bob Shaye, Sara Risher, and Rachel Talalay. So, I took this conference call, we chatted for a bit, and then I said to them, 'Okay, listen, I finish here on Friday morning, but I'm not supposed to travel home to LA until Saturday. If you change my ticket I will go straight from wrapping to the airport and you guys can pick me up.' And so, I met them in Beverly Hills, and we chatted further. Then I ended up meeting the director, Chuck Russell, on that Saturday afternoon because they were on night shoots that first week for some bizarre reason. Then I didn't hear anything until late Sunday evening, which is when I got hired, and I went to work on Monday night; that was when I first met Roy. We were shooting out in an area of Los Angeles called Sunland which had this big car dump, basically a wrecking yard, and we had to do all this stuff with the famous actor John Saxon and with Freddy. We had a lot going on that night, I was like, 'Oh, my God!' I had never heard of Roy before this night; I didn't know anybody on the project except for the woman who called me, Rebecca. They fired everybody on the Friday night: the cameraman, camera crew, grip, electric, and assistant directors—they were all let go. So, this new group started on Monday, and I was literally in the dark. I hadn't even read the script because I had been gone for fifteen weeks and I hadn't been home, and I was married at the time. I should never have taken the job after being gone for so long. It was my naïve loyalty. My father once said to me when I went to work on *All the President's Men*,

'Remember, there's no loyalty in this business. So just keep your eyes and ears open, your mouth shut, and just do your job.' And that has carried me through to this day. I've helped so many other people in this business and I don't get a Christmas card from them. That's fine. I've had a decent career; I've been able to put a couple of kids through school and whatnot. But when I took the job on *A Nightmare on Elm Street 3* I figured I could get through the first couple days and redo their board, figure out what was going on and what wasn't going on."

"I knew that they couldn't bullshit Dennis," Roy says, "A lot of times these studio people and producers will try to bullshit you and bully you, but they knew they couldn't do that with Dennis. He drew the line in the sand from the very first night. He saved my ass that night because I had a brand-new crew. I fired all the other crew because I said, 'No, I'm not working with any of those people.' When I got to that junkyard, they didn't even have any cable run. Nothing had been done. But Dennis gave me the time to do it and I got the whole place lit. Dennis trusted me enough to let me get that first setup. But, boy, that was a tough one."

"I found out on the very first night what their problem was," Maguire recalls, "and that was Chuck Russell. But the thing is that he *was* the project; he had written it with Frank Darabont, who turned out to be a huge success himself. So, the whole idea of this project for me was just to get it done in a very limited amount of time for what they were trying to accomplish every day. Another thing was that they had a very young, inexperienced group of people working on it. And this was New Line's biggest film to date, costing them $4 million. And it was their

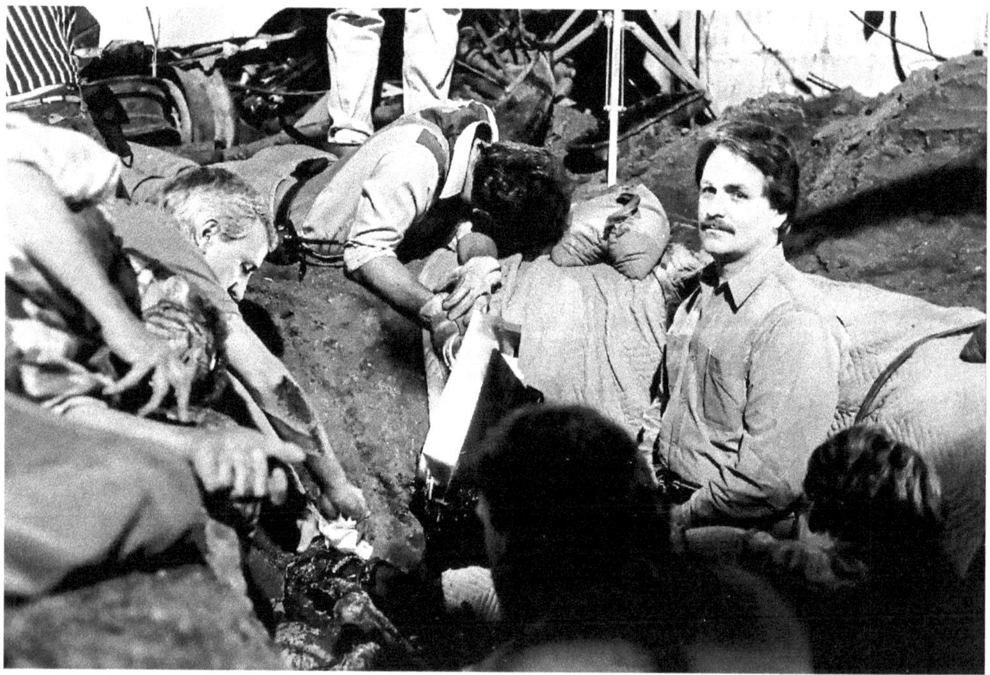

Roy deep in the Hollywood trenches on *A Nightmare on Elm Street 3: Dream Warriors*, 1987.

first time dealing with a DGA [Directors Guild of America] director, meaning Chuck wasn't somebody that they could push around because he had the DGA behind him and he also had written it. New Line wasn't used to that; they were used to making their little films and being able to do what they wanted and however they wanted to do it. But this film was a step up for them, and there were risks involved. So, I was shocked that night when I came in and saw how they were doing things. Chuck had never done anything of that stature yet, but Roy and I had a lot of experience, so we would say, 'Okay, we've got X number of shots to go...' because a lot of times Chuck didn't know what the coverage was, but Roy and I did. There were times when Chuck would want stuff that was not needed and I would have to step in and say, 'You don't want it and you don't need it,' and he didn't like that. We were in this screening place in the Olympic and Bundy area one night watching dailies and afterwards he asked to speak to me. He backed me into a corner, and he had a little hissy fit. He started to go off and act like he was a tough guy. And I just put my hand up and I said, 'You know what, Chuck, let's go back in and tell Niki and Rachel that they need a new assistant director tomorrow. I'm more than happy to go home if you're unhappy. I don't need this job. I'm here to help Rebecca. So, good luck!' He never had anybody ever do that to him, so he was in shock. Then he backed away. After that I knew he didn't have the guts to fire me. And from there on I just basically said, 'We're here, and then we're there. No buts. This is how you're going to make your days: you have got X amount of time to do this and X amount of time to do that. And we're going to march through these days. No more 16- or 18-hour days.'"

Maguire continues, admitting, "I didn't know Bob Shaye until that movie, I didn't know New Line. I didn't even know who Freddy was! On my first night in that junkyard, I was calling for the guy in the hockey mask, because I heard he was in makeup; I'm like, 'Put the hockey mask on him and get him out here!' And that pissed off everybody because that's Jason [from *Friday the 13th*], you know, big fucking deal! When I eventually read the script I found out who Freddy is, and I found the script kind of interesting. The horror genre was nothing I was familiar with. I was the nerd that would take high school friends to the theater on Wilshire Boulevard where they showed foreign films. That was my background. I was fortunate to have grown up on sets with A-list directors like Robert Wise and Elia Kazan, but I just felt responsible on the business side of filmmaking to get this done in a reasonable amount of time. It was imperative of me to allow Chuck to get stuff on film but also to control him; otherwise he would have just gone on and on and on. If we failed, New Line would have fired us because it would have been their only other recourse. I was always honest and respectful with the producers; I never bullshitted them like Chuck did. I gave them my opinion, as I've always done with hifalutin producers like Jerry Weintraub or Ed Feldman. You just tell them the truth. The smart ones know that the young guy is giving you the truth. He's not protecting the director. He's not out for himself. I was on their side. We were responsible to production and trying to be responsible to a director who was a first timer and who thought he knew more than he did; he had been used to pushing everybody around on the first week, but when he met us we were there going, 'Wait a second! No. The reality is that this is how you do it. We're going to be here, and while we're here, Roy's grip and electric are over there working also. And besides they're already lit here, so they're going to be over there pre-lighting and getting other things ready. We're not going to go over there standing around watching people work. This is how it works with the big boys, and we have got to be responsible.'"

Having someone of Maguire's discipline and experience meant an ally for Roy. Together they would get through the grueling shoot with some perseverance and a little laughter along the way. "Dennis and I didn't know each other," Roy affirms, "but I had been taught—and I know Dennis had been taught this too— that the relationship between a cinematographer and an assistant director is sacrosanct; you are both each other's best friend. And I think the way we survived that film was by becoming friends, and realizing we were there to protect each other and to get through this. That is so critical. A lot of young filmmakers don't realize how incredibly important the assistant director is. They are part of all the meetings with the cinematographer, the production designer, and so on because we're going to be saying things that are going to affect how he moves the company forward, including how much money things are going to cost. Dennis and I learned with the old tough guys, and they didn't put up with any bullshit, they knew exactly how to accomplish what they needed to. Our having grown up in the

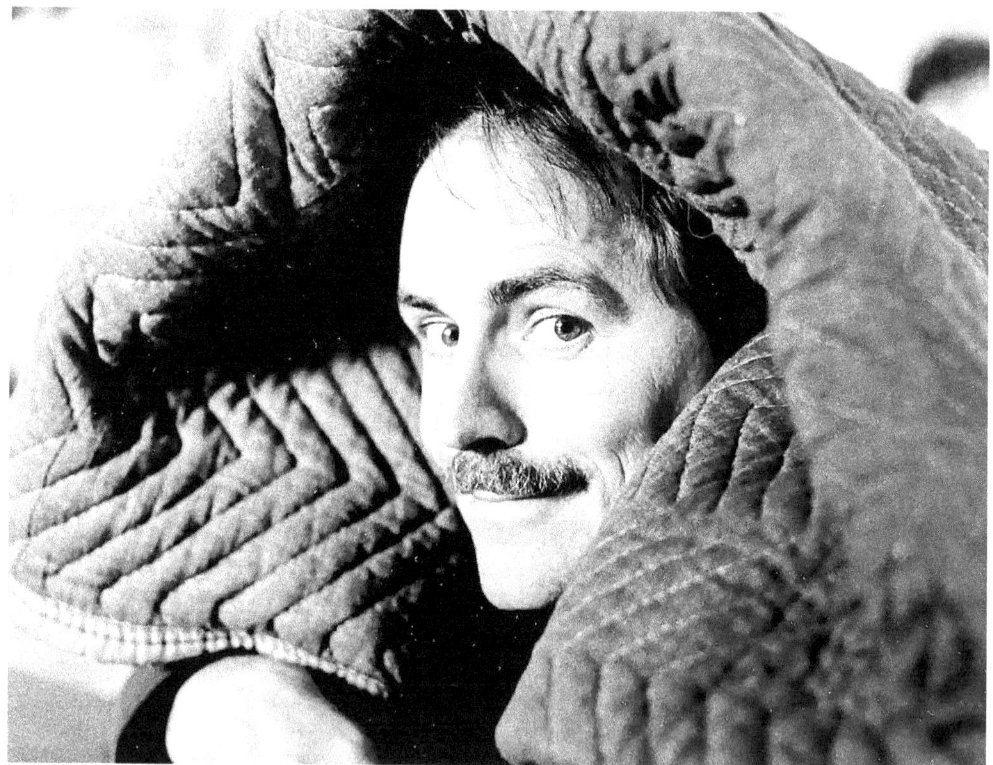

Roy covering up on the first night of shooting *A Nightmare on Elm Street 3: Dream Warriors,* **wondering, "What the hell have I gotten myself into?"**

studio system meant that we watched the old studio heads dealing with cinematographers and assistant directors, and we got to see them when they were all off the set. They were friends, they would do anything for each other, but as long as they were on set, it was their way and that was that. I heard Dennis say 'We gotta go, we gotta move!' many, many times. Dennis has had to be the tough guy, the guy that everybody loves to hate. But at the end of the movie, people walk away from it alive and safe, and the studio is happy. He has an incredible legacy; his father was an extraordinary assistant director and then a producer, so Dennis was sought out by every studio in the world. This is the legacy that I got to have on the first night of *A Nightmare on Elm Street 3*; I saw that this guy was the real deal. And he was a real partner. I knew I was safe with Dennis there. I knew the director wouldn't protect me; Rachel had hired me, but I knew she wouldn't protect me either. I knew that Dennis would protect me and that I would get through it based upon our relationship. Dennis was my coach; he was the guy telling me what needs to be done to get the day done. If you take offence, it's like taking offence to the guy next to you that's got a gun and is telling you to get out of the foxhole. If you are going to get into a foxhole in a war, your buddy is not the guy that's nice to you—he is the guy next to you saying, 'Watch out, look out, be careful.' And they may be shouting at you; they may be doing it unpleasantly. Hollywood has gotten to the point where everybody's got to be nice to each other. Everybody's got to be everybody's best friend. You've got to say all the right stuff to each other. Well, there were times when Dennis chewed my ass out, and the truth is that he was right. Absolutely right. And that is critical that you have that kind of partnership because it's like a marriage; you either survive or you don't. I'm astonished that I survived that film. It was a mess. But Dennis helped me survive it."

For Maguire, the feeling was mutual: "Having a DP like Roy there as a friend and ally meant I could say, 'Listen, this director is in trouble. We've got so much work to do. How can we help him help himself and get through this day? Because they don't want to fall behind anymore.' That's why everybody got fired in the first place. We had to reshoot 90 percent of what they shot the first week. Me and Roy being a team on the set made New Line like us, because we were getting them back on schedule. There were times when I had my doubts about what would work because of what I had seen leading up to it. The first time that the snake, or should I say that big dick, goes through the room and crashes through it, I had my doubts. There was always going to be the first fail, so I knew what Roy and I were going to do; I said, 'Okay, if this fails we're going to go over here and do something else and not lose time. We'll let them re-rig it, they've already got their sort of rehearsal—but they should have really rehearsed beforehand. And sure enough, it failed, so then me and Roy just looked at each other and said, 'Okay, we're going over here,' while Chuck was busy being Chuck. I did get in trouble with Rachel one time over a mechanical baby that cost a lot of money—something like $10,000—that was supposed to be in this film that we didn't use. The baby was articulated, and it took a couple of guys to run it. Chuck saw me looking at it one day and asked, 'What's wrong?' and I said, 'I don't know, Chuck, I think this is stepping over the line. I mean, a baby?' And unbeknownst to me, Chuck thought about it that night and then he went to Rachel and New Line and said, 'I'm going to cut it.' Rachel then found out that it was me who put a bug in his ear, and I said, 'I'm sorry, Rachel, but you can't blame me for this; ultimately, it's not my decision. Let's shoot it! If you use it, you use it; if you don't, you don't. It's built and ready to go.' But we didn't use it."

Having worked with some of the best cinematographers in the business, and his father having worked with legendary cinematographers, Maguire shares what he considers to be the common characteristics among those successful professionals: "It is the ability to understand exactly what a director—whether he's a first timer or an old pro—wants in a certain amount of time. When the director says what he wants and goes and sits back down in his chair, that DP goes and gets the work done. I mean, yeah, I've seen guys jerk around for hours lighting and at the end of the day you're going, 'What was the point of that?' The cost of that was the two or three other shots that should have been done that day. The key is if you're working with a DP who is on your side, he'll do whatever you want. John Seale was the cinematographer on a film I worked on in 1991 called *The Doctor* and he had been a very successful camera operator and then cinematographer. John's credits are unbelievably amazing. One day shooting that film we were on location at a real hospital in downtown LA, and we picked that location because we could be lit by the sun all day, but we got to the point when the sun was setting. Bill Hurt was the star of the film, and he was hung up whining about the script and the scene, and he was just beating up the director. So, I went to John and said, 'I guess I'm in trouble. I have to go to the producers and find out if we can come back another day." And he said, 'No, we don't want to come back here. Do we?' I go, 'Well, I don't want to come back here. But what are you going to do?' and he said, 'See if you can get me into a couple of those rooms down that other wing. If you do, I can make this work.' And I did, and he saved production; he saved my butt. We went a bit overtime, but I told the UPM it was better to bite the bullet and pay for the overtime, and to either charge it to Bill Hurt or call it a Bill Hurt overage. And we got it done because John understood the ramifications of production and what we can do and can't do. That doesn't always happen, because there are a lot some guys out there who will just say, 'Well, that's your problem, kid; now fuck off and leave me alone.'"

"To be honest, people like that don't have a very long career," Roy says. "It's very important if an assistant director comes up to you with a schedule and he is saying, 'I think we could flip this around and shoot this today instead of tomorrow.' There's a leap of faith that you must have in that moment. You can understand what he is saying and trust that this guy knows what he is talking about, and you can say, 'Okay, I will find a way of making this work.' My mentor Harry Stradling told me if you can't light a closeup in five minutes then you can't be a cameraman. That's how I learned to be fast. It is all about the support of all your partners. You are the one that makes a decision ultimately, but the truth is that there has been a countless number of times when I've been willing to go the opposite direction because I've had someone say, 'All right, don't do that. Do this instead. This is why I think we should do it...' And if you're smart you will listen.

The key to being successful in this business is fucking listening to people. You can be a master artist all you want but it doesn't mean a thing."

"The benefit of having Roy on that set was that artistically it gave Chuck such a great-looking movie on a shoestring budget," Maguire says. "Roy knew we had X amount of time and we had to keep this going, while also having to appease this guy and educate him on how it's all really done. And it's not like we had a massive crew either. I would have Roy shoot normal scenes and then have him running to the other part of the warehouse where we had this 40-foot by 60-foot blue screen and get him to shoot massive visual effects sequences. You must remember that they didn't give Roy an operator on this film. Everyone in that world back then always said, 'Oh, we'll get a DP-operator.' But they forget that while he is out there lighting, there's nobody on the camera saying, 'Keep that flag back a foot,' or 'Keep that light out, it's buzzing the lens,' all those kinds of things. So, not only would Roy have to light the set, but he'd have to operate at the same time. And I've always found that it doesn't save me time. I don't think it's a timesaver to have a DP who also operates, but other people do. However, with Roy it wasn't as big of a drawback because of his experience and knowing the frame well enough to say, 'Okay, the left side of the frame is over here, the right side is here.' So with Roy you don't start off by putting lights and flags in the frame and then moving everything back and reading the light. That was a plus. But every day was tough making that movie. I don't remember going in there on any day and getting to shoot an eighth of a page; every day there was massive stuff having to go on."

"The thing is that if you're on the camera then you can't be with the director," Roy states, "and you can't be with the script supervisor, and with all those people, the heavy breathers that are whispering things back and forth to the director; you don't hear that stuff because all you hear is the camera running. If you get a talented camera operator, then they can help you with the director; they can help you with all the superfluous things. They want to be who you are someday, so they're trying to make sure that they please you as much as they want to please themselves. So, if you get a great operator, they will do that job while I'm doing my job, which is to be with the director. My job is to be a partner with the assistant director and the director, to be part of that team; it's not to point the camera. I mean, that's the simplest job; being a camera operator is the best job on the movie set. But if you're the director of photography and the camera operator at the same time, then that is a different thing. I was never away from the camera on *Dream Warriors.* I would get home at night after twenty-one hours on set because I would go off to do the second unit after the first unit stuff. I would come home at night exhausted. Thank God I was young, but I was worn out and beaten up. I used to fall asleep on the camera because I would see that flickering image all the time. Those cameras had the mirror shutter, and I would see this hypnotic, repeatable flicker all the time. It would hypnotize you. So, I just don't agree with anybody who says that they are better for having been a DP-operator."

"I was trying to only give Roy like twenty-minute setups," Maguire says, "I mean, it just was like, 'we've got to get this done!' So, is it better to have it and then color correct things in post or to not get it at all? I didn't know anybody, and I just felt responsible for helping get a picture that was obviously going off the rails back on track, but you need everybody to be willing to do the work. Our lead girl, Patricia Arquette, was a pain in the ass. Roy was trying to be really nice and ask her about hitting a mark and all this stuff, and she made some crack at him, so I just stepped up and I said, 'Listen, here's the deal: if you don't want to be in the movie, don't hit the mark. You'll be in the dark. Your family won't see you. It's okay. I think at the end of the day, when the cameraman is asking you to help him light you, you should listen.' It took her a bit, but she got it. She was just being that young wannabe movie star and it's like, 'You're not the star here, Freddy is the star; Robert Englund is the star.' I didn't get to know Robert very well, but from what little interaction I had with him I think he had a good personality. He came to work every day and was never angry at anybody. I never saw him blow up or lose patience with anybody. But he was the star of that show."

"I have gotten hired again so many times because of a relationship with an assistant director, or a production manager," Roy says. "To me, if you can find that kind of partnership, then that's better than a marriage ... because there's no lawyers involved. Dennis and I haven't worked together for years and we're still friends. I would do anything for him because he was there when I needed him. It's critically important that we build relationships and that we understand the value of each other. It is very important that people understand how critically important bonds and relationships are in this business. Everything to me is like a scrapbook. I've done some crappy movies that people love and which I hate. But I look at the relationships that were made or which were developed on those productions; that is everything to me. If you mention *Return to Horror High* I think of the director, Bill Froehlich, who I love. When I think of *Witchboard* I think of the fun I had with my crew. We were up in Big Bear, and it was fucking crazy. It was basically a bunch of high school kids going out and making a movie. And we had Robin Oliver as our assistant director, who was Dennis's second A.D. on *A Nightmare on Elm Street 3*. I was so happy when I saw Robin on the set because we had such a good time on *Witchboard*. Dennis and Robin were both moving the company along. They were the ones who would come to you and say, 'we got a problem here...' If an assistant director has a great second assistant director, then you're made. Because they're protecting you. They're protecting production. And they see where all the dark dirty stuff is because they hear everything that's going on. Dennis and I used to have our names scratched and scribbled on the walls in every bathroom on *A Nightmare on Elm Street 3*, because we were the bad guys, the guys who came in and took over. But if you have a good team behind you, they can't do anything to you. So, if you hear me talking, I'm not talking about the movie. I'm not talking about the setups. I'm not talking about the lighting; I am talking about the relationships."

"That is how we got our jobs in the industry," Maguire says, "there was no IMDb, there were no fax machines, no cell phones; it was people. It was having an A-list first A.D., or when I was younger, an A-list key second, recommend you to someone when they called up saying they need somebody. It was all word of mouth. A lot of times you didn't even meet beforehand. When I was a P.A. I would

get called at nine at night from somebody introducing themselves and saying they
got my name from so-and-so....

'Are you working?'

'No.'

'Do you want to work?'

'Yes! When?'

'Tomorrow. Be at 6th and Spring in downtown LA at six o'clock in the morning.'

"And of course, I'd be there at 5 a.m. watching trucks get parked and looking
for a guy that was an assistant director type. I'd find him and say, 'Hi, I'm Dennis
Maguire. I'm the guy you spoke with on the phone last night,' and he would say
'Good! Find a camera truck, grab a walkie-talkie, I need you now.' That was how
it worked. It wasn't interviews; it was a phone call—'We need you now.' We would
get hired and just help get these movies made to the best of our ability. It was like
going to war. When I look back upon my time working with Roy on *A Nightmare
on Elm Street 3*, I'm just amazed at his ability to manage a film that was so out of
control. He made my job easier because I knew that he and I could get through
a day with a difficult situation, with a crew that maybe didn't like us, and I'm not
talking about the camera, grip, and electric guys, but the art department and special effects people that looked at us as the bad guys because their friends got fired.
But they got fired because they weren't good. I'm sorry about that, but we're just
here to do a job; they needed to raise their game because we were coming at it
from a certain level. And yeah, we expected a lot, we pushed people to get the
work done. And at the end of the day, I couldn't have done it without Roy, because
Roy controls so much of the film crew. So having somebody that's not out to fuck
me and who is not slow is always a benefit."

Despite the troubled production, *A Nightmare on Elm Street 3: Dream Warriors* has endured to become a classic in both the horror genre and within the context of the Elm Street franchise. Almost four decades after its theatrical release,
the film is lauded by both critics and fans as a sequel of rare quality, and one to
rival Wes Craven's lauded original. The film's thematic depth, with its psychological and sociological subtexts, allows for deeper engagements with the film
on an intellectual level, while its greater budget meant more elaborate, fantastical special effects, thus giving the film the feel of a grander cinematic experience.
That successful balancing of horror, fantasy, and darkly comedic elements must
be attributed to Chuck Russell's contribution to the final script and ultimately his
direction, as Wes Craven's original version of the screenplay was, in a style typical
of the horror maestro, much darker and abstract.

Roy recalls Craven's vision for the film:

"Wes Craven's script had no humor at all; he was a very serious man, an intellectual. However, Chuck brought this dark sense of humor of his which kind of
helped; it's a very sardonic sense of humor and he sees the funniest things in the
oddest places. Had we filmed Wes's script it would have ended up a very different picture. I love the film *Carnival of Souls* and I think Wes used that as a kind
of benchmark for his original *Nightmare* film, the idea of this awful decadence
of not really knowing what's real and what's not real, and the interesting thing

is that Herk Harvey knew as little about making films as Wes but their art, what they wanted to put on film, was in their soul and they were able to communicate that into their work, respectively. It would have been interesting to see what Wes would have done with a big budget *Nightmare* film. The tragedy about Wes is he never got to go as far as he could have gone, or should have gone, because he had the *Nightmare* baggage to carry throughout his whole career. That happens a lot; I knew Tobe Hooper and, similarly to Wes, I don't think he ever lived up to his first film because other people got involved and pressured him into doing certain things he really didn't want to do. If you look at *Poltergeist*, it wasn't really his film. This I know from having spent a lot of time talking with Tobe. Ultimately, *Dream Warriors* worked because of the humor that some of those other writers and Robert Englund injected into it. It meant you could laugh at somebody that you're afraid of. They ended up going way too far with that stuff in the later films and in pop culture. But I've always said that there is a thematic similarity between comedy and horror, and I think *Dream Warriors* was one of the first films to really use that—obviously there were the Abbott and Costello movies but I'm talking about using real horror and scary things while having a sense of humor. There are things in there which I still think are scary. But those who really made that film work were Bruce [Wagner], Frank [Darabont], and Niki [Marvin]—they are the ones who really made that script. Bruce was just this fucking dark guy, darker than Hell but with a great sense of humor; he brought the dark side of everything and that was needed, it needed a decadent, demented element—things like teasing the junkie with the needles on Freddy's fingers."

Roy continues, "Frank was a talented writer as well, but the best lines in that movie came from Robert Englund—Robert came up with 'Welcome to Prime

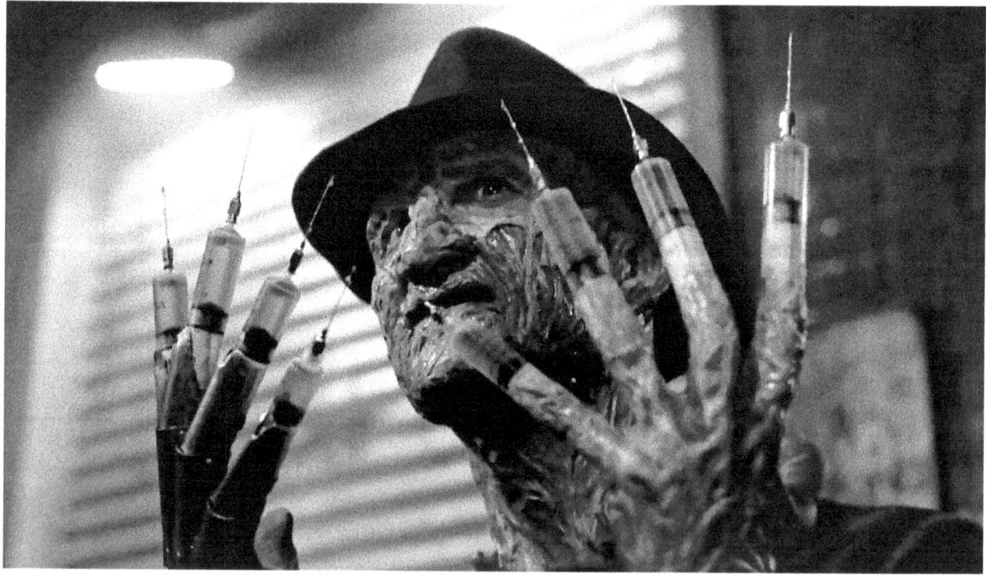

Freddy Krueger (Robert Englund) teases his junkie victim in *A Nightmare on Elm Street 3: Dream Warriors.*

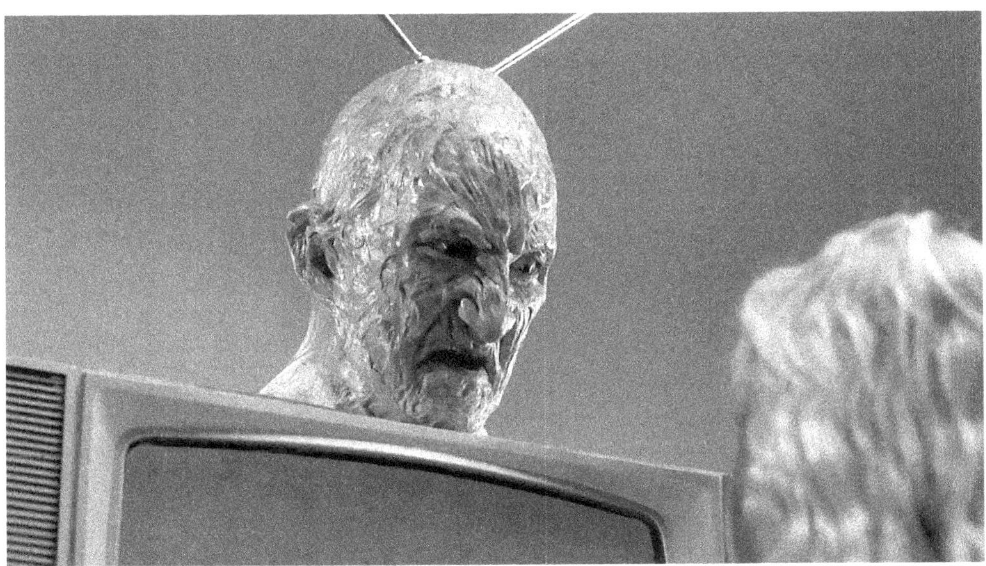

"Welcome to Prime Time, Bitch!" Freddy delivers the memorable one-liner, improvised by Robert Englund, in *A Nightmare on Elm Street 3: Dream Warriors*.

Time, Bitch!' on the set; that was not in the script. The funny thing about Robert is he came to it like a movie star. He walked into the set and wanted to know where his marks were and he did his work. I never saw any backstage issues with him at all. I've worked on other shows, which have massive problems with movie stars because they don't think they're getting enough recognition. I always say that this industry fails from the top down, never fails from the bottom up. However, the success in getting *A Nightmare on Elm Street 3* made is down to Niki Marvin—she was really the secret ingredient for that film, and by extension the secret ingredient to *The Shawshank Redemption* because she is the one who got Frank

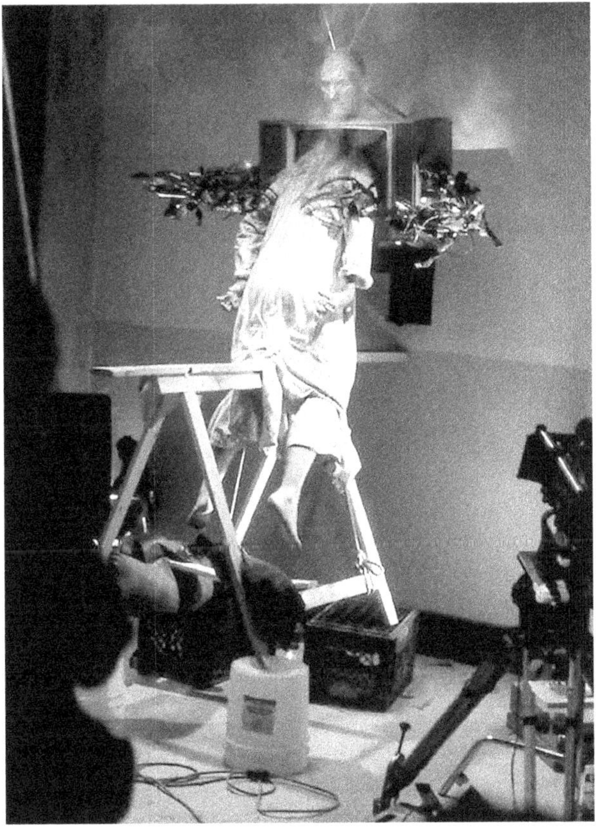

Behind the scenes of the classic scene in *A Nightmare on Elm Street 3: Dream Warriors*.

Darabont to write it; she was the producer on that and if it hadn't been for her, who knows how Frank's career would have gone. That film was a big deal for him. Niki was fucking smart; she was British and had worked for the BBC. Whenever we couldn't solve a problem we would go to her, and she would solve it; there was nothing she couldn't figure out. Dennis and I went to her countless times."

As *A Nightmare on Elm Street 3* made a significant impact at the box office, it was only natural that further sequels would be swiftly put into production. Bob Shaye realized the potential of his new cash cow and duly made sure that Freddy Krueger and the Elm Street brand made its presence felt in every facet of pop culture: music, television, toys, clothing, etc. As Freddy-mania reached its peak in the late-eighties, Shaye became a formidable player in Hollywood, and New Line Cinema became colloquially known as "The House That Freddy Built" as it ascended the film industry to become a mini major studio to be reckoned with. An assistant director of much experience, Maguire was more than aware of the risks that New Line Cinema was taking with their first big budget effort:

"The first film was like $1.1 million, the second one was around $2.5 million, and then all of a sudden they leaped up to $4 million. For New Line to spend that much money to make this movie they were probably mortgaged to the hilt. So, it was a stressful environment and I didn't feel like it was going to be a commercial steppingstone for the franchise. Roy maybe felt it more than I would because I was so disassociated with the horror genre. I thought we were delivering something which was going to be okay for what it was, but I had no idea what it was going to become. There were lines going around the block at theaters in Westwood on opening weekend, and that was a big deal. Then I saw on the news that it had taken $10 million on opening night which was huge back then; it was a big deal to open like that—it's about $30 million in today's money. I remember receiving a delivery from New Line which contained a bottle of Dom Perignon and a VHS tape of the film, thanking me because I was one of two key people who helped get that film made. The success of the film led to more sequels and helped New Line become a mini major, but that's probably what hurt them. They went to a level that they probably should not have; they should have stayed in their lane. Bob Shaye only came by a couple of times on *Nightmare 3,* but I worked for him again after when I did a movie called *Torch Song Trilogy,* which was based on a very famous play that was written by Harvey Fierstein and which starred a very young Matthew Broderick. New Line produced a film version of it that came out in 1988, and I worked on that. So, I met Bob Shaye again and he was happy to see me in New York; in fact, he was very kind to me in front of a lot of people, he said nice things that he didn't have to. I thought that was generous of him."

"New Line were kind of desperate when we were making *A Nightmare on Elm Street 3,*" Roy recalls. "They were terrified that this was their last chance to make something good and something that would sell. They couldn't rest on the fact that they had a hit with the first Nightmare movie because they blew it with *A Nightmare on Elm Street 2.* They realized the errors that they made with that film by making it too bright and making Freddy too visible, so [production manager] Gerry Olson was constantly telling me he wanted it darker. They didn't want to see Freddy because they showed too much of him in the previous film. I've always been considered a dark cinematographer, so telling me to be darker is kind of dangerous. So, I made it darker."

"Roy wasn't afraid of the dark," says gaffer Brian Crane. "*A Nightmare on Elm Street 3* was such a funky film, and I only worked with Roy on it briefly, but I saw how obsessive and precise was. I remember Roy's first night on the job, which is in that car junk yard, and he was running around the entire night; he would be like, 'Get a light over here, get a light over there! Give me a PAR in here!' and this type of thing. Having Roy around was a big difference from earlier on in the show when it was a different camera crew and cinematographer. Prior to Roy joining the production, it seemed as if we would set a light, move it, put all the diffusion in front of it, and then there would be nothing happening for a little bit. But when Roy came on, things started moving and instantly the set became more dynamic. He was 100% involved in every aspect, and that is not just so he gets his fingers into every piece of it, but so that he can help make a better film. I've seen him take some very low-budget things and turn them into masterpieces compared to what they could have been. And even after shooting we would go and watch dailies and do color timing. So even though my day was fourteen hours on set, there would be another two hours with Roy color timing or whatnot. I can't tell you how many a director's ass he has saved, how many productions he saved, bringing them in on time and helping rearrange the schedule to make deadlines. *A Nightmare on Elm Street 3* was one of those."

"That movie would not have been made if it hadn't been for Dennis and me," Roy admits, "It just wouldn't have. It was survival of the fittest, and it was a struggle. I started out on big features with my mentors, and I also had a lot

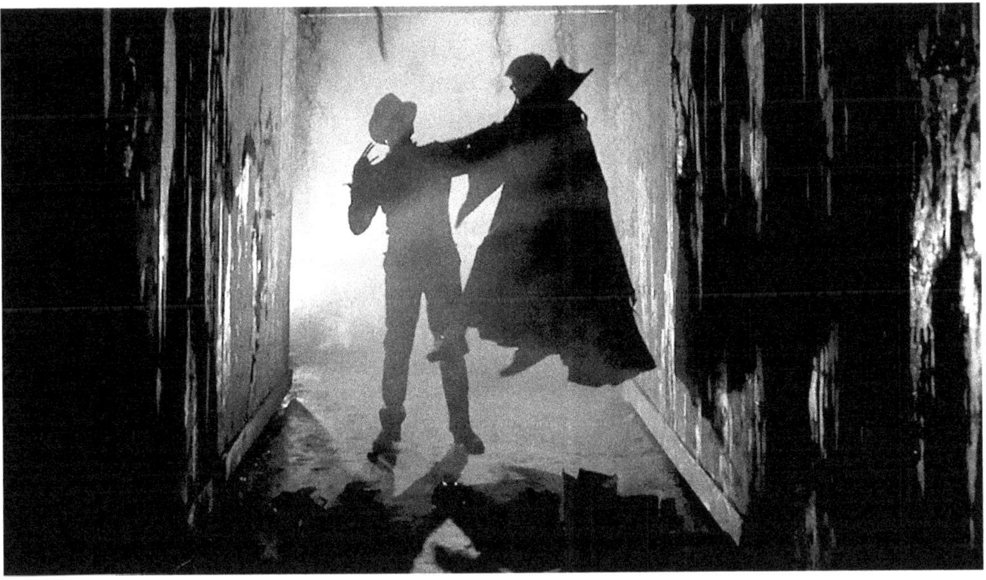

Roy put Freddy (Robert Englund) back into the shadows for *A Nightmare on Elm Street 3: Dream Warriors*. Also pictured: Ira Heiden as Will Stanton.

of experience on low-budget productions, so I was familiar with how both sides of Hollywood worked. Dennis was a studio kid, and he knew how it was really done. The training and experience that we had saved that film, and it became very successful. A lot of people involved in it went on to have great careers. It not only kept the Elm Street franchise going but it made New Line Cinema a very powerful studio; after that film they became a mini major. They started out with films like *Pink Flamingos* and all that kind of crap, but they went on to make arthouse films and big commercial movies like *Lord of the Rings*, which made a huge amount of money and won many Academy awards. Bob Shaye put out some really low-budget cheesy stuff early on, but he was wise enough to surround himself with the right people who helped steer the company in the right direction. I mean, Sara Risher was an extraordinary, valuable resource to Bob. She was the class act. Bob could scream and yell and be crass, but Sara was really a very decent and kind person."

"I haven't watched *Dream Warriors* in years," Maguire admits, "but I remember seeing it for the first time and going 'Wow!' When you're filming you don't know how it is going to turn out, but then I saw it on a big screen in the movie theater and the visuals just blew me away. Roy really gave it a great look and that was a contributing factor to its success. For that genre it was very good, and it shows because today everybody talks about the first one and the third one. The diehard fans went nuts about it. It was after *Dream Warriors* came out that they started selling Freddy Krueger costumes for Halloween. The first two triggered that but it was after the third one came out when everyone went, 'We should be Freddy for Halloween!' The thing I remember the most about it is that Roy and I laughed, despite them all. And I think that drove people crazy, because we made our fun, even though there were times when I just wanted to throw my hands up and say, 'Fuck it! I don't need this. I don't need the money, the grief, or the aggravation.' But I was responsible, and I was committed to the show, and I stayed on it, so at the end of the day, I hope I made a decent film."

"The release of *A Nightmare on Elm Street 3* was a significant moment for me," Roy says, "because after thirteen years of busting my ass doing crappy ninja films and starting on terrible low-budget horror films that never got finished, I now had three movies in the theater simultaneously. On the weekend that *A Nightmare on Elm Street 3* opened the theaters were also showing *Witchboard* and *No Man's Land*—the Charlie Sheen film that I shot second unit on. So, I had three films that I shot on release at the same time. That meant I was considered 'successful,' even if I didn't necessarily feel like I was. It was only when someone whom I admired greatly said it that I felt some kind of achievement: around this time Billy Fraker spoke at the AFI [American Film Institute] and a kid in the audience asked him who are the upcoming cinematographers to look out for, and Billy said, 'Roy Wagner.' When I heard this, I thought, 'I'm no different a person from before he said that,' but because Billy Fraker said it, that meant that now I'm somebody—now I'm a bigshot."

Burglars, Beasts,
and the Beauty
of Second Unit

William Fraker's words at the AFI were not just paying lip service to a trending young cinematographer who was making his stamp in the industry, for the eminent Fraker showcased Roy's work to the world when he hired him as the second unit director of photography on the Whoopi Goldberg action comedy *Burglar*. The film was directed by Hugh Wilson, who created the successful CBS sitcom *WKPR in Cincinnati* and wrote and directed the first entry of the massively popular *Police Academy* franchise. Set in photographically friendly San Francisco, Goldberg plays Bernice "Bernie" Rhodenbarr, a retired thief forced back into the criminal life upon being blackmailed by retired policeman Ray Kirschman (G.W. Bailey). Once back to burgling, Bernice becomes embroiled in a contrived murder plot involving a dentist trying to retrieve valuable jewelry from her ex-husband's apartment, and she ends up becoming not only a witness to murder but the chief suspect in such.

After a decade toiling in the low-budget independent film realm, this was a change of scenery for Roy: a high profile, big budget studio film, working with the best crew people money could buy. And it shows onscreen. The film is beautifully framed by Fraker, who memorably photographed the likes of *Bullitt* (Peter Yates, 1968), *Looking for Mr. Goodbar* (Richard Brooks, 1977), and *Sharky's Machine* (Burt Reynolds, 1981), and he brought Roy onto the production of *Burglar* to shoot the intricate downtown chase sequence, which is in its own way a nod to Fraker's noted work on *Bullitt*. Roy recalls filming on the vertiginous streets of San Francisco:

"I'm really proud of *Burglar*. I was so happy to be there, and Billy [Fraker] really protected me. It was thanks to him that I worked on this movie; he made all that happen because he recommended me to Jim Arnett, who was the second unit director. This was a big Warner Bros. movie, so we had lots of time on that movie; there was no pressure whatsoever. It was great fun shooting the chase scene, even though there were a couple of close calls. Debbie Evans was Whoopi's stunt double and when she performed the big bike leap she couldn't stop the bike when it landed, so she ended up tumbling all the way down the hill and got a concussion. Thank God it wasn't worse than that. Debbie went on to do *The Matrix* and has done a lot of bike work in movies. There were some great car stunts as well, so we put the cameras in some interesting places. The shots from the view of the cars came by way of my key grip, Al LaVerde, who had been the key grip on *The Dukes of Hazzard* series. He had these mounts that he could put on the sides of cars, but they never jumped them like this before. So, I had them re-manufactured and we did a bunch of jumps with these mounts on the side of the cars. The best one we did was when they tore open the inside of the car and put a front surface mirror underneath it and pointed the camera straight down so that when the car jumps off the road you can literally see the wheels, you can see the city in the background, and you can see when the car comes down. Everybody was applauding when they saw that shot."

Roy continues, "One day Jim Arnett said to me, 'We're doing this big car crash, but we don't have a crane. The only crane that's available is the one Fraker has on the first unit, and he won't let us have it. You need to go talk to him about that.' So, I went to Billy and said, 'Billy, is it possible for us to borrow your Chapman Titan crane for a day to do this stuff?' He agreed to give it to us on the condition that we had to return it the next day. I went back to Jim and told him what Fraker told me, and he said, 'Oh yeah, no problem. We'll get it back to him the

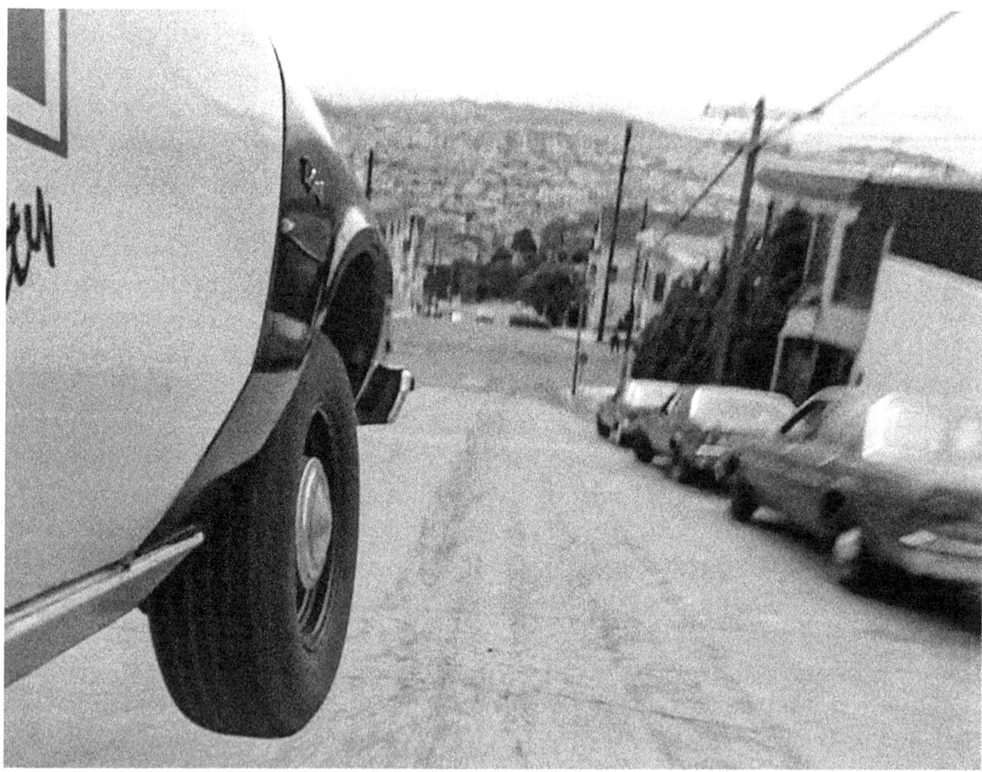

The unique framing of Roy's second unit work on *Burglar,* 1987.

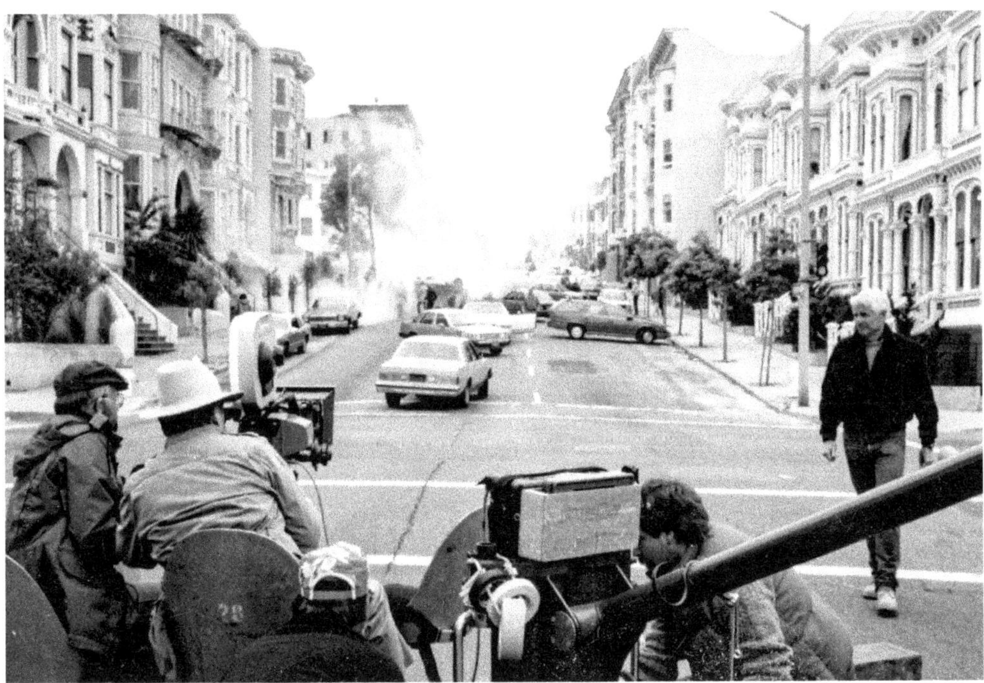

Shooting *Burglar.* From left: 1st A.D. Richard Meinardus, Roy, key grip Jon Gutteres, second unit director Jim Arnett.

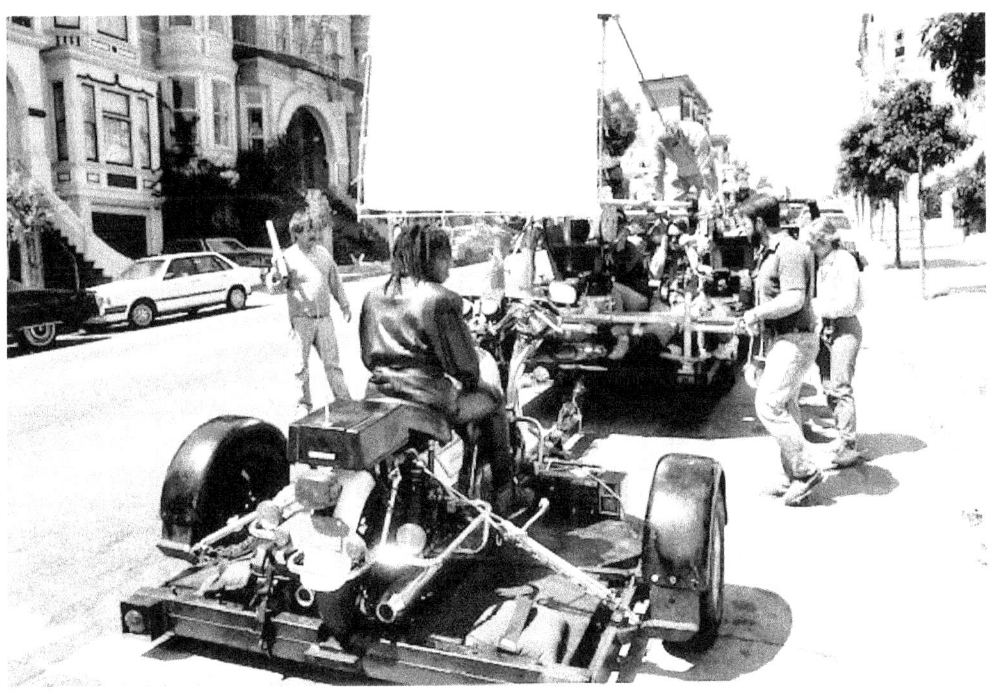

Whoopi is ready for her closeup on the chase scene of *Burglar.*

next day.' So, we got the crane, did this big stunt, and it only took us the morning, it didn't take a whole day at all. It was the scene at the end where all the cars are crashing and Whoopi drives through it on the motorcycle and the crane rises; it's a cool shot, it was the first shot that Mike Benson did for me after my first camera operator was fired because the director hated him. So, I got a very good operator when Fraker recommended Mike Benson, with whom there was no bullshit. And I just trusted him. So, we got the shot on a Chapman Titan crane with a 150 millimeter lens on it, and once we cut I turned to the crane drivers and said, 'Okay, you can button up the crane and send it back now.' And Jim said, 'Why are you doing that?' I said, 'We promised Billy that we would get it back to him.' And he said, 'Fuck him. I'll talk to Fraker. He can

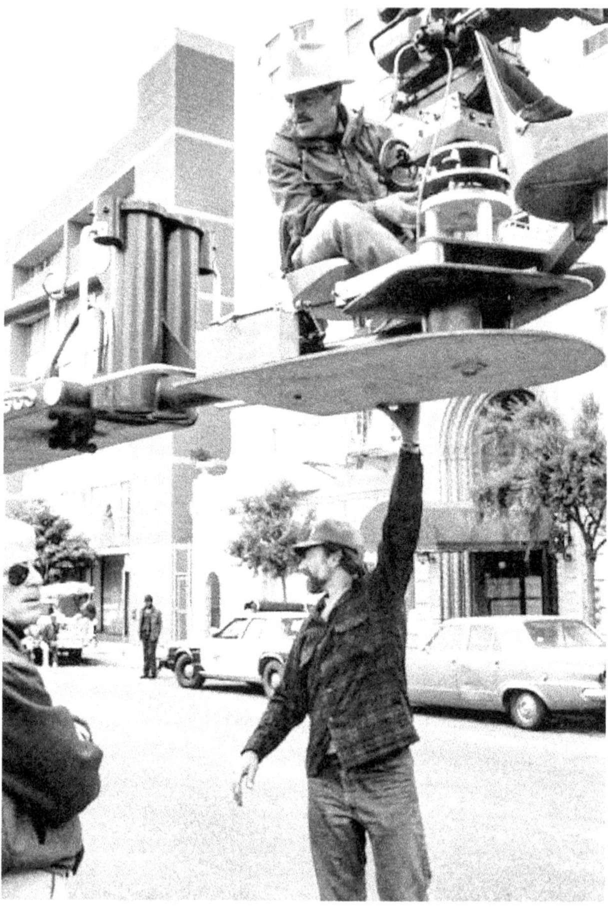

Roy converses with second unit director Jim Arnett (left) as he gets ready to roll on *Burglar*. John Guterres, key grip, is under Roy.

get it back as early as I want.' I just thought, 'Okay, all right. He's the director. He can do whatever he wants.' So, we kept the crane.

Later that evening we went to watch dailies and while we're sitting there in the dark I hear Billy Fraker coming in and he said, 'Where's that fucking Roy Wagner?' And now I'm thinking, 'Oh, God!' But it's okay because Jim Arnett is going to cover for me. But Billy is standing in silhouette in the doorway, and he says, 'Where are you, Roy? I want to talk to you.' This is a guy who helped me, but he could fire me in an instant. He comes in and says, 'You told me you were going to get the crane back to me. Why didn't you get it back?' And Arnett says, 'Billy. I told him he really should have got it back to you, but he wouldn't listen to me.' Are you kidding me?! And with that Arnett looked at me and winked. I'm like, 'Motherfucker ... you just destroyed me!' Fraker is there screaming and yelling at me in front of everybody, and then he sits down next to me, turns and gives me a giant wink, then puts his arm around me and says, 'Fuck you, Wagner.' It was all a horrible practical joke on me. But that was Billy. He could be tough on people. He was tough in a way that most of those old men were and that's the way they were all taught. And once they saw that you could put up with them, then they loved you. They would do anything for you. But that's the way it was for these guys, just bantering back and forth all the time. If you were sensitive, you didn't make it. Someone said to me that I was always an old man and I think that's the truth. I was raised by my father, but he died when he was fifty. So, I was raised by the Old Hollywood cameramen Joe Ruttenberg, Harry Stradling, and James Wong Howe. So, the first portion of my journey was to be the tough guy cinematographer. The old men were all tyrants and tough guys, and they were thought of as Gods at the studios. They were inscrutable. So, I tried to be like that, but it didn't work out too well because they weren't really tough guys, they thought they were, but it was an act; when you would go to the ASC, they sort of bluffed themselves, 'Well, I did this and that.' But that was not the way they really were. Russ Metty, 'Curly' Linden, Lenny South … if you ever got them alone, they were the nicest people, but on set they had this gruffness about them. I used to hang out with Leon Shamroy and he would scream at everybody on the set and then turn and wink at me like it was some big game. I thought, 'Oh, man, this is scary.' I never wanted to be a part of that."

Director John Badham, who hired Fraker for his 1983 tech thriller *War Games* and with whom Roy would work later in his career, got his start at Hollywood studios at the tail end of the Golden Age, and he clearly recalls the old man mentality that Roy refers to:

"They did have mean attitudes. It was hard to find one that was reasonably polite and fun to work with, like Al Edens. He was just a sweetheart. But [Lionel] 'Curly' Linden would bite your head off. That was all coming out of the pressure from production, from having to work so fast, especially in television. Back then they were doing one-hour shows in six days, and with much longer scripts than we do in a one-hour show now; they were doing 50 to 53–page scripts, whereas now we're doing like 42 to 45. And trying to do those 53 pages in six days meant there's no room for any error."

Roy's stellar work on *Burglar* was appreciated by Arnett, who also took him on to his next production, which was the Charlie Sheen film *No Man's Land*, a youth-oriented crime picture directed by Peter Werner and written by television legend Dick Wolf. Here, Sheen plays Ted Varrick, a yuppie criminal who deals in stolen high-end vehicles behind the façade of his Porsche auto garage. Ted befriends his newly hired mechanic, Billy Ayles, who is in fact a rookie undercover San Diego police officer named Benjy Taylor (D.B. Sweeney). Benjy has infiltrated Ted's business posing as an auto mechanic whiz kid with a particular skill for German cars, but his goal is to gather enough evidence for Lieutenant Vincent Bracey (Randy Quaid) to uncover Varrick's lucrative grand theft auto scheme.

For Roy, it was another opportunity to have fun working on the second unit of another mainstream film, which meant enjoying the benefits of a production with money while not having to bear the responsibilities of a first unit director of photography: "I loved working the second unit. You were working with some

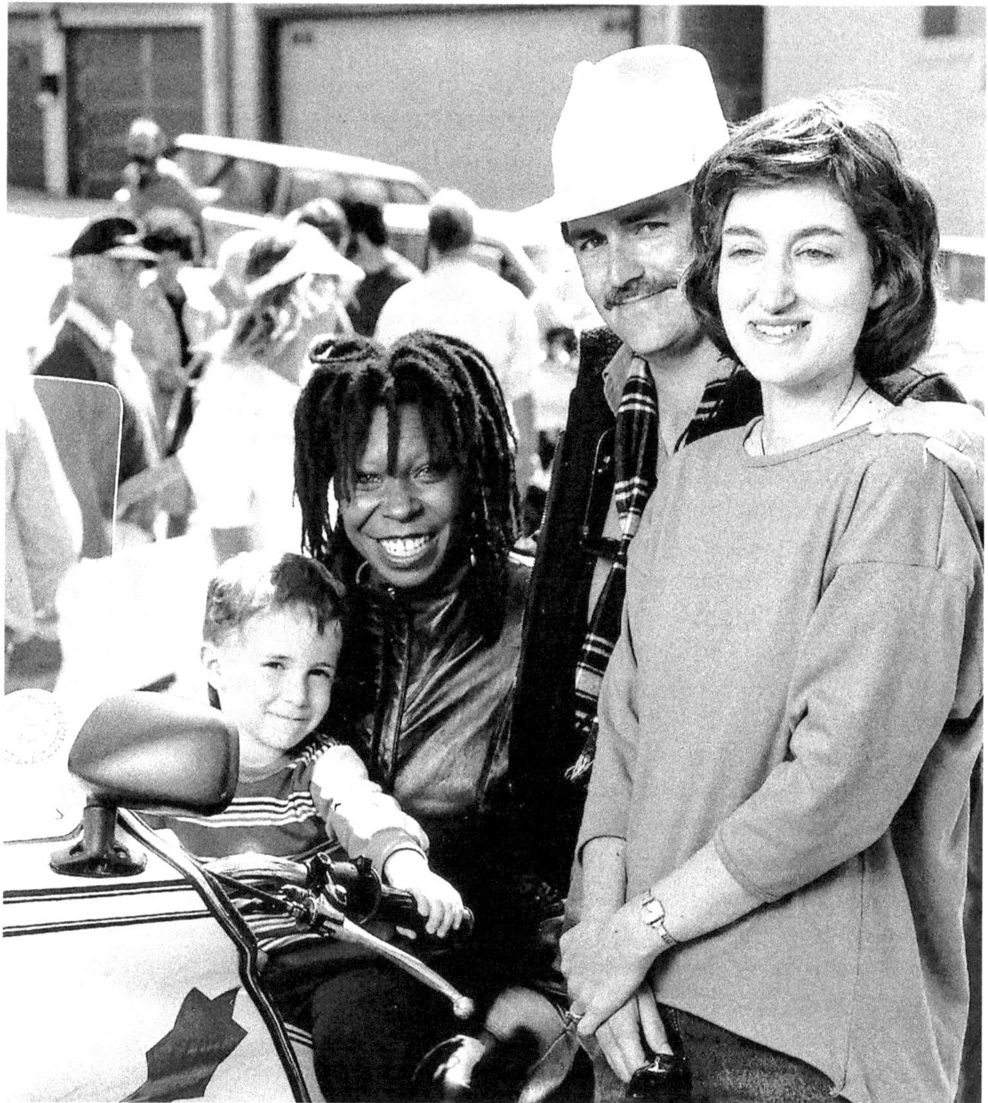

Whoopi with the Wagner family—Wagner, his son Phillip, and first wife Wendy—on the set of *Burglar.*

of the best people in the world. They are like a gypsy family that sticks together. If I didn't love lighting so much, I would probably have stuck with second units because I just love the camaraderie of the people. They are so much more fun. The second unit doesn't come with the same risks because the actors are not involved. Generally, you don't have egos on the set. Being a first unit director of photography means always dealing with drama—someone in the cast doesn't like something or the director doesn't like something, or a production manager wants you to do it this way, or the A.D. is coming to you and saying, 'We don't have time for that!' Frankly, first unit is a pain in the ass. So, I was very happy to do the second unit on *No Man's Land.* I was doing all the car chases—the car going through the truck, splitting the truck in half, all the interstitials, and the steel mill stuff, a lot of night work. I also did all the car interior stuff with Charlie [Sheen], who was a very good guy; I've worked with every one of the Sheens: Martin the father, and the two sons, Charlie and Emilio. The director, Peter Werner, knew everybody, so we got the best people working on that film. We had all the top stunt people, including Buddy Joe Hooker and Hank Hooker, as well as Terry Leonard who did *Raiders of the Lost Ark*; that was the kind of quality we had on that show. It was a lot of the same people who had been on *Burglar* because Jim Arnett brought over those that he liked. So, it was just like an education for me. I thought I was a big hotshot because I had done all those ninja films, and I knew how to do it, but not the way these guys were doing it. They were doing it the right way."

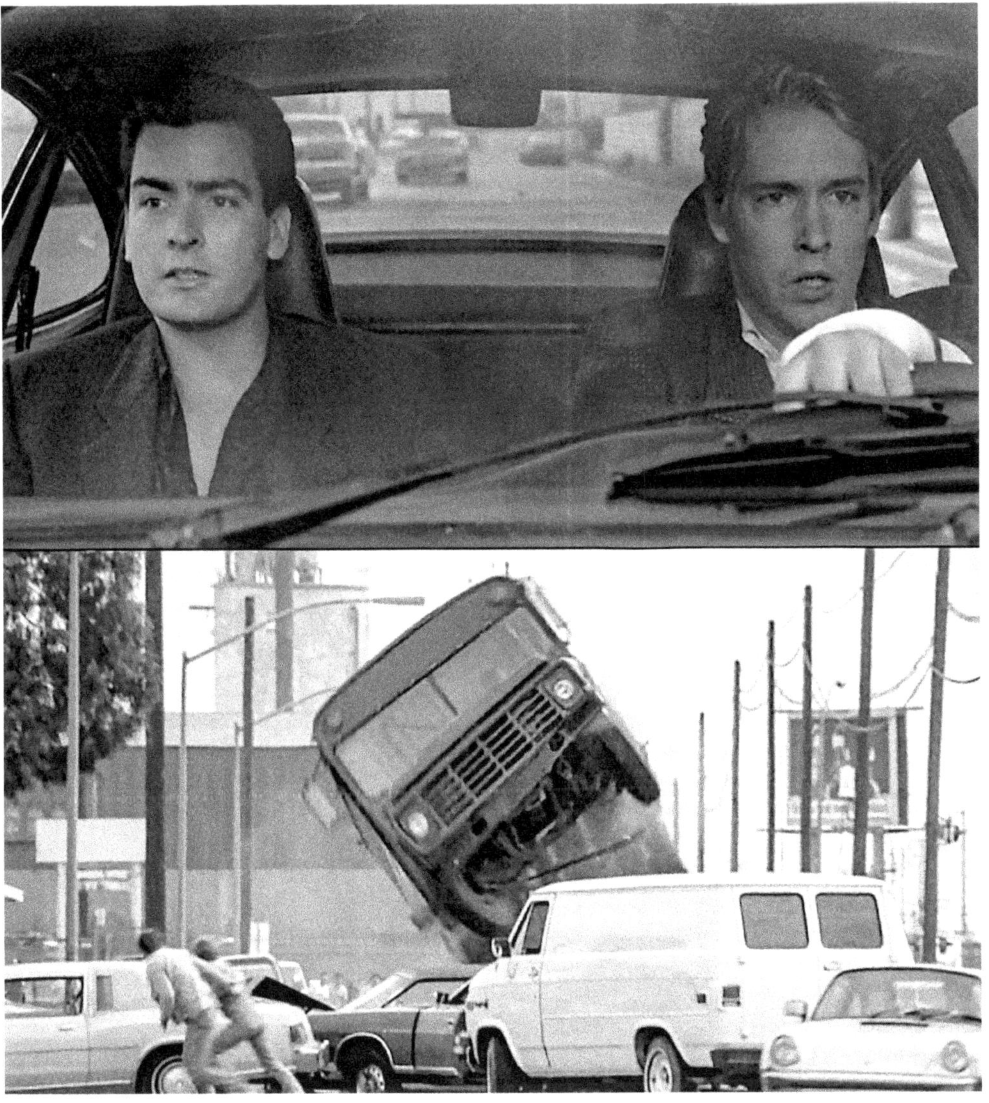

Scenes from *No Man's Land*, 1987. *Top:* starring Charlie Sheen (left) and D.B. Sweeney.

The second unit material for *No Man's Land* was filmed in four weeks, which was a significant amount of time given for a second unit at that time. With up to fifteen cameras running at once, filming often took a full day of lighting, staging, and setting up for one shot, not to mention the rehearsing and practicing required to see if those shots actually worked. Fortunately for Roy, the first unit director of photography Hiro Narita had all the confidence in him to pull it off successfully and allowed Roy the freedom to bring his vision to the screen. However, while enjoying being part of the second unit gang on *No Man's Land*, Roy received a call from filmmaker Richard Franklin, director of *Roadgames* (1981), *Psycho II* (1983), and *Link* (1986). Franklin was preparing to helm the pilot episode of a new CBS television series called *Beauty and the Beast*, a contemporary adaptation of the famous fairytale. This modern fantasy was set in, and below, New York City and based around the burgeoning relationship between corporate attorney Catherine Chandler (Linda Hamilton) and the leonine underground dweller, Vincent (Ron Perlman). Catherine was rescued by Vincent after being attacked in Central Park in a case of mistaken identity; after Vincent nurses her back to health she promises to keep her savior and his subterranean sanctuary a secret from the rat race above. She leaves her job at her father's law firm to join the Manhattan District Attorney's Office as an investigator, and whenever she faces

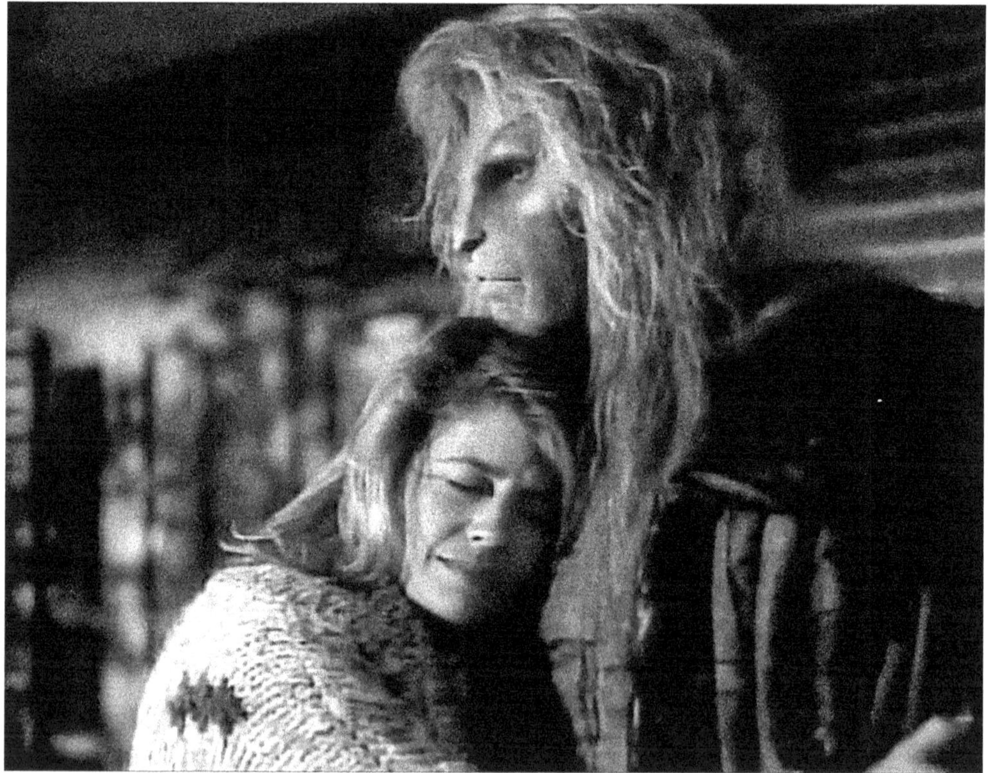

Catherine (Linda Hamilton) embraces the beast, Vincent (Ron Perlman), in *Beauty and the Beast*, 1987.

danger in her duties, Vincent surfaces to assist her. Soon their forbidden romance blossoms as the man-beast's inner beauty is revealed to her.

Franklin had previously tried, though unsuccessfully, to hire Roy on *Psycho II* and was now seeking him out once again to shoot the pilot for *Beauty and the Beast*, a tantalizing potential project for Roy as it would be his first opportunity to shoot a major studio show as the first unit director of photography. This would be a massive career move for any ambitious cinematographer. However, Jim Arnett had other ideas, as Roy recalls:

"I was on *No Man's Land* probably a month or so, and I was having a lot of fun on that when Richard called saying, 'Roy, I've got a pilot I want you to do called *Beauty and the Beast*.' I'm going, 'Oh my God, it's my first opportunity to do a studio project!' I asked him when he wants me to start, and he gives me the date and it's the date after *No Man's Land* stops, which meant no time for prep. So, I went to Jim Arnett to see if he would release me, he said, 'No, you're here. I'm not releasing you.' So, I'm in trouble here. *No Man's Land* was my second big studio picture, after my first being *Burglar*, and you don't want to get a reputation for walking off the shows. So, I went back to Richard and told him my dilemma and said, 'I want to work with you really badly, so what are we going to do?' And he said, 'Well, that's too bad, I've got to have you for prep.' I said, 'Richard, he's not going to release me but I'm willing to do it after hours and I'm willing to come to the set at the weekends.' Richard agreed to letting me try doing it at weekends, so we would work all day Saturday and Sunday prepping *Beauty and the Beast*, but it really wasn't the kind of prep you need for something like that. I never scouted anything. Not a thing. It was my first television pilot, first major TV show, and I had no prep, yet we did incredibly well. I was just very lucky to have come into a group of people that were kind to each other, and we had a really good producer. But then it changed once it became a series, as do most; though I didn't know that at the time. But Richard was the best. He knew exactly what he wanted, but he allowed you to be who you are. If you work with a person who has a theory or a plan, yet they will allow you to move forward in that plan, I think that is the best of both worlds. That is what ended up happening with me and Richard, he became an incredible collaborator and contributor. If there was a problem with Richard as a filmmaker, it was because he was so ensconced in having been mentored by and devoted to Alfred Hitchcock. Because of that he never really became completely himself as an artist, and that was too bad because Richard was amazing. He was a huge talent who made some incredible movies like *Link*, and his Australian film *Patrick* which displayed his childlike innocence yet was imbued with all the sophistication of Hitchcock. So, I was very happy to finally get an opportunity to work with him, and if he hadn't agreed to accommodate my situation with *No Man's Land* then I would not have done *Beauty and the Beast*, but he did and it changed my life."

Just as Roy accepted the job on *Beauty and the Beast*, a call came in from legendary special effects maestro Stan Winston, who was about to make his directorial debut with a low-budget monster movie called *Pumpkinhead* that he wanted Roy to shoot. *Pumpkinhead* is a brilliantly realized fantasy horror that would

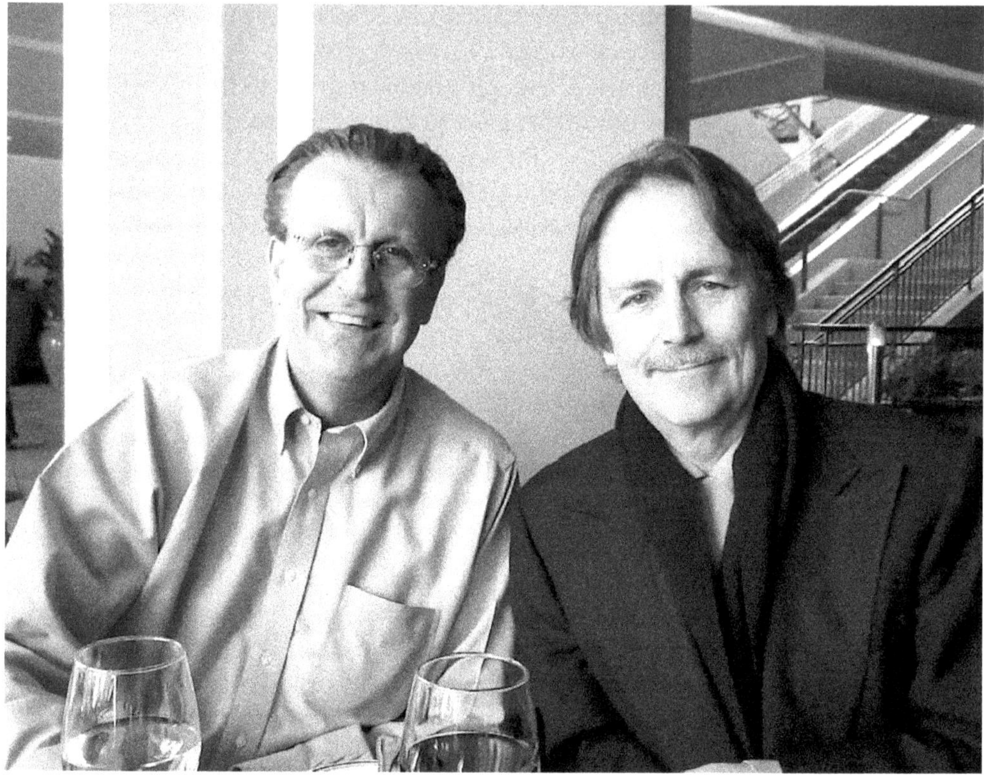

Director Richard Franklin (left) with Roy, sometime after *Beauty and the Beast*.

ultimately be shot beautifully by Montenegrin cinematographer Bojan Bazelli. However, Roy wisely followed the advice of his mentor Harry Stradling which dictated that the best way to make it as a studio cinematographer was to just keep working, regardless of whether one liked the project or not, and a particular way to obtain consistent studio work was to get onto a hit television series. On that advice, Roy decided to forego *Pumpkinhead* in favor of shooting another monster:

"It was such a weird thing that I got the offer for *Pumpkinhead* right around the same time that I got the offer for *Beauty and the Beast*, but that was a nine-month guarantee of work for a major TV studio. I got a phone call from Stan Winston saying he loved what I did on *A Nightmare on Elm Street 3* and he really wanted me to shoot *Pumpkinhead*. So, he sent me the script and I read it, but I couldn't imagine how the hell they were going to make that monster work; and with me not knowing who Stan was, I said, 'This is going to be impossible, or it's going to look hokey.' And I've never seen it, so I don't know if it's good or bad. Who knows what would have happened if I had worked with Stan Winston on *Pumpkinhead* instead of *Beauty and the Beast*. I didn't know who Stan Winston was at the time and I had no idea where his career was going to take him. You just never know where your career is going to take you. But I loved the idea of working all the time, and that is why I ultimately decided to stick with *Beauty and the Beast*. And after that Richard wanted me to work on another movie, *F/X2*, but I couldn't do it because he was filming it in Canada, and I couldn't take my crew. I had a full-blown crew that I was working with all the time. But not doing it was a stupid mistake on my part; I should have gone with Richard to do that film ... and I didn't."

Having decided to stick with the opportunity that a television series would afford him, Roy began work on *Beauty and the Beast*, instantly bringing a sumptuous visual quality to this romantic fantasy, imbuing the mise-en-scène with rich contrast of light and shadow. In an aesthetic sense, this is top television. However, not everyone at CBS appreciated the caliber of work that was giving their show its greatest quality. Alas, it wasn't to last for Roy, as he ruefully recalls:

"I had never done television before. When making features you always answer to the director and I assumed it would be the same in television, that I would be answering directly to the creative people. But after the pilot, Richard was no longer directing, so the person I had to answer was the creator of the show, Ron Koslow. The line producer, who physically ran the show, and his production manager didn't like me; they had someone they liked much better, so they used subterfuge to try to get rid of me from the very beginning. I understand why they were trying to do that; they knew someone that they could trust, and they didn't know who I was. I was probably a loose cannon anyway. So, they decided to undermine me from the beginning. There was an executive of CBS whom I had been a production assistant with at MGM, and his name was Les Moonves. He came out on the set one day when we were filming the first episode and he said, 'Roy, this stuff looks beautiful. It's just gorgeous.' And I said, 'Thanks a lot, Les.' I thought he was paying me a compliment, but he said, 'Why? Why are you doing all this? You know that all you're doing is shooting the filler between the commercials, right?' And I never thought of it that way. But he was serious. There was a lot of that mentality in episodic television, this idea of, 'Why try so hard? It doesn't mean anything.' But being my mother's son, I was always going to change the way things are done. Everything had to have a meaning for me. Everything. I got to come from such a small place without any chance of ever making it, so when I finally did make it, it had to mean something. I've got to care about everything. I probably cared too much too many times in my career. And I don't think anybody understood that. They may have been frightened of me or they may have thought that I was tough, but I was being tougher on myself than I ever was on anybody else."

It was while shooting the third episode of *Beauty and the Beast* that Roy really irked the suits at CBS. Having arrived at the Long Beach shooting location without having previously seen and inspected it, he immediately heard that it was not fit for the purpose, proving too dangerous for his crew, who were unwilling to risk their lives for the sake of a paycheck. Little did Roy realize that standing up for the basic health and safety of the crew meant that he would end up going through one of the darkest periods of his career:

"I heard this was going to be a tough location, and when I arrived in Long Beach the crew was already there because they were to lay cable and get everything ready for the day. It was an abandoned building with a lot of lead-based paint and a person died there the week before. They fell to their death in an elevator shaft. Well, I didn't think anything about it, because I was kind of new to the studio, and being a director of photography in the studio system I thought, 'They will take care of all that.' I had been used to doing independent features, so I was sort of roughshod, but I didn't feel like I had to do it here. The problem is if you were standing up for the crew, the suits saw you as the in-between for the studio and below-the-line. I stood up for the crew on *Pray for Death* and they nearly fired me and then it began happening again on *Beauty and the Beast*. The crew refused to go into the building because the lead-based paint is dangerous in the air and there were no lights. People would have hurt themselves in there. So, I went to the producers to tell them that the crew are not going in and they said, 'Well, you're going to have to tell them to do it, or it's your career.' I said, 'I can't tell them to do it. I don't know anything about it. I'm no safety officer.' All this time I'm remembering *Pray for Death*, and that's why I was trying to stay away from this and not get involved. I just said, 'Look, bring down a safety officer or somebody that knows something about this. I'll go talk to them, but I'm not management; I'm below-the-line. I'm a director of photography! I can't tell them to do anything. I can't fire them. I can't hire them. I can recommend things, but I can't do any of that.' And the producer said, 'I don't care. You have to tell them.' So, I went out to the crew, and they said, 'Roy, don't even start. Don't even try. We're not going in there!' I then went back to the producer, and I said, 'The only opportunity here is for you to bring in a safety officer and a fire marshal; they can look at it and say, 'it's okay, work away,' or they will say, 'no, it's dangerous, you can't do it.' Well, they weren't going to do that. I was naïve, I thought that they would work it out and everything would be fine. But it wasn't fine. They had shut down the show for the day and that was a huge deal. It wasn't the crew's fault. It was the producers' fault. And this was long before the safety measures that now run the motion picture industry."

The result of Roy's standing up to the producers meant some devastating news waited for him in the following days. While slugging along making the day at a location in downtown Los Angeles, a crew member told Roy that word on the grapevine said he was to be imminently fired.

"He had just heard it from the Teamsters," Roy recalls, "and the Teamsters are always the first ones to hear anything. So, I immediately call up Ron Koslow, the creator and owner of the show, and said, 'Ron, what's going on here? I'm hearing these rumors…' He replied, 'Oh, don't worry about that. Nothing's going to happen. Everything's fine.' But the rumors persisted throughout the day. They got to Linda Hamilton, they got to Ron Perlman, and they're saying to me, 'You're not going to get fired, this is not going to happen. We love you. We're going to keep you on.' It was dreadful, I kept hearing these rumors all day long, as well as assurances from the creators of the show saying that all is okay."

Then, at the end of that particularly long day, Koslow apologized to Roy for the rumors he was subjected to hearing and offered to meet for breakfast the following morning to have a discussion about it all, a moment Roy remembers vividly:

Beauty and the Beast   * * * M E M O * * *

```
TO:    ALL CAST & CREW

FROM:  PRODUCTION

RE:    Long Beach Location

DATE:  August 24, 1987
```

The following is excerpted from the location agreement provided by the owner of the Long Beach location: "Disclosure of Danger and Hazard. The property has been condemned by the City of Long Beach. The condemnation resulted because the improvements located on the property are of a dangerious and unstable condition. An individual died from a fall down an elevator shaft. The property has not been improved since the purchase by Cificap and continues to exist in a dangerous and unstable condition that could cause serious physical injury on any person who enters onto the Property and which could destroy any equipment and/or personal property located at the Property."

The building was once a beautiful building and in disrepair has the fascination of a Haunted House. But it is dangerous.

PLEASE DO NOT WANDER AWAY FROM THE COMPANY.

PLEASE DO NOT LEAVE THE COMPANY WITHOUT CLEAR INSTRUCTIONS OF HOW TO EXIT, OR A GUIDE WHO IS FAMILIAR WITH THE BUILDING. CHECK WITH THE LOCATION DEPARTMENT OR A.D.'S.

PLEASE DO NOT GO ANY WHERE WITHOUT ADEQUATE LIGHT TO SEE WHERE YOU ARE GOING.

If you are not comfortable working under these conditions, please notify your department head or production, and we will replace you for the 2 days.

Thank you.

Safety memo from *Beauty and the Beast* outlining the issues with the Long Beach location.

"We went to The Copper Penny, which was across from Warner Brothers. I went in, sat down, and Koslow fired me. I was devastated. I was told that I'd never work again, that I was done in this business. I went home devastated. That night at around three o'clock in the morning, I was sitting there thinking to myself that I'm the only one in my family that knows about this horrible news that all my hopes and dreams were doomed, that I'm not working anymore, and all our plans are gone. It was late and it was weird, but I called Billy Fraker. He was like my father to me, so I called him, waking him up in the process. He asked me what was going on and I said, 'Billy, I just got fired.' And I was thinking that he would say something like, 'Oh, I'm so sorry, Roy. It will be okay.' But what he said was, 'Congratulations, you can now call yourself a director of photography.' And I said, 'But, Bill…' and he snapped back, 'Fuck you! This is part of it. You are going to get fired many more times. Don't worry about it, just go to bed.' That was Billy and that was the way he dealt with things. I was looking for more sympathy than that obviously but didn't get it. Billy loved me, but that was his way. That was his sense of humor. I didn't know what I was going to do with myself. It took a long time to overcome that feeling of loss because it was my first big television series, the first thing I've ever done on television, and to have gotten fired off it hit me hard. This anxiety went on for weeks, I was just sitting there not knowing what to do with my life. And then the show came on the TV. I was sitting there watching the first episode and crying my eyes out because I'm not there anymore. I felt like a failure; I have failed my family, and I failed my career.

"One of my crew members said I needed to file a complaint against the show because this wasn't right. So, I went to the camera local, and they said, 'Forget it. You will burn bridges and never work again. Ever.' So I went to the electrical union, which is Local 728. I talked to them, and they said they would support me. I went through the labor board, and I told them the story and they agreed to take it on. But it went on for a year or two. It was dreadful. But I had another fight on my hands, as I had a Pay or Play contract, which meant that I got paid for the rest of the year, but I argued that my crew should be paid the same thing. The studio said, 'That is not part of your agreement.' But I told them that my crew had reason to believe that they would be able to collect the same thing. I fought tooth and nail, and a year later my crew all got paid for the whole term of my contract. And that was when I started getting these phone calls in the middle of night telling me, 'You're never going to work again. You're done.'"

Then, an angel in a suit emerged: Seymour Friedman was a veteran of both World War II and Old Hollywood. As a director Friedman made many films throughout the forties and fifties, including low-budget thrillers, films noir, and horror pictures such as *Bodyhold* (1949), *Chinatown at Midnight* (1949), *Counterspy Meets Scotland Yard* (1950), and *The Son of Dr. Jekyll* (1951). While his filmic output is largely inconsequential in the trajectory of Hollywood history, he eventually ventured into television by joining the executive ranks at Columbia, for which he had made many of his movies. When Roy received a call from Friedman, a lifeline if ever there was one, this former B-movie director was now Head of Production at Columbia's Screen Gems television division. His reputation preceded him as a tough, hard-nosed executive, but he saw something in the images created by Roy and knew this was a talent worth saving. Friedman told Roy he heard that he was fired from *Beauty and the Beast* for all the wrong reasons and wanted to offer him an olive branch. But it came with a caveat:

"I had no idea who Seymour Friedman was," Roy admits, "nor did he know who I was, but he called me up and said, 'You certainly caused a lot of trouble, but you should not have been fired.' I told him I didn't cause any trouble, and then I asked him who exactly he was, and he said, 'I'm Head of Production at Screen Gems.' I found out that he had been Frank Capra's assistant director and that he'd been with Columbia Pictures all those years but now he was the head of the whole thing. He said, 'Look, come over here with me and I'll offer you a seven-year contract. But if you ever fuck up, you'll never work in this business ever again. It doesn't matter what anybody else says—I'm Seymour Friedman and I have the power to ruin you forever.'"

Roy's *Return to Horror High* director, and television veteran, Bill Froehlich recognizes the rarity of Friedman's outreach:

"There are some tough sons of bitches in this business and Seymour Friedman would fall directly into that category. Seymour was a legend. He was someone of power and someone you had to contend with. Not someone you wanted to get on the wrong side of. This man was talented, he was smart, he was sharp, but he could be a tough character. So, to have someone like that recognize the quality of the principles behind which Roy made his decisions and the quality of his work is also testament to what he was able to see. And sometimes in our business the best results or the best actions can come from somebody you never would have expected that from. And here Seymour Friedman helped to raise Roy back up and give him the opportunity that he needed when he could have easily just buried him. There's so much fear in our business, it is at a level of insanity, but within that insanity is an element of truth about the nature of the entertainment business. When you want to do good artistic work you have to keep in the back of your mind how to roll with those punches."

"I'm still in awe of it," Roy admits. "Seymour didn't know me at all, he just heard the story from one of the producers on the show who said, 'We just fired this guy and I think we made a mistake.' It's just so unlike Seymour to have done that, but he took me under his wing, and I did a lot of work for him. Seymour was this guy that everybody hated; they were afraid of what could be a monster. But he loved me; he saved my life. To this day, I have a huge black mark on me that I'm a troublemaker, that I'm a tough guy, or that I can be cantankerous. Most of the crews that have worked with me for years will say that is not true at all. But that's the rumor in the legend of Roy Wagner. It's too bad because I don't think I'm that person at all. I just don't put up with bullshit but that was the reputation that the *Beauty and the Beast* situation gave me. Seymour is the reason I've had this career, he thought that something had been done to me that was wrong and he allowed me to continue. So, I did everything he sent my way. I always worked very hard and very fast. If you look over my career you will see that I've done a lot of work for Columbia Pictures. That's because of Seymour."

Appreciative of this second chance, Roy knew that his new career path in some ways echoed those of his Old Hollywood mentors who also worked hard and fast, and most importantly, often. He immediately began filming pilot episodes and taking over for reshoots on troubled productions. Friedman tested him, giving him the toughest assignments to see if he could survive and be worthy of the support he provided. And then, a moment of exquisite karma occurred at the 1988 Emmy Awards. Despite his unceremonious firing from *Beauty and the Beast,* the executives in attendance at the ceremony saw the gong for Outstanding Cinematography for a Series be bestowed upon Roy for that very show.

Picking up the award in their presence was a sublime moment of acknowledgment, and a moment of art and the artist emerging triumphant from industry indifference to such.

"When Emmy season came along, I didn't know enough to nominate myself. The studio had nominated me. So, we went to the ceremony and were sitting in the back of the hall when they called my name. I had not prepared for anything because I had no expectation that I could win. I was like, 'Oh my God, what am I going to say here?' So, I'm walking through all these people, and everybody is congratulating me, and the last table I passed through was the *Beauty and the Beast* table. Tony Thomas, who was one of the producers, turned to me, grabbed me, and said, 'We fucked up, didn't we?' And I replied, 'Yes, you did.' I went up on stage and said, 'I just want to thank Tony Thomas and Ron Koslow for all their support and help.' And everybody knew what I was saying. But I meant it sincerely, I wasn't trying to diss them at all. The funny thing is that they tried to call me back three other times to get me back on *Beauty and the Beast* after they fired me. But I was not available."

"Roy's story is central to how you survive in the entertainment business," Froehlich says, "and it does force you to know who you are, and to continue to stand up to that. It reminds me of the Rudyard Kipling poem—'If you can meet success and failure and treat them both as imposters, then you are a balanced man, my son.' Because many times what people in this business call failure is exactly what you need to move you forward. They were so wrong to fire Roy off *Beauty and the Beast*. Roy was doing feature level quality work as a cinematographer on that show, it's just stunning. He is an example of how you ultimately have to believe in yourself, because when you hear those words, 'You'll never work in this town again,' after doing the best work that you could do at the time, it can destroy you if you are not able to take a deep breath and say, 'I still believe in myself and I'm going to continue to do the right thing.' Roy was able to do that because not only was he a terrific cinematographer who was going to grow into a great cinematographer, but is he is also a great human being."

Roy survived the *Beauty and the Beast* debacle and immediately began honoring Seymour Friedman's belief in him, taking on the job as director of photography on the CBS crime drama *Houston Knights*, filming thirteen episodes of the show's second season. It was on this show that he would meet Dale Alexander, who would become Roy's long-time key grip. Alexander has worked closely with Roy prolifically throughout his career, from television series (*Christine Cromwell, Nasty Boys, CSI: Crime Scene Investigation, House M.D.*) to feature films (*Drop Zone, Nick of Time, The Pest*) and has seen the best and worst of his friend and colleague. Alexander was working at Warner Brothers on the TV series *The New Gidget* in 1987 when his future boss turned up on set to survey a potential new key grip. He recalls an inauspicious introduction:

"Roy needed a key grip for *Houston Knights*, so he came to the set to meet me, but he felt I was too young and too inexperienced. I was probably 21 years old at the time, and he was about ten years older than me. So, he left to do this show, but he hated the key grip that he ended up hiring, so he came back to meet me again and offered me the job. From that time on I worked with him for eighteen years, almost full time. There were very few projects where I might have been on a different show for a little bit of time, but then we'd go back and work together again. We loved working together. It was a love-hate relationship. The key grip and the cameramen are always in a love-hate relationship. When I first met Roy, I found that he was quite charming, but then I soon realized that he was also extremely challenging. I loved that he challenged me to constantly come up with solutions. He would say, 'I need this right now!' And I'm like, 'But how do I do that?' He drove me into situations where he made me solve the problem; he would say, 'I know you can do this.' That was one of my favorite things about working with Roy, but conversely that was also one of the things I hated about Roy. You almost never had a break with him because he is a very intense director of photography, but he uses his intensity on trying to get the best out of everybody. He would challenge you to do things and you must use your own creativity to get to that point. From the very get-go I knew Roy was the most talented cameraman I ever worked with. His vision was unbelievable."

Having emerged from *A Nightmare on Elm Street 3* relatively unscathed and now busy finding his footing in the television world, Roy briefly returned to his low-budget film origins for an absurdist black comedy called *Mortuary Academy*. Coming across like the offspring of the unholy communion between *National Lampoon's Animal House* and *Eating Raoul*, the film tells the story of two young men, Sam and Max Grimm (Christopher Atkins and Perry Lang, respectively) who inherit the bankrupted Grimm Mortuary and Academy from their recently deceased uncle. However, before they can claim ownership, it is stipulated that they graduate from a mortician course, or else the business will remain under the control of incumbent owner, and resident necrophiliac, Paul Truscott (Paul Bartel). The academy accepts a roster of clumsy and irreverent students whose wacky hijinks are closely watched by Paul and his sultry assistant, Mary (Mary Woronov).

Roy's work on *Mortuary Academy* goes back to connections made during his time working as a projectionist while trying to make a name for himself as a budding cinematographer. He was working the booth as the chief projectionist at the Nuart Theatre in west Los Angeles, the owner of which was Kim Jorgensen, the president and proprietor of the arthouse cinema chain, Landmark Theatres. Jorgensen would branch out into filmmaking, executive producing modest independent cult comedies such as *Kentucky Fried Movie* (1977) and *Bad Manners* (1984), as well as Sydney Pollack's *Out of Africa* (1985). Despite working on a high-profile Oscar-winning studio film such as the latter, he would return to the spirited anarchy of the former two comedies on *Mortuary Academy*. When the film ended up in trouble with a cinematographer who wasn't cutting it, Jorgensen remembered his old projectionist who had gained a reputation for being able to bring complicated productions in on time and on budget.

"That was one of those situations that ultimately comes down to relationships," Roy says, "I met Kim Jorgensen when I worked for him as a projectionist at his Nuart Theatre. It was one of those niche movie theaters that showed old

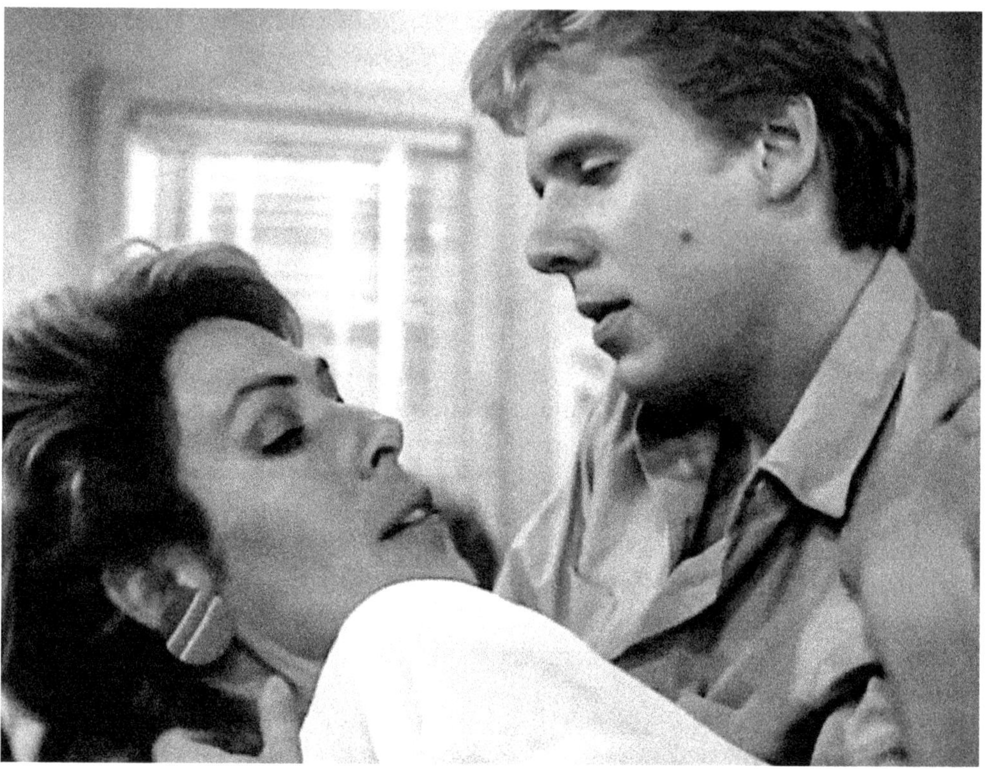

Mary (Mary Woronov) seduces young Sam (Christopher Atkins) in the classroom at the
Mortuary Academy, **1988.**

movies and cult films like *Pink Flamingos* and *Thundercrack!* I was a struggling
cinematographer at the time, but I did whatever I could; I was a reader for MGM
and I worked as a projectionist, which I was still doing when I was shooting *Meatcleaver Massacre*. And I loved doing that. I love the idea of the presentation, of
opening the drapes at the proper time. I ran every theater in Los Angeles at one
time or another. However, I was not getting to be who I wanted to be, which was
to be a cinematographer. But then a few years later when I was approached about
doing *Mortuary Academy* I saw Kim's name attached to it and I thought, 'Oh,
great. He's just done *Out of Africa*. This is my big opportunity.' He was a huge deal
and he remembered me from my days as a projectionist when they were doing this
movie. So, I got the note to go see the producers whose names were Zane Levitt,
Chip Miller, and Alain Silver. I went to the old David O. Selznick studios, RKO
Culver City, which was where they had done *Gone with the Wind* and *Citizen
Kane*, and I'm thinking, 'Finally, this is going to be a real job.' Then I walked on to
the set and saw what I was actually going to be doing, and I went, 'Oh, Jesus, how
is this happening?' Because it was being shot at Culver studios and the producer
was making big movies, I thought this was going to be a significant studio project, but it was nothing. It was a little tiny movie. But it was work and it was not
bad work, in fact it was really good work. I was told I would be replacing another
cinematographer who they fired four days into filming because he was too slow

and because of that they were running behind schedule. But I don't think that the original cinematographer was the problem, I think it was that the director Michael Schroeder was going too slow. What ended up happening is what always happens in this situation: they always fire the cameraman first, not the director. I think Michael was wary of me at first because I was replacing his original choice of cinematographer, but after the second day we became good friends."

The film is most memorable for the wonderfully absurdist performances of Bartel and Woronov, a formidable screen duo who displayed their fine comic sensibilities previously in Bartel's *Eating Raoul* (1982). And while *Mortuary Academy* displays nothing near the subversive nerve of *Eating Raoul*, it does get by on Bartel and Woronov's delightfully eccentric sexual chemistry.

"Paul Bartell and Mary Woronov were the stars, but I didn't know who they were," Roy admits, "I had not seen *Eating Raoul* at that point, but from what I was aware, *Mortuary Academy* wasn't anything like *Eating Roaul*, which was very esoteric; this was crasser and sillier. I think that Paul's crowd probably was looking for something a little more alternative, and it wasn't there in *Mortuary Academy*. Paul and Mary were so much fun to work with; there's no way I can ever tell you how much fun they were. Paul obviously is very gay. And I'm very not. But I've had this legacy of working really well with gay people. And gay people love me, for

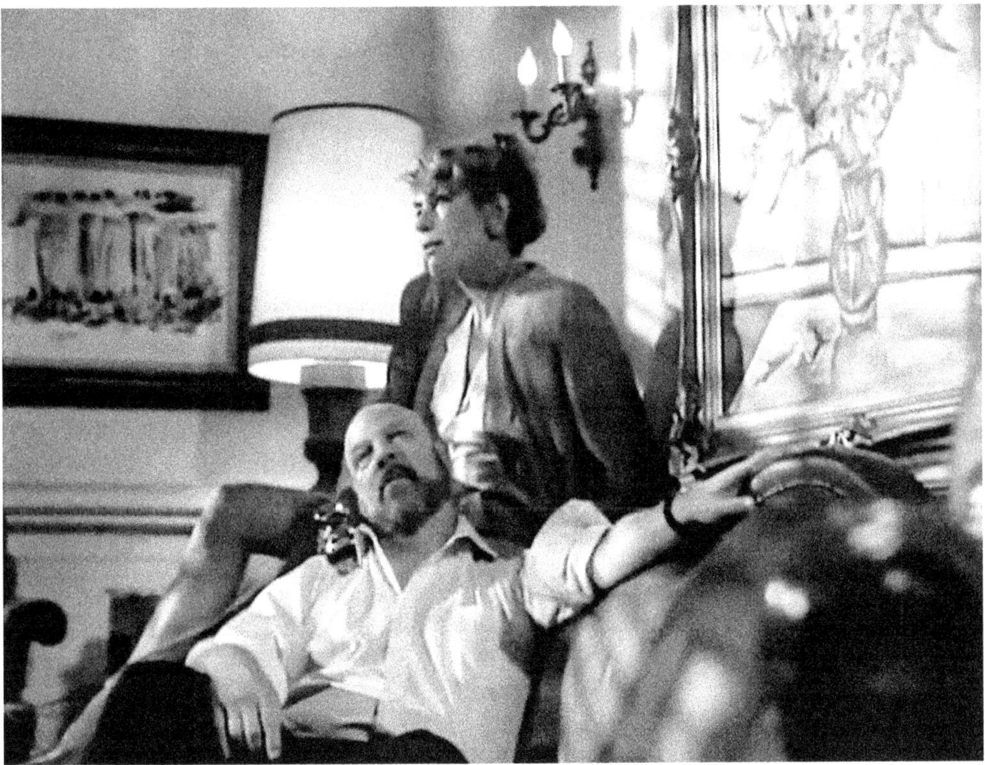

Mortician Dr. Paul Trustcott (Paul Bartel) and his cunning assistant Mary (Mary Woronov) conspire against the brothers Grimm and their impending inheritance of the academy in *Mortuary Academy.*

whatever reason. And Paul used to say, 'Roy, I want you to come to set every day with a smoking jacket and a pipe.' I would say, 'Paul, I don't smoke, I don't have a smoking jacket.' 'I will provide everything! Just come and tell me stories.' He was just great fun, and he had his eye on me throughout the movie, but he was a wonderful guy. The person you saw on camera in *Mortuary Academy* is who he is. I would have done anything to work with him again. He was fantastic, an incredible character. And all the actors were just remarkable. I do like *Mortuary Academy*. I love that kind of dark sense of humor. I'm surprised that it turned out as well as it did. It became something of a cult classic that people kind of discovered after the fact. The script was smarter than the film that we made. I wish Paul could have directed it; he would have really made something special out of that script. Michael Schroeder did a good job, and I would have done another movie with him, but he couldn't get arrested after that film. I don't know why because he is talented. But that has happened to me quite a bit—I will rescue someone by getting them out of a difficult situation and then they don't get another movie."

Hits and Misses

Taking a Leap Into TV

"I was taught by my mentors to never say 'No' to a director."

Roy kept his word in delivering for his savior Seymour Friedman when a new science fiction project went into production for NBC. The series was *Quantum Leap* and starred Scott Bakula as time-hopping physicist Dr. Sam Beckett and Dean Stockwell as his equally temporally fluid friend, Admiral Al Calavicci. The series was created by Donald P. Bellisario and became hugely popular across its five-season run. Having been assigned the job by Friedman, Roy had another opportunity to prove that the power player made the right decision in giving him his second chance, though not everybody saw the value of the show's ambitious, and expensive, premise:

"When we met to discuss the pilot, I was in the boardroom with Don Bellisario, the production company people, and all the department heads. Harker Wade, who was the production manager, said, 'We don't have the budget for this. We can't make this show.' And Don said, 'Well, how can we please the studio?' because they weren't going to sign off on the budget. We were really frustrated because we had to build an X-2 and many other sets, and Don said, 'Look, give the studio the budget that they want. Just tell them it is going to cost this amount of money.' And Harker said, 'Yeah, but they will see that we're going to go way over budget.' Don replied, 'Screw that. If it's good they will allow us to continue; if it's not good, it won't matter what the budget was.' That was a giant learning curve for me to know that if you're over budget, but you do good work, typically they will love you. But if you do horrible work and you're still on budget, it won't matter because you will never work again. So, I was never willing to compromise the look of the show."

Production began, though things got off to an inauspicious start when Roy found himself working with a director under the influence. David Hemmings had been a British Cinema teen idol in the early 1960s before assuming his most remembered role as the lead in Michelangelo Antonioni's 1966 countercultural masterpiece *Blow-Up*. Further supporting roles ensued in major studio pictures such as *Camelot* (1967) and *Barbarella* (1968) before he turned to directing in 1972 with *Running Scared* and then following up with *The 14* (1973) and *Just a Gigolo* (1978). Upon moving to Hollywood in the early eighties, Hemmings became a journeyman television director, helming episodes of *The A-Team*, *Airwolf*, and *Magnum P.I.* He would also be hired to direct the pilot of *Quantum Leap*, but it didn't take long before problems arose behind the scenes, as Roy recalls...

"David Hemmings was a good guy, but he was also incredibly tough to work with; he was a complete alcoholic and was doing cocaine. David would have mucus coming out of his nose from the cocaine and I'd say, 'David, you should blow your nose.' I was so insensitive and naïve because I didn't know anything about any of that stuff. Despite being a wonderful guy, and a very funny guy, he was his own worst enemy. He was a friend of Don Bellisario, but they had a falling out because David couldn't stay on set. So ultimately, Don came in and directed for about a week."

Quantum Leap displays some of Roy's most intricately designed work, and it is evident for all to see that he approached the smaller canvas of a television frame much the same way that he would approach the larger format of the cinema screen. In the seven episodes that he shot, Roy used many physical optical illusions that he learned from his Old Hollywood mentors to trick audiences into believing the show's time-traveling concept.

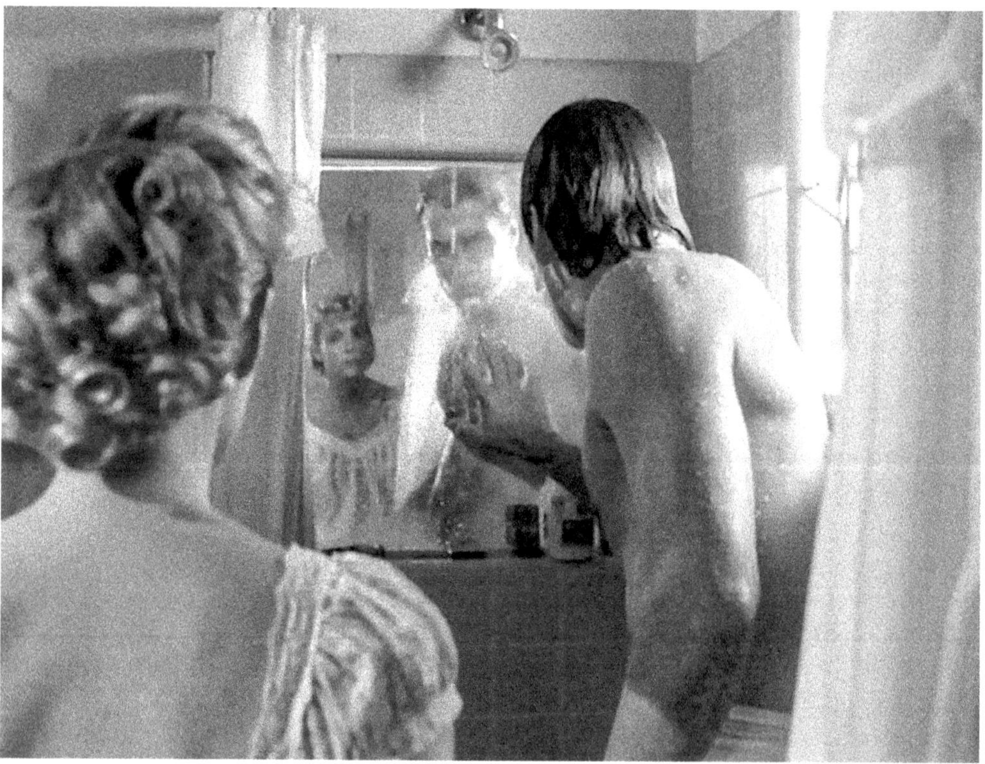

A scene from *Quantum Leap* showcasing Roy's use of reverse sets to give the impression of a mirrored image. From left, with their backs to the camera: Jennifer Runyon and Scott Bakula. The actors in the mirror are not identified.

"I didn't look at television as being different to features. I was working on a major studio lot following in my mentors' footsteps. In fact, shooting television shows like features got me in a lot of trouble because everybody used to say, 'Your stuff is so dark,' and I would say, 'Well, I don't do bright stuff.' Having done *Beauty and the Beast* and all the horror films, I really did not have any knowledge of how to do bright, airy, funny, pretty stuff. So, for me, whether the project was destined for television or for the cinema, I was always trying to make the story look more interesting and more theatrical. And so, the lighting on *Quantum Leap* is pretty theatrical and old fashioned; it is quite rinky-dink in some ways. I have always found working with blue screen, CGI, or any kind of special effects boring; I just want to light, and anytime I had a chance to do things in-camera I would pitch the idea of doing that. *Quantum Leap* is probably the penultimate project that I did that was all done in the camera. There is something about doing things that are in front of you; they have a kind of physical and emotional and mental reality about them that you can't get with CGI or with optical effects. There's always something that takes you out of the story when you're watching a blue screen shot or a CGI shot; something that tells your brain that this isn't real. I love the idea of Heather Langenkamp falling through the chair on *A Nightmare on Elm Street 3* because that was real and happening in front of you. On *Quantum Leap* we had a top special effects man, but he was never there, so I was always pitching ideas to Bellisario. The whole notion of looking directly into the mirrors—that was my idea. Originally, they were going to do it with a blue screen."

Roy continues, "I did things physically that they didn't believe would ever work, and then they worked so well. That happened a few times. When he looks in the mirror at the beginning for the first time, that was all my idea and I kept saying to them, 'Why do you want to spend money on these effects? You're not going to be able to see the effects until it's already out on the air because you won't be able to deliver them that quickly. Why don't you let me try to do this and see if it works; and if it does work, I'll do as many as I can.' And so, I pitched the idea for the mirrors which weren't really mirrors at all—they were picture frames. I wish I could say this was my idea, but it came from *Peggy Sue Got Married*. I was friends with Jordan Cronenweth and I asked him how he did that and he said, 'Oh, that was a great idea! It's just a picture frame.' And the biggest and best of those shots happened later when we shot the one where Scott appeared to be a black man. Our production designer, Cameron Birnie, built the set of the diner on stage and we had this big mirror over behind the counter; we literally had a duplicate of that set on the opposite side and what was so much fun about it was that everything was in reverse—the clock that he made was printed in reverse, as well as all of the pictures and anything else you could normally see in the restaurant. I love that sequence because we did it all in-camera and made it so organic. The director could look at it and go, 'Oh, that looks great,' and then move on because he didn't have to worry about whether it was going to match. The simplest shot that I did was the one where Dean walks out from this bar and opens the door into the night. We were right in the middle of the desert and shooting on film, and you never could light up a desert like you can now on digital; it was impossible. But I had learned a trick whereby if you lifted a light straight up above the camera and you put up a flag so that you took all the lights that the hit the set, then it was lit with the atmosphere. There's a lot of dust particles in the atmosphere at night and what ends up happening is if you use a tungsten light, it's warm; if you use an arc or an HMI, it's blue. Well, we used an HMI and so all that night became blue. I didn't light it at all; I just put that one light on Dean where the door was supposed to be. I asked them to bring a door frame to the location and he said, 'That's ridiculous; it's not going to work.' But it worked perfectly. All we had to do was lock the camera down. In the shot he walks up and we lock the camera; he stops, then we slide the door in and then he opens the door. And it's all gone. It's just a locked-off shot. They printed the stars in it afterwards. This is my favorite stuff: nice shading, beautiful lighting. I mean, how could you not love all that. That is what I'm most proud of, these fun little things that are there because you have a little secret. I'm not a true magician but we were doing that stuff all the time which are essentially magic tricks."

Roy is somewhat sanguine regarding the look of the show these days, as he recalls the technical processes the print went through in making it to broadcast.

"Universal was the last studio to finish shooting on film. That was fine, but the bad part of it was we went from a camera negative to an interpositive, which is very flat; it has no contrast whatsoever. And that was in the early days of transferring film to electronic; it wasn't called digital back then. So, you had to be right on top of the colorist to make sure that they were adding the contrast back in. I find it sad when I look at it now because it does not look like how the show is supposed to look. It is supposed to have grain and other elements. The guys who cared would always go in and fight for it, but when the guys didn't care it would end up just flat and ugly. But I cared. I always fought for the work, and that made me a hero to some, but it also made me a pain in the ass to others. I knew that the only cinematographers that survived are the ones that fought for their work and fought for their career; they did whatever they could to survive. I had an incredibly good relationship with all the vendors, including Panavision, so I could go to them and say, 'I only have this amount of money in the budget, but I need this amount of stuff.' And the fact that I was working all the time meant they knew I was giving them repeat business, so they would say, 'Okay, whatever you want, we will give you.' Having that fighting spirit probably helped me more than a lot of other cinematographers. I'd like to say that it was because I was the better artist, but I think it was simply because I worked more and fought harder for everything I was doing."

Despite the stellar imagery that Roy was capturing and the immense effort in doing so, things turned south when production began falling behind—and the reasons for such being circulated implied that it was because of Roy's camera crew not pulling their weight.

"I left *Quantum Leap*. I got fired on *Beauty and the Beast* and I wasn't going to get fired again. The problem was that Don Bellisario overwrites every one of his projects. They were always too long. And instead of blaming Bellisario—who had a contract with the studio—who do they blame? The director. And then the director blames the cinematographer or the A.D. So, I began to get these notes about having to work faster, 'You have got to do this. You have got to do that.' I said, 'It's not my fault. You need to alter your show. It's slow because of the way you've written it and the way you've scheduled it. I'm not going to be blamed for this anymore.' So, I went straight to Bellisario and said, 'I'm done. I quit.' He said, 'You can't quit. I'm going to make you a director. I really like what you have done. I want to work with you more, you can't quit.' I just said, 'Harker Wade is saying he wants to fire my gaffer because he thinks he's causing the company to be slow. But if they are blaming my gaffer, then they are really blaming me. If he is slow, it's my fault, not his fault.' He said, 'No, I'll fix that.' I replied, 'Yeah, right. You're going to fix that? I've heard that story too many times.' So, I quit."

And with that, Roy took on his first project for Wolf Films, *Christine Cromwell*. The glossy crime drama was part of ABC's Mystery Movie lineup that consisted of four episodes which were broadcast in late–1989 and early–1990. Jaclyn Smith plays the main character, a Harvard Law School graduate and former public defender now working for a prestigious and powerful San Francisco law firm who represent the rich and famous who end up in various nefarious situations involving murder and skulduggery. The series, which also co-starred Old Hollywood stalwarts such as Celeste Holm and Ralph Bellamy, remains a favorite of its contented cinematographer, and for good reason...

"After I quit *Quantum Leap* I ended up getting this reputation that you couldn't push me around and in a way that was a good thing because it protected me from certain people that were just doing junk. So, I started working with Dick Wolf and doing quality shows like *Christine Cromwell*. I am incredibly proud of that. I did that show at Universal and it means a lot to me on a personal level because that is how I met my second wife, Jill; she was Jaclyn Smith's best friend and still is. It was simultaneously one of the best experiences of my life and one of the worst experiences of my life because my son Michael nearly died around this time. So, it has mixed memories for me; on

Roy in 1989 accepting his second Emmy award for his work on *Quantum Leap*.

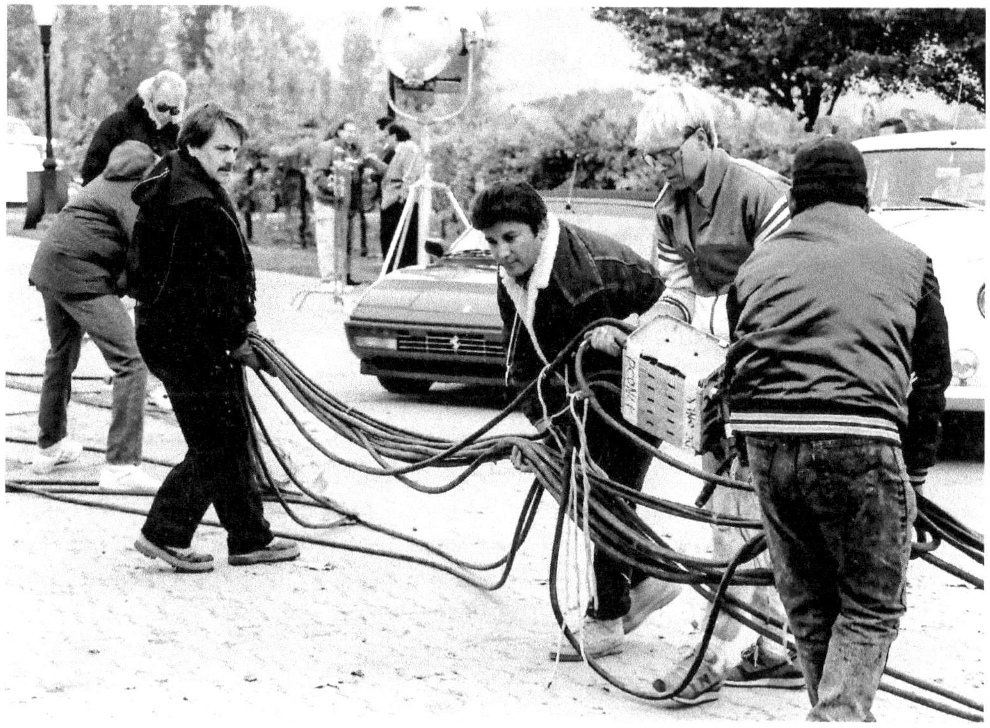

Roy (left) pulling cable with his crew on *Christine Cromwell*, 1989.

one hand warm, wonderful memories, and on the other hand frighteningly tragic memories. But I did some of the best work of my career during that period. *Christine Cromwell* is probably my best lighting up to that point. It was dark, but it was also glamorous, which was not something I was used to doing. I was trained to do that, but it was not something I was ever asked to do."

Another show which took Roy into the nineties was the ill-fated Steven Bochco musical police procedural *Cop Rock*. Bochco developed the concept after

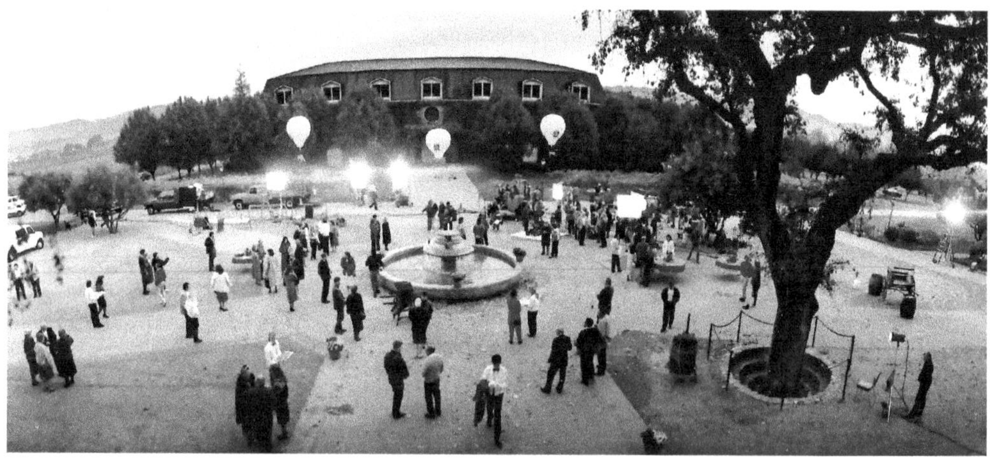

Filming *Christine Cromwell* at the Coppola vineyard in Napa Valley.

he was approached about turning his iconic television series *Hill Street Blues* into a musical for the Broadway stage. That idea was never going to work, but he did consider the notion of turning a musical into a police procedural, but it was also going to be a risky proposition for any willing network open to the idea. Ultimately, it would prove to be Bochco's first series for ABC as part of a major deal with the network.

"The show was Steven's wife Barbara's idea," Roy affirms, "she loved musicals, and she played the mayor in the show. Truthfully, it should have been a Broadway production. It would have been perfect on stage, but as a TV show it was a technological nightmare, mainly because someone had sold Steven on the idea of recording the music live. And this was back in the days when we were using Nagras for recording sound. I worked on huge musicals before, and it was always done using playback. But in this case, they'd sold him on the idea of recording the sound on the stage at the same time we were shooting it. And there was so much movement that you couldn't do it with a boom, you had to use wireless microphones, which to this day are not very good, but back then they were horrible because there was always frequency response, popping, and hissing. Things would not work when they were supposed to. We had the finest sound mixer in the world, and everything was recorded to a 24-track truck from The Record Plant. This huge semi-truck would pull up to our location with two-inch quad tape and they would be recording sixteen or eighteen tracks of sound all at once. When we stopped rolling at the end of a song we had to wait for them to play the song back in the 24-track truck. The thing is, it could be a perfect take for us but if it wasn't perfect for them, we had to do it all over again. They had also convinced Steven of the idea of doing a linear pass, meaning you couldn't break up the music, so if the director wanted more than one camera angle or cut in the scene then we had to have more than one camera. I was not going to give up on movement at all, so you can see when you look at some of those episodes that we were moving a lot; but to move a lot meant that we had to have a Steadicam, and not just one, but many. There were times we were shooting with five or six Steadicams."

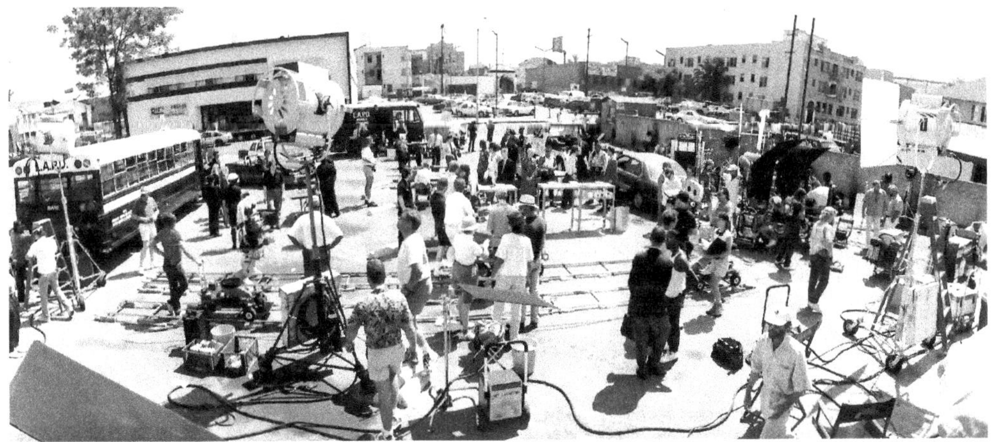

Three cameras filming a musical number on the set of *Cop Rock*, 1990.

Roy continues, "We shot some of the sequences on a soundstage at 20th Century–Fox and they had to find a way of flying the walls and flying the back end in the middle of a take so that they could allow the camera operators to get in there. And it was incredibly complicated. And even more so with the music and dancing. At the same time, we were getting the crossing over shots and the master shot. But if you're in the police station and you're walking down the hallway—and it's a real hallway—they've got all these cameras moving at the same time making all that noise, plus the actors each had a wireless microphone which would pick up all the noise they were making while moving. It was a nightmare. An absolute nightmare. But I loved the idea of this challenge. I love the idea of doing complicated things where you don't see the seams. I get easily bored with doing straightforward, simple things. I mean you look at most of my stuff you will see that it is pretty complicated; it's never just the camera pointing at something, the camera is always moving and doing something that hopefully is driven by the story."

Despite the unique premise and the immense effort that went into production, the show couldn't withstand the critical mauling and commercial underperformance for more than a single season. After eleven episodes which showcased a wholly original, if perhaps bizarre, marriage of the gritty and the glamorous, the show came to an end. Not a surprise, according to Roy…

"I used to refuse to talk about *Cop Rock* because I thought the premise sucked, but I am proud of some nice stuff in the show. If you look at some of the episodes they don't work as traditional television storytelling, but the camerawork is complicated and pretty. Unfortunately, everything on *Cop Rock* was the wrong idea. Had we used all the disparate elements in the right combination, we could have been amazing. Or if we had focused on a single element then it may have worked. If it had been just the cop show it would have been okay; if it had just been a musical then it might have been okay. But women didn't like the police procedural element and men didn't like the musical element; and kids didn't like the songs either because they were complete shit. There is a song in the show called *Bumpty Bumpty* and it is the most embarrassing thing I have ever heard in my life. After that, I knew we were going to get cancelled. When I saw that song, I went to the director and said, 'You know what, we're done. This is our last episode.' And it was our last episode. We had all these incredibly talented performers, almost all of them are fine singers, but that was just so embarrassingly bad that I knew it was the end of us."

After Roy's dismay at both the confused aesthetic of and negative reception to *Cop Rock*, he soon returned to work for Dick Wolf on a project which could at times be equally unusual, but which at least functioned within the realm of a well-defined genre: science fiction. *Mann and Machine* was a very short-lived series that premiered in the spring of 1992 and starred Yancy Butler as the gynoid police officer, Sgt. Eve Edison, the artificially intelligent partner of the flesh and blood Detective Bobby Mann (David Andrews). Set twenty years ahead in futuristic Los Angeles, the show stayed true to the generic formula of pairing a mismatched cop duo for comedic effect as they carry out their criminal

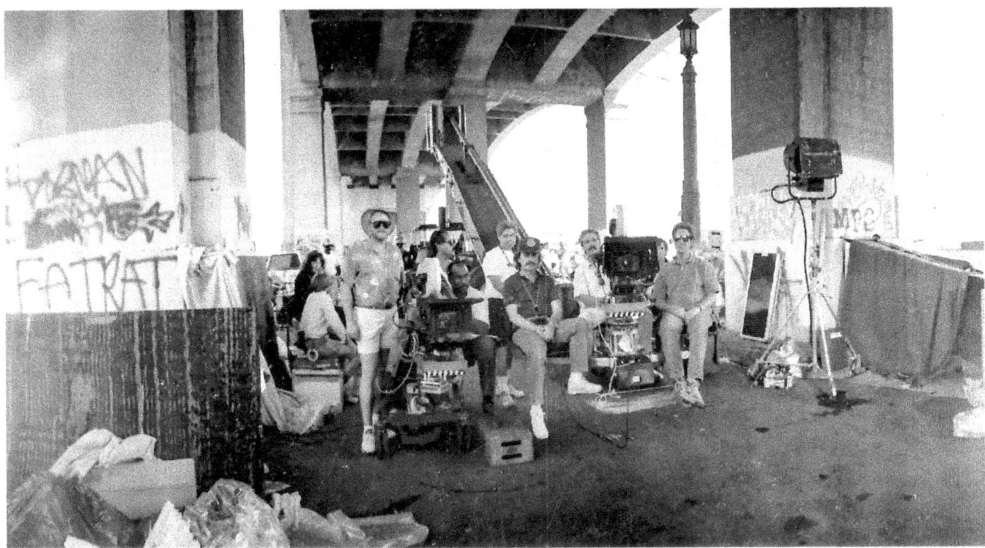

Roy and crew under the Third Street Bridge, shooting *Cop Rock*. From row, from left: John L. Wagner (Roy's brother and first assistant camera), Norm Langley (camera operator), Roy (director of photography), Gary Huddleston (camera operator), Tommy Klines (first assistant camera).

investigations; only here the clichéd culture clash is not one based in racial or ethnic contrast, but one between—yes—Man(n) and Machine.

"That was another Dick Wolf show, but they didn't have the right amount of money to do it. Nobody ever has the right amount of money to do anything. The production designer had built a beautiful futuristic police station, and it cost $20,000 a week for backings outside of the windows. And they said, 'Wow, that's crazy! We're spending way over my budget just on backings.' So, I said, 'Why don't you just paint the windows? Just paint them so I can light them, so that they're translucent but you can't see outside. Because in the future there may or may not be anything to see. And besides that, it might look kind of silly when we realize how rinky dink it all looks with the backings. So, she painted all the windows, and it became sort of the style of that show; we used a lot of source lighting, but it did not come from anything specific. That was the show where I really decided that I was not going to be trapped by having a Steadicam. I had never liked using it that much before. I was trained to look through the eyepiece and light through the camera, but when the Steadicam came along you couldn't do that anymore because the camera could float anywhere. So, I was reluctant to use Steadicam for a long time; I used it on *Cop Rock*, but I decided not to use it on *Mann and Machine*. So, we did everything on the dolly and that was incredibly difficult—I had the camera operator sometimes doing 360-degree moves and there was only one set! It could get really complicated at times, but *Mann and Machine* was a fun show to do."

Unfortunately, with low ratings the show was cancelled after four episodes. But Roy would soon find satisfying work with an auteur filmmaker who was coming off a series of massive hits with *The Lost Boys*, *Flatliners*, and *Dying Young*. Joel Schumacher brought his distinctive style to television and was the creative force behind the prime-time soap opera *2000 Malibu Road*, an attractive Aaron Spelling production the premise of which sees four young professional women—a prostitute, a lawyer, an actress, and her sister—all living in a beach house and navigating life, love, and lecherous men in sunny Malibu.

"I loved working with Joel," Roy enthuses, "he was one of my favorite people. I regretted that it was not successful, I would have had a long relationship with him. It was me who convinced him to direct every episode. And he did. He directed all of them. It was very glamorous and stylish, every one of those actresses was wanting and having to be beautiful, so that was a big part of it. And we were shooting in summertime, just extraordinary. There was a lot of camera movement on that location in Malibu; I did some big, complicated dolly shots outside of the house and we didn't have a Steadicam—it costs a lot of money to have a Steadicam operator. All those complicated moves in *2000 Malibu Road* were done by my wonderful key grip Dale Alexander. It was just amazing stuff."

Alexander recalls the effort: "We just had to be Roy's right-hand and left-hand; we were executing what his creativity had already come up with. How we got there was up to us, just as long as we got there and gave him the finished product that he was looking for. By the time Roy gives us the information that he took away from his meetings with the director, he already has in mind what he wants; he has already seen everything, and though we could give him input it is really about executing what Roy wants. He was incredible with lighting but when it came to rigging that's where Roy couldn't really accomplish. He could ask for

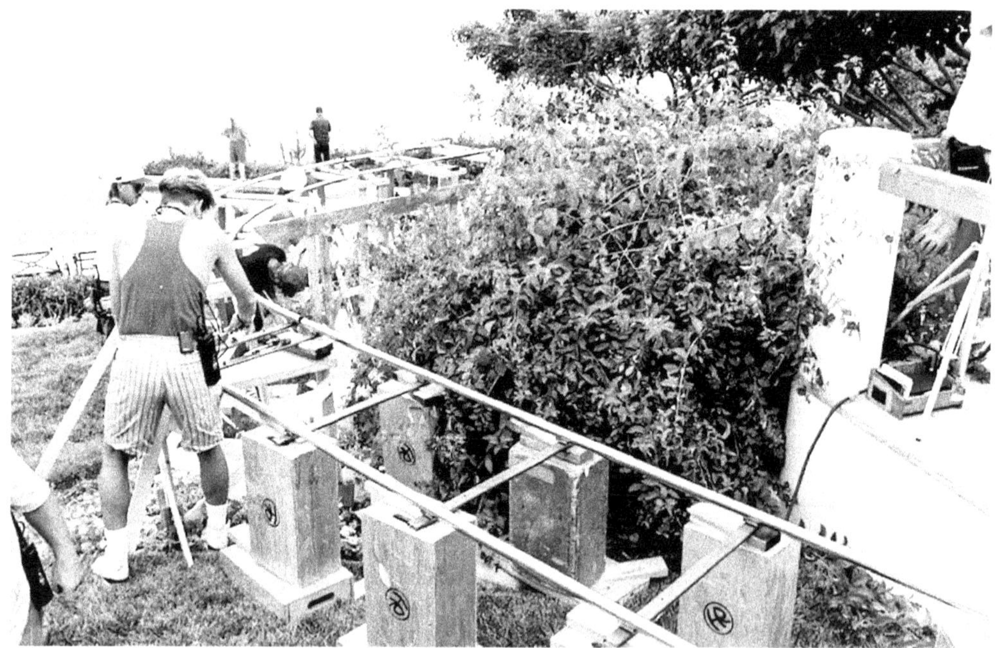

Setting up shots on location for *2000 Malibu Road*, 1992.

things, but he wouldn't know how to achieve it physically himself. That's where he and I got along so well. I could get anything he wanted done in little time."

"Aaron Spelling could be incredibly cheap," Roy states, "but Joel really made sure that I got the time and the money that I needed to do whatever was necessary and we still did it on budget. Joel had style but he was a minimalist. There was one particular scene where Joel completely redesigned the look of the set. We had a wonderful production designer named John Walker who came into this house and dressed it beautifully, just beautifully, but Joel came in and said, 'No, I don't like it. I don't want to do it this way.' I was already lit and ready to shoot it, I was so in love with it. I just couldn't believe it when Joel said that. And then he came in and redressed the set himself. This is the scene where they're all sitting around the fireplace at night. It's gorgeous and there's nothing there. Literally nothing there. So, I used a big camera movement with them at the fire, giving it a sense of place with a big wide shot, and with the light the way it was it looks far better than what we originally planned. Joel had been a window dresser at the big department stores in New York; that's how he started. So, he really had a sense for design and aesthetics."

Roy continues, "Working with Joel was like a marriage. You always want to please your mate. And for me, as a cinematographer, I didn't want it to be a Roy Wagner show; I wanted it to be a Joel Schumacher show. Whoever I work with, I always want it to be their show and for me to find my way into that. That is because I always learned so much more by stepping out of my comfort zone and doing things that other people wanted to do. I was always open to change. I was

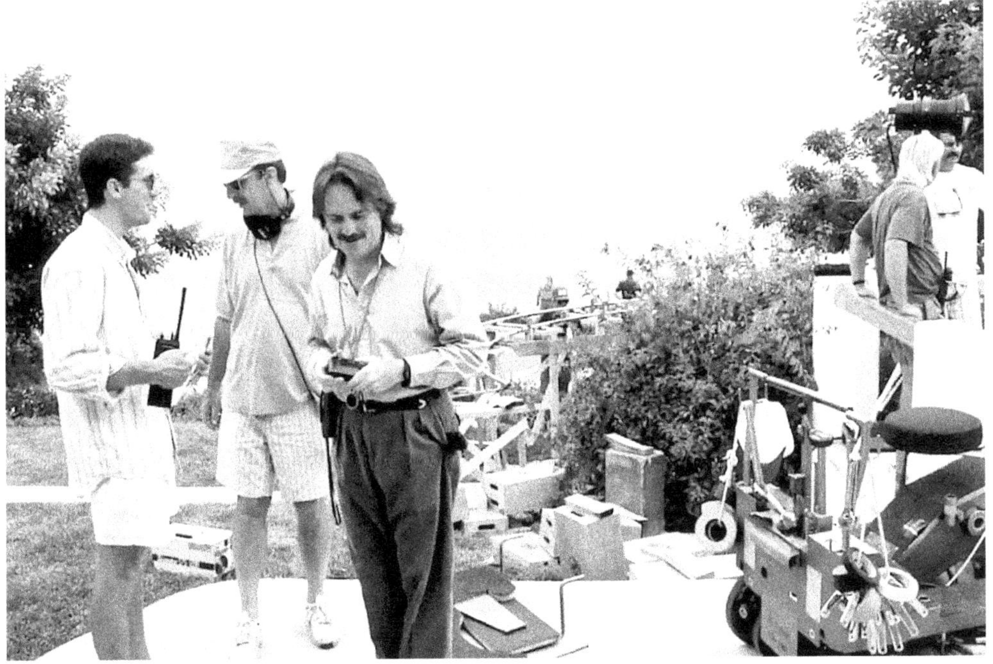

Roy (third from left) and crew on set of *2000 Malibu Road*.

taught by my mentors to never say 'No' to a director. The only time I would ever say 'No' is if anybody's safety was in question. On *2000 Malibu Road* I really tried to find my place amongst the actors, the director, and the studio. I don't go in thinking I have to bring the Roy Wagner style to it, whatever that is anyway. I wish I could say that Joel and I had these big, large conversations about the aesthetic of the show, or that we had conflict that would make it more dramatic and theatrical, but it was not like that at all. We were collaborators in the sense that Joel would tell me the feeling of what he wanted, and then I would go do it. He had incredible taste and knew exactly what he liked and what he didn't like."

Despite the gorgeous stars, glamorous setting, stylish photography, and tasteful production design, the series only lasted six episodes. "Aaron pulled his own show! *2000 Malibu Road* was a CBS show, but he had a contract with Fox for his other show, *Melrose Place*, and the problem was that *2000 Malibu Road* was doing great; it was getting better ratings than *Melrose Place*. It was really growing at that point until Aaron pulled it. We would have kept going because the cast was amazing and the writers, Kimberly Costello and Terry Louise Fisher, were just exceptional. But Aaron killed his own show in an act of self-sabotage so as not to rival his bigger show. He was a partner with Joel on *2000 Malibu Road*, but he owned *Melrose Place* entirely, so he had a much bigger interest in that being a success. It was a great experience working with Joel, but I never really cared for Aaron's work; I think they are cheesy shows, and I didn't want anything to do with them."

Party of Two

Crucial Collaborations

"It's a contact sport. If you don't want to get hit, don't play the game!"

After an unfortunate run of short-lived TV shows throughout the first few years of the nineties, something far more significant was to come for Roy. *Party of Five* was a Fox family drama which premiered in 1994 and featured an ensemble cast including Scott Wolf, Matthew Fox, Neve Campbell, and Lacey Chabert as the four recently orphaned siblings of the Salinger family who are tasked with looking after each other and raising their baby brother, Owen (initially played by Alexander and Zachary Ahnert). The series lasted six seasons, the first two of which being shot by Roy. The show proved to be an opportunity for Roy to make some crucial connections as he would forge friendships and secure future opportunities in the process of its production. Enter Peter O'Fallon. A veteran of the commercial world, O'Fallon had also accrued his episodic television directing experience working on critically acclaimed hit shows such as *Thirtysomething*, *Northern Exposure*, and *American Gothic*, a resume that made him the ideal candidate to come in and save *Party of Five* after an inauspicious pilot episode left producers nervous as they moved into the series. O'Fallon recalls: "I was a very young man at the time, and I was busy doing commercials. I kind of felt loyal to the commercial people but they had done the pilot for *Party of Five* when they called me up and said they didn't like what the pilot looked like and told me that they would like me to come in to help. So, I went in. Roy didn't do the pilot, and when he came in I learned that he likes to work fast, which was great for me because having done television commercials for years I like to work fast too. You see, in commercials you get paid; they give you a deal where you make a percentage of the overhead if you save money. So, I ended up getting to be very quick on those; I would shoot a thirty-second commercial in four days. I like to move very quickly and make things happen. I think it's better for the actors and Roy was so into it with me that I was actually shocked. I ended up loving the guy immediately. I was like, 'Can we do this?' and he would be like, 'Yeah, we can do that.' 'And can we do this?' 'Yeah, we can do that.' That's the kind of willing collaborator Roy is."

Party of Five now benefited from the collaboration of a young visionary director and a cinematographer of much experience and authority, and while this meant for aesthetically interesting television, having two men of distinct artistic sensibilities and strong personalities meant for some bureaucratic battles with their edgy producers.

"Our line producer was very difficult to work with," O'Fallon says, "I mean I liked the guy, but he was difficult with all sorts of things. And Roy had very specific ideas on how we wanted things done too. So, we came up against production at times. The Technocrane had just come out and we had one for *Party of Five*. One day, Roy was setting up a shot that I really wanted which required a platform that could lift this 10,000-pound thing and the line producer was freaking out that we were taking so much time to set it up; he walked in to where Roy and I were sitting and started yelling at us saying, 'I told you this thing was a waste of time and a waste of money! If you guys don't get this shot in the next half-hour, we're going to pull the plug.' And so, we get the whole thing down, we're rehearsing it, and it looks as cool as I thought it would look. Then we roll the camera, the operator comes down and then comes up, but then it shook a little bit and I turned to Roy like, 'What the fuck?' And then Roy walks up and pushes the guy out of the way and says, 'It's a contact sport. If you don't want to get hit, don't play the game!' Then Roy sat down at this thing, we called the second take, and Roy nailed it perfectly. I loved it. I turned to the line producer and said, 'I got it!' And he goes, 'All right, then let's wrap.'"

O'Fallon continues, "There were too many times throughout our career where people would challenge us not to be able to do the things we were supposed to do. The great example of this is when Roy got fired from *Party of Five*. I

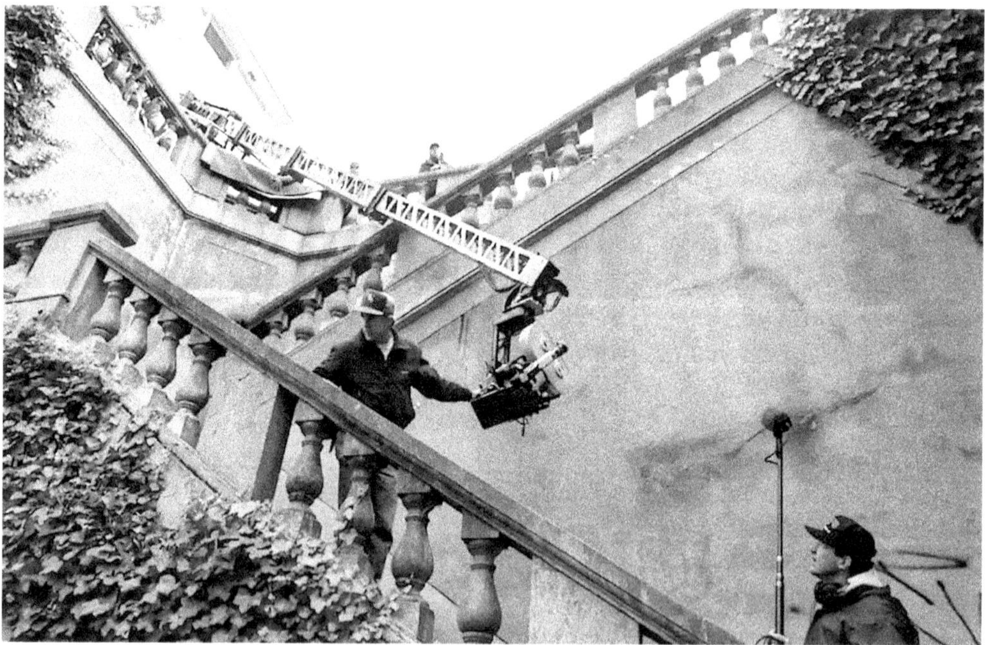

The telescopic crane used for a "walk and talk" scene in *Party of Five*, 1994.

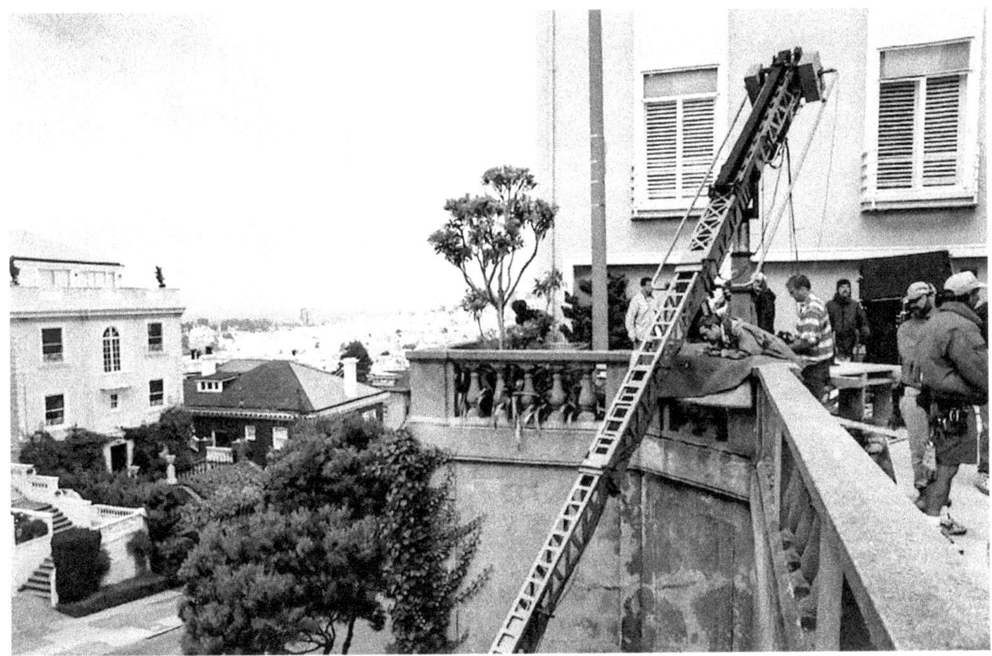

Crane set up for a complicated shot on the set of *Party of Five*.

wanted to do this whole thing in the ice-skating auditorium, a 360-degree shot on the Steadicam, but to do that meant you would see the entire audience, but they couldn't afford that many extras, so Roy goes, 'I've got a plan!' Give me twenty minutes.' When I came back to Roy he had gotten around thirty or maybe fifty extras, had four slashes of light, and he put all the extras just in the light. Everything else was pitch black. So, the auditorium looked full. And we finished the whole thing."

Key Grip Dale Alexander recalls the ingeniously simple solution that Roy provided to what should have been an expensive and complicated set up: "For that episode we had the little girl, Lacey, doing this on the ice skating rink and Roy had me build something where I had the camera on the ground and she was able to hold on to it and the dolly grip could make it spin and do all the stuff on the ice. And this was all at the last minute. Roy said, 'Okay, Dale, this is what I need you to do...' and I was like, 'Really? Right now?' He expected it, and we got it done. He always came up with these genius ideas and techniques."

"Roy pulled it off," O'Fallon says. "We got to do this 360-degree amazing shot and do all this other stuff, which is huge for television, but then our line producer walks in and goes—I'll never forget this—'I just want you to know we're going to fire Roy.' And I go, 'Are you fucking kidding me?!' At this point we had just got done at three-thirty after a nine-hour day, and I go, 'Why?!' and he says, 'Roy sent one of his assistants to fix his car.' And I turned to this guy and said, 'I don't care if Roy sent his whole fucking crew to fix his car! This is insane! Why would you do this? You're always worried about money and yet every time Roy and I shoot, we do it in nine-hour days and we get incredible stuff. I do not understand what you're doing. This seems stupid to me.' And he's like, 'I don't know what to tell

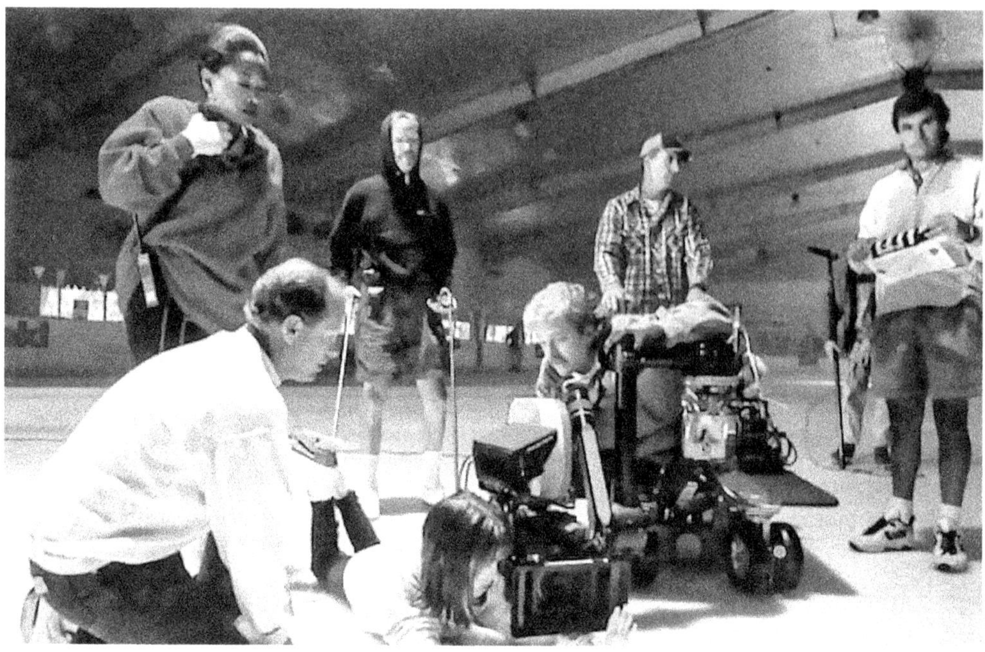

Shooting *Party of Five* at the Burbank Ice Rink. From left: Eric Jewett (assistant director), Vicki Jackson-Lemay (assistant director), Lacey Chabert (actress, on ground), Grover Austin (grip), Gary Huddleston (camera operator), David Buchanan, and unknown crew member.

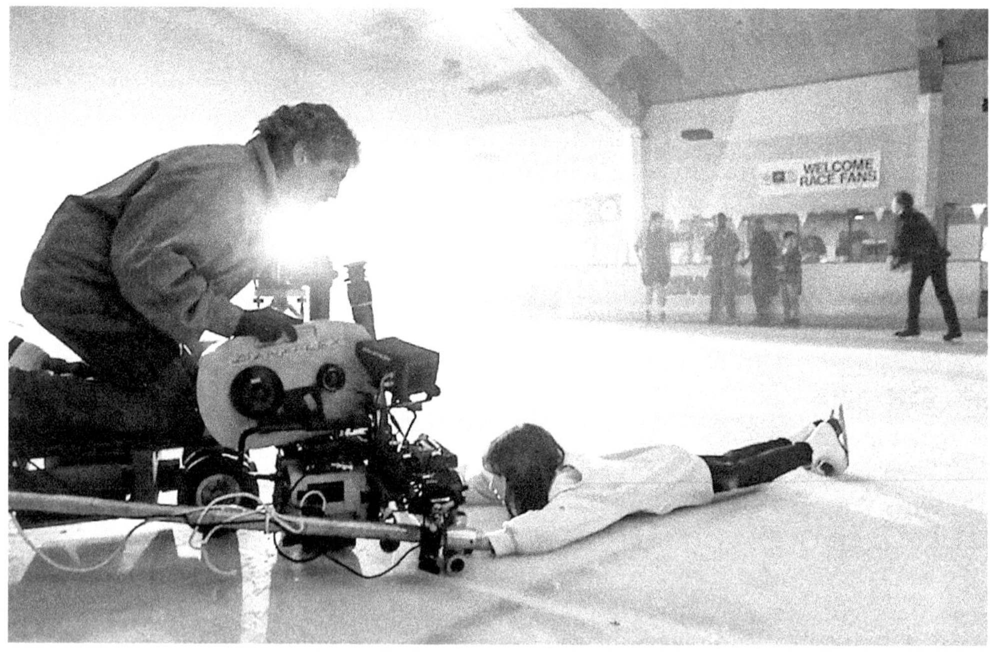

Camera operator Gary Huddleston shoots actress Lacey Chabert on the ice in *Party of Five*.

you, Peter.' I guess he just had something for Roy, So, I went directly to the show runners, explained the situation, and then Roy got back on the show."

"I was not always the greatest diplomat," Roy reveals, "'nor is Peter incidentally.' Everything with Peter is, 'Fuck it! We're not doing it that way, fuck it!' He can be like a bull in a china closet; you are going to do it Peter's way, one way or another. But if it hadn't been for Peter, I wouldn't have been brought back to *Party of Five*. And then they tried to fire me again because I was always bringing my kids to the set. I was divorced and so my kids had no place to go. I had grown up with cinematographers who didn't know their children, and I felt that if my children don't know who I am, then it doesn't matter how good a cinematographer I am—I'm screwed. So, they always came with me to the set, and they were not a problem whatsoever, but they wanted to fire me for that because it was an insurance issue. Peter saved my ass plenty of times. If it wasn't for him, I would not have had the career I've had. On *Party of Five* we like were these two bad boys, but the thing that irritated them the most about us was that they couldn't claim that we were slow or that our work wasn't good, and we always did what they wanted us to do. In fact, Peter became a big superstar on *Party of Five* because he was able to do the impossible."

With Roy back on the show, he continued to push the stylistic boundaries in a medium not known for breaking from convention. However innovative, not everybody appreciated Roy's artful aesthetic on the show, as he sharply remembers, "There was a famous critic who said, '*Party of Five* would be a very successful show if it wasn't for Roy Wagner's dark photography,' and we had been on the air for two seasons at that point. It was never supposed to be a dark, brooding show, but it was about five kids who lost their parents, so how can I make this a pretty, happy show?"

Gaffer Brian Crane recalls Roy's style being somewhat challenging to studio suits and the show's producers who were not so used to such artistic formalism: "It was the kind of ingenuity you don't see a whole lot of on TV, especially back then. Because it was such an odd and rare thing to do, they were skeptical at first. But once Roy showed them how it could be done, all those directors who worked on the show appreciated what he brought to the sets, things that you would never think you could shoot in that way. He wasn't afraid of space at all. I've never heard him say, 'Can we move this?' He just would just yell to his grip to get him a front-surface mirror."

"On *Party of Five* Roy wasn't afraid of the blacks," Alexander says, "he wasn't afraid of pushing the edges, and going without fill. But he did put a little glint in the actors' eyes; he would always put something somewhere in the frame that gave a little sparkle in their eyes. God, that was such a fast-paced show to work on, but Roy was able to bring an amazing intimacy to the characters with his photography. His work on that show is jaw dropping."

"Roy learned a long time ago that I don't like the word 'problem,' because it creates this tension," Crane says, "so I prefer to use the word 'challenge," so everything with him was a challenge, like, "Change the light up there! Let's see if we can do this in thirty seconds." That type of thing. One memory that sticks out from *Party of Five* is when he would say to me, "Give me five lights," and I'd go and set them, and then he would say, "Give me another five lights," and so I would set those, and then it's another thing, and so on. So, I finally went up to him one day and I said, "Roy, you can give me more than five lights at a time, I'm more than capable of remembering this." So, what we ended up doing was he wound up walking me through the entire downstairs set of the *Party of Five* house, and the complete upstairs set, and then to the bar set, and the bar had all these lights with various colors, I would say probably about eighty lights in total with gels and everything else. And when he walked me through there it was really quiet, and Roy looks up and he goes, "That's yellow. It should be orange!" But because I had my guys listen to him, I was like, "No, Roy, it's supposed to be yellow.' And he was impressed that I could remember that. I think ever since that moment he knew he could trust me with any number of lights and that I was more than capable of lighting more than one set at a time for him. That became an asset to him on future shows because I could go ahead and pre-light a look for him that he could walk into and then just finalize. It was good for our speed too."

While *Party of Five* took a couple of seasons for the viewing public to catch on to its charms, Roy didn't stick around long enough to enjoy the show rising to the profile of peak '90s programming. Crane recalls Roy's rising frustrations which led to his premature departure from the show:

"Roy had difficulties with some of the younger, inexperienced directors who were coming in. He almost lost his shit with a few of them because they didn't understand what was going on. They would be like, 'I want everything like this, this, this, this and this,' and Roy would say, 'If you just shoot everything *this* way and then shoot everything *that* way you would be done with it. Or shoot with two cameras.' The way these directors worked could be frustrating for him, and the other frustrating thing is that after working on a TV series for about two years he has already lit everything every which way that he could, and so he gets bored at that point, and I think he becomes edgy. But it's mainly boredom. Many of us have tried to convince him to do more features because of that. There's such a short window with features that he would be able do everything he could with it and then move on to the next project on which he could do something completely different. But I think it's the downtime in between features which frustrated him, whereas with television it just ran and ran and ran. And he liked that. He liked to be busy, he liked to light, he liked to be doing what he was doing. But once he lit everything you could see the boredom setting in; there was nothing like, 'Oh, we'll do this, and try that.' The fun was gone for him and that's when the boredom affected him."

"I never stayed on shows that long," Roy affirms, "which was stupid because I could have made a lot more money if I stayed and settled, but I was afraid that if I settled onto one show for a long time then I would just do the same thing over and over again. I was in the middle of the second season of *Party of Five* and I was working with the same beautiful sets and one day I ran into a wall, literally in my mind I ran into a wall. I thought I was so smart as to be able to get myself out of the box and figure out another way or another approach to doing something, but suddenly I realized I was doing the exact same thing and I said, 'Oh my God, this is horrible,' and I thought that no matter how talented you are or how artistic you are, there's a point where the doppelgänger catches up with you and now you have been found out. And I didn't want to find out who I was. It was during that show where I realized that you can have a plan but you can always break the rules of the plan, and that was for me where I would be watching rehearsals and my hands would be clenched thinking, 'Oh God, don't let that actor go over there, that's where I'm going to put a light; I don't want him to be in this part of the house because I want to put a camera there.' I had all these pre-conceived notions, and I thought my ideas were always better because I could formulate them, put them in a little box, and make them safe and comfortable because I knew exactly how to survive them. One day I was having anxiety attacks and really getting stressed out and I asked myself a series of questions to help me understand what I was going through: 'What the hell is wrong with you?! You say you love cinematography, and you say that you love being the director of photography, but what is it that you love? Here you are watching rehearsal, the most creative moment in the process where everybody is finding their space and figuring out what they are going to do, and you're terrified! And if people don't do what you want them to do you try and force them to be where you want them to be. Why don't you flow with them and find out what they're doing so you can be organically connected with the actors and organically connected with the director and find this combustion between yourselves?'

"And in asking myself those questions I came upon an answer: that I might find out amidst this chaos a happy accident. Something that I did not have any idea was there because I was so myopic, having locked myself in this place where I felt safe. I thought, 'You keep telling yourself that you're trying to be outside of the box but you're not outside of any box, you've boxed everybody in with what you're doing.' That was the length of time that it took for me to reach that realization, and it was that simple. Suddenly it was like somebody lifted something off me, and everything from that point forward was about experiencing openness— the actor wants to go over there? Okay! And if it wasn't right, it was about finding an organic way to fix it. It wasn't about telling people what to do and what not to do, it was about everybody finding their own way and being part of that orchestra and getting to the end of that piece of music. It was such a beautiful experience. It wasn't just about 'pretty' photography, it was about being part of the storytelling. I had this revelation because I met Peter O'Fallon on *Party of Five*; he was a huge part of that transition for me."

◆ ◆ ◆

Roy would reunite with O'Fallon again at the turn of the millennium, this time working with the larger canvas of the cinema screen. *A Rumor of Angels* is O'Fallon's feature debut, a heartbreaking melodrama based on Grace Duffie Boylan's 1918 novel *Thy Son Liveth: Messages from a Son to His Mother*. The film is centered around the deep bond that develops between twelve-year-old James Neubauer (Trevor Morgan) and an elderly recluse named Maddy (Vanessa

Redgrave). The pair, both lost souls without much personal connection in their lives, first meet after James crashes his bicycle through Maddy's fence and she demands that he return to repair it. James has been emotionally lost since the tragic death of his mother in a car crash. His feelings are exacerbated due to his rarely present and emotionally barren father Nathan (Ray Liotta) who is often away on business. He also endures a strained relationship with his stepmother Mary (Catherine McCormack). However, James forms an unlikely bond with the mysterious lady in the house on the hill, both helping each other come to terms with bereavements which have blighted their lives.

O'Fallon recalls the origins of what proved to be a long and arduous project to get from script to screen:

"When I was in Denver—before I went to Chicago, then New York, and then LA—a good friend of mine invited me to a reading of a play that was based on a book called *Thy Son Liveth*. So, I watched this play and I thought, 'Oh my God, that's great. I love this thing! Do you want to make a movie out of it?' And he goes, 'Sure!' So, he and I rewrote it. And then I rewrote it about nine more times after that. Then this old-school big-time producer picked it up immediately and he arranged for me to meet with Sophia Loren to play Maddy. So, we went to Sofia's big giant home in Calabasas and her husband Carlo Ponti met us there at the door. I walked into the room and there was Sophia; she was probably 60 at the time and still gorgeous. She was wearing a dress, and she had her legs crossed with one leg coming out of the slit in the dress. She just looked incredibly attractive; I felt like Carlo had told her to look good for the director. I loved her, and I thought we would make it happen, but then it fell apart. I can't remember why. Then we tried to put it together again and that's when I met Lisa Hansen. She was a producer and worked for a company which was making really cheap dumb movies, so she wanted to change the name and change the company. So, she optioned the film and we spent forever trying to get it going. And then this is the weird luck of Hollywood: I was with the William Morris Agency and someone in the

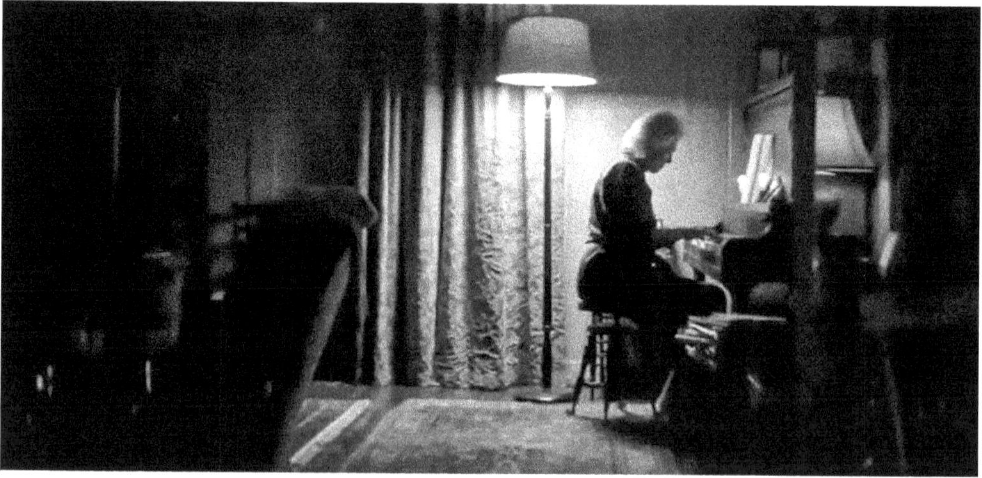

Vanessa Redgrave sparsely lit in the opening scenes of *A Rumor of Angels*, 2002.

talent department read the script and said, 'My God, I love your script!' And I was already kind of jaded to the point where I was like, 'Yeah, okay. Thanks, man.' And he goes on… 'I'm thinking about getting Vanessa Redgrave.' And I shrugged it off, like, 'Yeah, go ahead, you do that. Go for it.' And then he called me up about a week later and said that she read it, loves it, and wants to do it. And I was like, 'You're kidding!' And then he goes on: 'I'm also thinking Ray Liotta…' So, he gives it to Ray Liotta and now Ray wants to do it. I absolutely couldn't believe it. This guy was a young brand-new agent in the talent department at William Morris and after *A Rumor of Angels* he quit the business. I asked him why and he said, 'Because I thought it would always be like what we did—I read a script that really moved me, I talked to the actor, it really moved the actor, and they wanted to do it. It wasn't about how much money they were going to get paid and all that. Then I started to realize that the way we did it on *A Rumor of Angels* was not the way that it always was going to be.'"

With some actors committed, O'Fallon proceeded to set up the film to shoot in Oregon, but things didn't go to plan, which meant for a delay in production moving forward and a change in location. Ultimately, shooting would proceed in a scenic maritime province further north. Production was moved to Nova Scotia, which would provide various locations such as Lunenberg and Crystal Crescent Beach to fill in for the Maine-set story. O'Fallon recalls the practical, financial, and aesthetic benefits of such:

"Nova Scotia offered us a credit that basically paid for the money that I had spent in Oregon trying to get set up, like 250,000 bucks. The greatest thing about Nova Scotia is its magic three hours—it's not a magic hour like it is everywhere else; the sun gets low and stays low. And it hovers around the horizon before it drops. Beautiful. So, I went to Nova Scotia and immediately called Roy, and I told him that we were going to shoot on 16mm, which I really did not want to do. But Roy came back and said, 'Okay, I can get you 35mm, I can get you anamorphic, I can get you this and that…' And I was like, 'Anamorphic? You're fucking kidding me!' So, thanks to Roy we used an anamorphic lens, and we were shooting wide open and using available light. I wanted it to be as natural as possible. I think it's a good movie, but in the big picture it is the look of the film that makes it work; it's the mood that Roy brought to it with his photography."

"Peter kept saying, 'Go through the muslin!'" Roy recalls, "And I'm going to do what he wants, so I went through the muslin, and it was beautiful. It gave it this nice, soft, beautiful light. Nova Scotia was a brand-new filmmaking community, and they had this chip on their shoulder; they didn't want anybody from the outside to come in and help them with their movie. But we brought in a lot of people from outside of Nova Scotia and now they've all been trained by us. They've got some great crews up there now. We brought in a first assistant camera guy called Jayson Clute, who was the assistant to a Steadicam operator that I worked with on a film in Toronto. Jayson is still to this day probably the best assistant I've ever had. And the Steadicam operator was just as good. They both were like me and Peter; they never said no about anything, they would just say 'Okay, we'll figure it out.' Photographically, it is probably

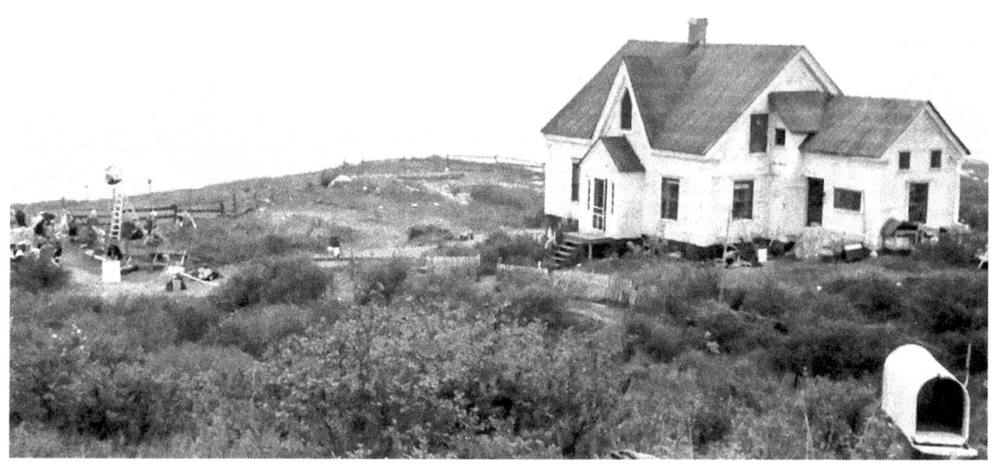

The rugged Nova Scotia location for *A Rumor of Angels*.

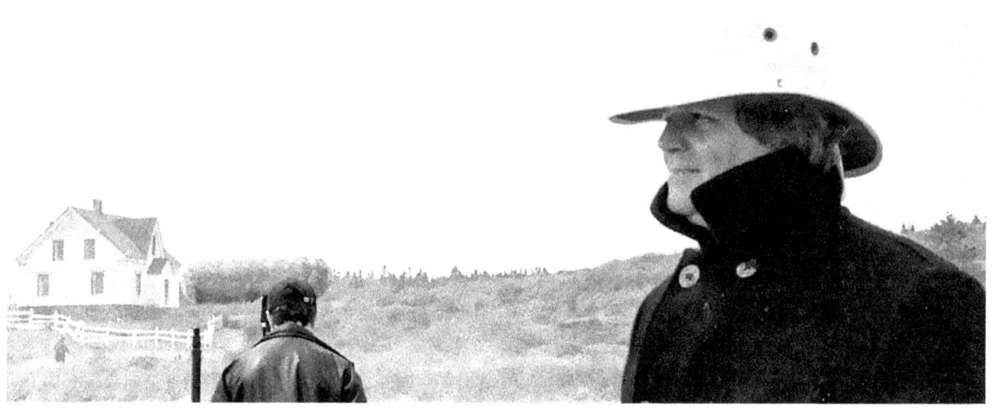

Roy surveys the photogenic landscape of Nova Scotia for *A Rumor of Angels*.

my favorite movie, and my favorite image in the whole movie was also the simplest to achieve: a shot of the piano at the beginning which was just lit by the candle. But the real reason I wanted to do *A Rumor of Angels* is because there was something about working with Peter. He is Irish, and he's got that fearlessness about him. He's like a bulldog and won't give up. But when Peter and I initially spoke about the doing the movie he just told me, 'I don't think we can afford you.' And I asked him, 'If you can afford me, can I do it?' and Peter said, 'Of course, you can do it!' So, I found out how much they were going to pay the cinematographer and how they had for camera, equipment, and film. Originally, they were going to shoot it on 16mm, but I went to Eastman Kodak and they gave us 35mm film stock virtually for free. Deluxe labs even gave us a certain number of prints for free. For the cameras I first went to Panavision who said they would do it but then they defaulted, so I went Denny Clairmont and he said, 'Tell me what you want to do.' I told him, and he said, 'I'll do that.' So, I got the cameras plus anamorphic lenses for next to nothing. That was unheard of. By that point I'd saved them so much money that they could have paid me $10,000 a week and still save money. So, they allowed me to come in and shoot the movie. The problem was the production designer, Stephen McCabe, who did incredible work, spent the entire budget of the movie before we even started! They spent all the money building this grand house set that was constructed on a sled which meant we could pull any of the walls when we wanted to. But by the time that set was built we had no money left in the budget."

"Stephen spent all the money, but he did an unbelievable job," O'Fallon applauds. "We built the house in such a way that the sunlight came in for the scenes set in the morning and then in the afternoon the light came in the other side, we could pull the walls in this giant set. One weekend I went to the location to figure out what I was going to do, and I found him there by himself with a paint can and I said, 'Oh my God, Stephen, what are you doing?' and he replied, 'God, they all suck up here. I have to do it all myself.' He was busy making the paint look aged and weathered, but I remember being so mad at him. I was fuming, and I said to Roy, 'Stephen has spent all the money!' And then I went out to the location a second time and there he was again painting by himself. I walked up to him and said, 'Stephen, I'm so fucking mad at you right now I can't even stand it!' But then I looked around the house and it was so damn good. It looked like he had been there painting the place for a hundred years. And to his credit, he was unflappable. He had this great British sense of humor. I was yelling at him about having no money and he is just like, 'Well, Peter, you will have to figure that out, and I'm sure you will.'"

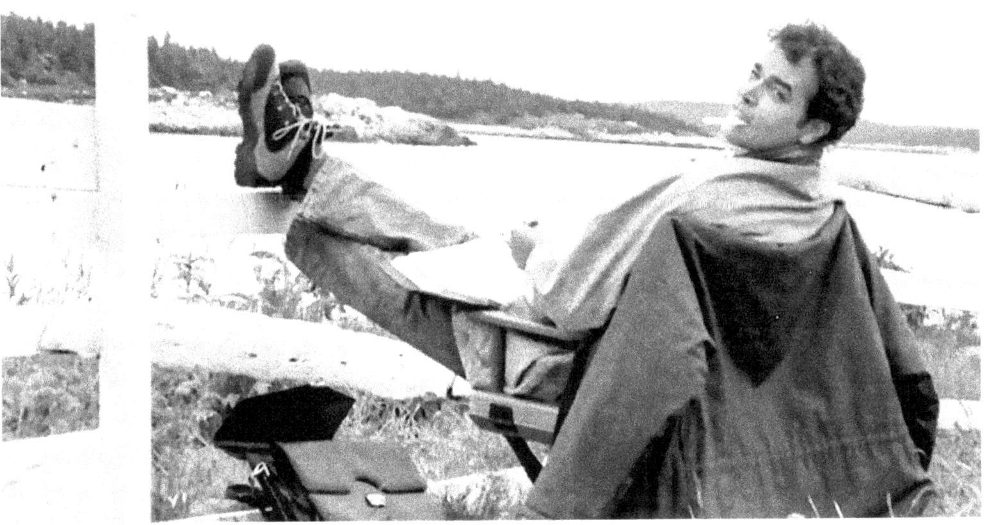

Ray Liotta takes time out between takes in *A Rumor of Angels*.

O'Fallon continues, "It was one of the greatest times of my life, but making this movie was a nightmare for me. Everything was incredibly difficult. We were some of the first people up there in Nova Scotia and we had a lot of problems with the crew. One of the reasons they brought in the money to Canada was because the fisheries had collapsed, as did the coal industry. So, a lot of the people up there had been on the dole for a long time and a lot of crews kept saying 'No' to us. They would be like, 'I'm busy doing my garden tomorrow,' And I'm like, 'Are you fucking kidding me? You're doing your garden tomorrow?!' The greatest one was one day where I had this incredible scene all set up with Vanessa Redgrave and the kid out on the beach and it was supposed to rain; the producer, God bless her, walked up to me and she was like, 'Okay, do you want the good news or the bad news?' I go, 'Alright, what is the good news?' And she said there isn't any, so I go, 'What's the bad news?' And she says, 'The fire department was going to come and make the rain for us, but they have decided not to come. And I go, 'What do you mean? Do they have a fire to attend to?' And she said, 'No, they just decided they didn't want to come.' So, Roy comes up and says, 'Don't worry, Pete, we got this. Do we have a garden hose?' We got a garden hose, and we shot the scene with that making the rain, but it looked terrible. But then Roy goes, 'Wait, I got it...' then Roy went and got a black background, and we shot the water on a black background. And then we put the rain into the sea. Is it perfect? No. Did it work? Fuck yes! It saved our ass."

Further contention occurred on set, but this was less of a production issue and more to do with differing approaches to delivering an appropriate performance. This very chasm occurred between O'Fallon, who was used to the more yielding casts of television productions, and the classically trained stage stalwart, Vanessa Redgrave. The actress brought immense gravitas and emotion to the film, as well an exacting method for enveloping herself in the role, much to O'Fallon's chagrin.

"Don't ever hope that you get what you want," Roy cautions, "because Peter dreamed of getting Vanessa Redgrave and he got Vanessa Redgrave. She was tough; she would never let the bone go. She was so tough on me, so I stayed away from her, but she was even tougher on Peter. She hated working with him because he was so accustomed to working in the television style where the actors just do what the director wants. Peter was accustomed to talking to actors and hearing, 'Oh, okay, I got it,' and getting his way, but with Vanessa he had to hang in there with her and put up with all this stuff she brought with her from the Old Vic. We all think she's kind of instinctual and she just lets things happen, but it's not that way at all—it's very procedural. She wanted to explore and understand everything about her experience. She had to have an answer for every single thing. At one point she said, 'Why am I lying in his bed?' And Peter said, 'Because you're tired,' which was very cute and funny, but she really wanted more than that. I had to walk out because Peter was there talking to her for an hour and a half before she was ready to do the scene. Once she gets all that, then she's amazing. But Peter had to wade through all of it. So, it was contentious. But the truth is, I think it was a good contentious. We ended up doing a better movie because of that."

"Vanessa is the opposite of me," O'Fallon affirms, "and we had too many arguments. If I'm the Grateful Dead, she's a symphony orchestra. I'll jam and see where the music takes us, but she wants to have everybody play the exact note they're supposed to play when they're supposed to play it. When I would set up a scene with Vanessa I would have to map out exactly what she was to do: 'Alright, Vanessa, walk over to the table. Pick up the cup, take a sip from the cup, set the cup down on the table, sit back down, say your line, stand back up, walk towards the door, open the door, say your line.' She was being directed, but that's just not my style. And we annoyed her even more because we scouted exterior angles that we wanted but we needed to wait for the right light to shoot them; so, we would be inside doing something else and then somebody would come over radio going, 'It looks pretty good!' So, we would run out and look at it and go, 'No, no, a little later.' Then we'd go back in and shoot some more until all of a sudden we'd hear, 'Alright, we're going!' And we would run back out and shoot in this perfect light. Vanessa hated that. What I will say, though, is that she was genius in this movie. Absolutely genius. And she was incredibly kind to young Trevor. So calm, it was like a mother and this cub. But with everybody else she was quite difficult, so much so we had some guys go to a hospital. One guy for an asthma attack and one guy for anxiety because they had to drive her to the house location every day, and we built the house on the edge of this thing because we were shooting anamorphic, but the village was a mile away and they had to drive her in and out every day."

"The cast that Peter assembled was unreal," Roy says, "Ray Liotta was

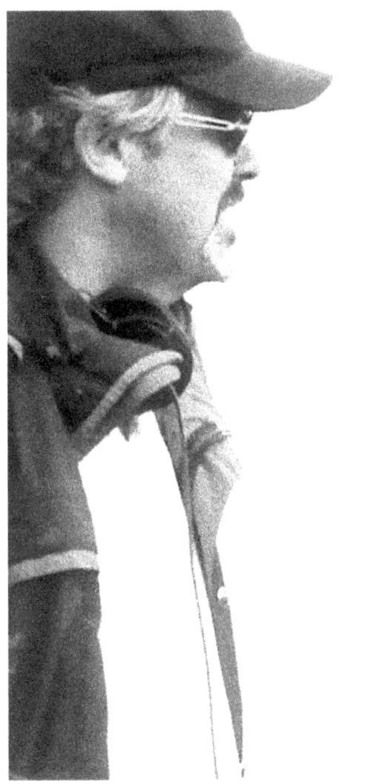
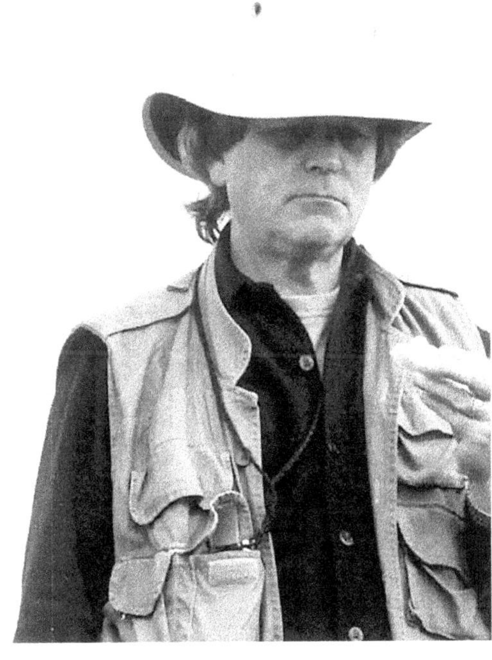

"Let's wait for the light." Director Peter O'Fallon (left) and Roy on set of *A Rumor of Angels*.

absolutely wonderful. I loved Ray. He would sit in his director's chair reading a script and smoking a cigarette. And then there was a brief bit of chaos when Catherine McCormack was cast. She was chosen on the basis of the way she looked, and when she came to the set we realized that she had cut all of her hair off."

"A classic agent story," O'Fallon laughs. "Catherine is an incredibly gorgeous woman and she had just done *Braveheart* in which she had long hair hanging down. But she called me and said, 'Hey, by the way, I cut my hair.' And I said, 'Oh, well, okay, send me a picture.' So her agent sent me the picture and her hair was down to her shoulder. Okay, I thought, it's shorter, but still kind of long. But when she showed up her hair was the same length as Roy's! There was some talk of using wigs but then we just decided to embrace it. And then, God bless her, when we screened the movie in Vancouver she sat next to me and afterwards she was crying her eyes out. And I asked her, 'Why are you crying? Were you moved by the movie?' But she looked at me and said, 'I ruined your movie! I am so sorry.' Of course, she didn't ruin it."

After all the pressures and difficulties of making the film, O'Fallon met with further stresses when it came time to test the film with an audience, as he recalls: "By that time, I was in a major depression about the whole thing, thinking how bad the whole experience had gone. Then the company involved with the film decided to test it in Santa Monica. And I thought to myself, oh my God, we're going to die, we're going to have a bunch of film students going, 'I hate it! This movie sucks!' But we screened it and when the movie finished they put twenty people up in front of the screen where they did all of the research. So, they asked this crowd how many of them would recommend it to their friends, and nineteen out of twenty of them raised their hand and I was like, 'Holy shit, this is unbelievable!' They saw things in the film that the critics completely missed; they said it's the kind of film that Hollywood doesn't make anymore—it's happy, it's sad, it's funny … it's life! It shows life. And I was freaking out going, 'Oh my God, this is so great.' It tested very well, something like 86 or 83, which is huge in testing. So now I'm thinking, 'This was all worth it.' And I turned around to some people from MGM and said, 'Hey, guys, what do you think about these scores? This is great news!' And one guy turns to me and says, 'You heard them: it's happy, it's sad, it's funny, it's this and that … how the fuck am I going to sell this movie?' And then I said, 'Well, how about you sell it like a good movie?' And he goes, 'Tell me how the fuck I'm supposed to do that!' And I said, 'I don't know. Do I have to tell you how to sell the movie now too? How about *Driving Miss Daisy*?' Then the guy got really irritated."

If the executives saw a film which was difficult to define, one notable audience member saw beyond marketing strategies to be touched deeply by the emotional core of the narrative. Conrad Hall, the revered cinematographer, hero of O'Fallon, and friend of Roy, came to see the film and offer his opinion. Roy recalls his reluctance of receiving the unreserved opinion of his mentor…

"For some fucking odd and stupid reason, I called Conrad to invite him to see the movie. The reason this was a stupid thing to do is because Conrad had this problem where he had to be totally honest with people. If you asked him a question he would tell you the truth. And that's not such a bad characteristic, but he could tell you exactly what he thought of you, and people don't always want to hear the truth about themselves. I once said to Conrad, 'Gee, Conrad, I wish I could do the big movies like you've done.' And he said, 'What big movies have I done?' 'Well,' I said, '*Day of the Locust, Cool Hand Luke, American Beauty* and—' Then he stopped me and said, 'What are you talking about? Those were low-budget movies; they only became big movies after they were released. I didn't get any more money for them, and I didn't get treated any better on them.' That's the kind of thing Conrad could say to you. But I respected his opinion, so I invited him to the screening and he said, 'Yeah, I'll go.' And as soon as I hung up the phone. I went, 'Oh, shit. What did I just do. I invited Conrad Hall to come see a movie and if he hates it he will tell me and I'll be devastated.' That would have killed me. So, with this playing around in my mind I was just miserable all the way through the screening. I could not bear the idea that as soon as the film was over he might tear me apart. But then at one point during the film my daughter kept nudging me in the arm and she whispered to me, 'Dad, Conrad is crying.' When the film finished, he did something which was not typical of Conrad at all—he turned to me and he gave me a hug, and he said, 'This film has touched me more than any film I've ever seen. This is the best photography you've ever done.' And I said, 'You're just teasing, right? And he said, 'No, no, this film deeply affected me.' He said that in front of the whole audience that night at the AVCO cinema in Westwood. I was blown away. The audience thought he was just being gracious, but Conrad was not a gracious person when it came to the work. He told you the truth. It really was an emotional experience for Conrad. I didn't know that Conrad was going to die in less than six months."

"I was sitting next to Roy during that screening," O'Fallon recalls, "and he was sweating the whole time, knowing that Conrad is sitting there watching the film. But then I was standing there with Roy when Conrad told him that he deserves an Academy Award."

Return to Horror High director Bill Froehlich similarly applauds his friend's work, "*A Rumor of Angels* is a prime example of how the work of a truly gifted cinematographer can elevate a film to an entirely higher artistic level. You really see Roy's quality as a cinematographer come across in that film. All the elements that he pulled together were so connected to the depth of the story and helped to elevate the characters and their relationships. Roy's photography was entirely in service to the film. He is not commanding the audience to look at him, there isn't a nanosecond of that in this film. It was just unbelievably gorgeous. And the key to being great at anything is that spontaneity, that connection amongst all the different people that are working with you. When you're in an orchestra, you may be a great, great musician, but it's how you respond to those other musicians that makes you so great. The relationship between the director and cinematographer is critically important. And it's also critically important between an actor and the cinematographer—where they go, how they move, where they look, how they respond to a certain point where they are within the frame, all those things are very valuable to both. I'll tell you flat out right now, I think Roy Wagner is one of the great cinematographers. He doesn't always want to admit that because he is a man of humility. But his work on that movie is staggeringly brilliant. It is an amazing work of art. It bolsters and resonates and helps the storytelling and is completely devoid of ego. He is painting with light, and it is just amazing."

"There are maybe three or four movies in my whole career that I think of as personal films," Roy admits, "films that I really care about. And oftentimes as filmmakers it's not necessarily about the movie itself, but the experience. Well, for me, *A Rumor of Angels* is one of those. So many people love *A Nightmare on Elm Street 3*, but that was torture. There was constant battle with the producers, they didn't like anything we were doing. But with Peter, even on the worst day we were still making our movie and he never lost sight of that, even though he got his ass kicked a lot. The opening shot is a testament to Peter because I was trying to light it and Peter just said less, less, less. So that big wide shot with Vanessa is not really lit. That's one light, that candle, and exposure. That's what really informed my style in that film, just listening to Peter. That is the key to me, always listening to the person. I can be a pain in the ass, and I can be obstinate, and Peter knows that, but he is like my brother, I feel like I can talk to him. I'll go further with Peter sometimes until it pisses him off and he has told me to shut the fuck up. We will argue, but there's not a lot of directors you can do that with, but Peter understands that I'm not there to hurt him."

When it comes to what O'Fallon looks for in a cinematographer, he makes an interesting analogy to one of the great improvisational jam bands of the counterculture era...

"It's almost embarrassing to say now that I'm such an old man, but I'm a Deadhead. Which is to say that I like The Grateful Dead. And one of the things that I liked so much about them is the jam. Roy is like a great lead guitar player. He is always willing to go to new places and bring us with him. It's like the difference between a studio musician who plays perfectly off a sheet and the guy who just plays instinctually. For me that is way more fun and more exciting. In a way I'm like a sheep herder, I'm trying to get to the top of that hill and we kind of go

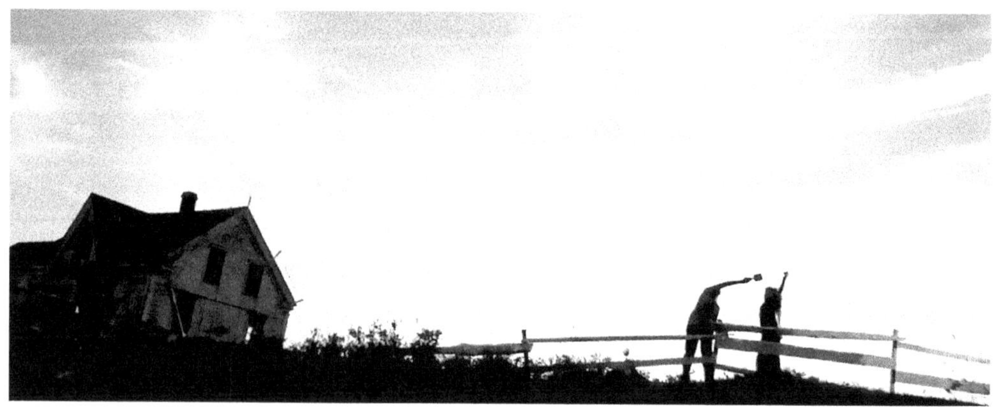

A painterly image from *A Rumor of Angels*.

this way and then we go that way. And then we go another way. All I want to do is get to the top of the hill, though I'm not sure exactly how we're going to get there. But with Roy I know we will get there."

"I have always felt like Peter runs better on instincts instead of intellect," Roy says, "because he is racing past what he knows." And that makes you better because suddenly you discover things that you didn't know about yourself, or what you are capable of doing; every time I worked with Peter I walked away with so much more knowledge and courage. *A Rumor of Angels* was a labor of love, but it was hard work, and it was harder for Peter. I mean, he wanted to quit. He was having to answer to Lisa, having to answer to that French production manager, and he was trying to be civil to Stephen McCabe, who was doing an extraordinary job. I remember riding with Peter in the car when we found out how much Stephen was costing production; it was not pretty. I feel like I have become a bit like Billy Fraker, who worked with a lot of young directors who were more casual about what they were doing; that way I could be—and I hate to say this—sort of like their co-director and help them get through it. This happened with Peter, and I overstepped myself many times on *A Rumor of Angels* because I felt like I was more of his branded partner than just his director of photography, even though Peter had very specific ideas about what he wanted it to look like; the way that movie looks is pretty much because of Peter and what he wanted it to look like. Had it been up to me I probably would have used more hard light. But when I see it now I realize how beautiful it looks; Peter was absolutely right to do it the way he did. But I loved the idea of not being the same all the time, always working with someone that challenged me to do something that wasn't safe. I didn't like safety, and I don't like 'Look at me!' moviemaking. I don't want to do a movie where you go, 'Oh, wow, look at that photography.' I want to be engaged with the movie, I want to fall in love with the characters, the story, and the themes of the movie. That's the kind of movie I want to be involved with. The kinds of movies we all grew up on. *A Rumor of Angels* is that kind of movie.

"My ultimate memory of *A Rumor of Angels*, when I close my eyes for the last time, will be standing on the beach in the twilight with Peter saying, 'Slow down and take your time, Roy. This may be the only time in our entire life we get to wait for the light. We will never get a chance to do this ever again ... just waiting for the light.' I've never forgotten that. And that was coming from someone who was always saying, 'We gotta go, we gotta go!' That, to me, is my most extraordinary memory of my film career; just he and I standing there working on this very special personal movie of his, knowing he was getting inundated by the bond company and being told, 'No more money! No more.' Just getting his ass kicked everyday by everybody. But there we were in that moment in time and he is saying to me, 'Roy, let's just wait for the light.' I will never forget that."

♦ ♦ ♦

Roy's first association with director John Badham came about in 1991, when he was brought on to photograph the second unit material of the action comedy *The Hard Way*. The film functions delightfully as a mismatched buddy police picture resplendent in the verbal byplay of Michael J. Fox's pampered movie star Nick Lang and James Woods' hard-bitten New York City cop, Lieutenant John Moss. Lang is studying and shadowing Moss for a potential role in a credible cop movie called *Blood on the Asphalt,* but Moss isn't happy with this arrangement as he is busy on the trail of a psychotic killer known as The Party Crasher (Stephen Lang); the last thing he needs is a high-profile Hollywood ego diverting his attention and getting in his way. Roy was brought in by the film's producer Rob Cohen, with whom Roy had worked in 1990 when Cohen directed an episode of Dick Wolf's cop show *Nasty Boys.* Roy was tasked with shooting the scenes from Lang's film-within-the-film *Smoking Gunn,* which resembles a kitsch parody of Indiana Jones–style adventure and low-budget martial arts exploitation, the kind with which Roy was very familiar thanks to his experiences on *Nine Deaths of the Ninja* and *Pray for Death.* As the shooting of these scenes required several days' work, the first unit was unable to fit it into the busy schedule, and so Roy was brought in to apply his skill and economy.

"There are a few people who really changed my life. Seymour Friedman was

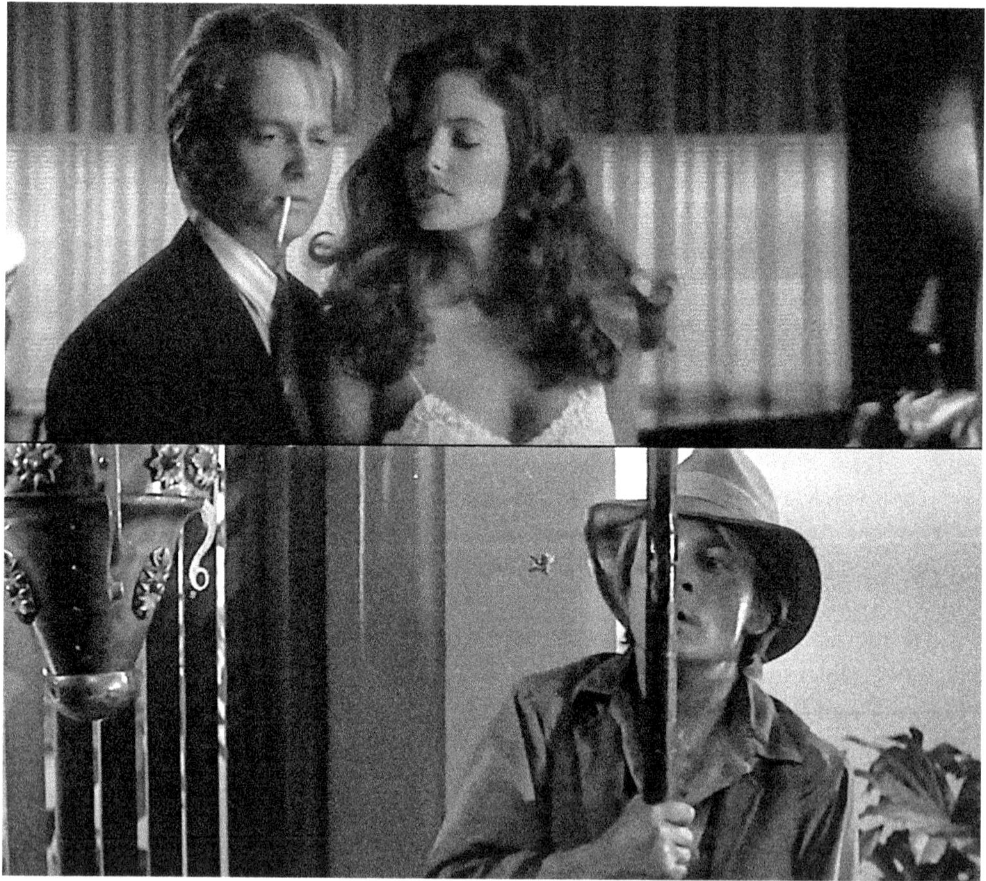

Michael J. Fox stars in *The Hard Way,* 1991, as actor Nick Lang, who plays "Smoking" Joe Gunn in the movie-within-the-movie. Also pictured: Holly Kuespert.

one; Billy Fraker another. And I would say Richard Franklin for bringing me in for the pilot of *Beauty and the Beast*. Peter O'Fallon for believing in me as many times as he believed in me. And of course, John Badham. I thought I was going to be stuck in television the rest of my life until John came along and took a chance on me. We have ended up working together many times since *The Hard Way* and that all happened because of Rob Cohen, who was John's producing partner. And I hate what happened: Rob worked with me on the television series *Nasty Boys* and he loved me and what I did. So, he recommended me to John and because of Rob I got hired to do the second unit on *The Hard Way*. I went to New York and didn't ever have any connection with John whatsoever; the connection was with Rob. And then I did the pilot of another project with Rob and a couple of other things. And then Rob left John; they were no longer partners because Rob went out on his own. I think Rob felt that I was his cinematographer instead of John's. So, when John started hiring me all the time, I think it pissed Rob off. I have a letter that says that, and which broke my heart because I really liked Rob. But before that happened he called me in to shoot a martial arts movie that he was doing with Rafaella De Laurentiis (*Dragon: The Bruce Lee Story*), but it was going to be non-union. But it took me so long to get into the union that I didn't want to get out of the union or to take the job even if it was for a big movie. So, I turned it down to work on an NBC miniseries instead and I don't think Rob ever forgave me; that's when he wrote that letter. But he had recommended me to John Badham, and I went in and met with John, but he never said a word to me. He just let me talk. I'd never met John before, so I didn't know if he liked me or didn't like me, or whether he was just bored with the meeting or whatever. It wasn't that he was intimidating, but John is a man of very few words; the thing is that he listens, which is very unusual in today's world. I have worked with people in my life who would charm you to your face and then stab you in the back. John was not that person. He was very clear about whether he liked you or not. And I admired that about John because you knew exactly where you stood with him. All the time. And he was very tough in a friendly way. But tough, because he had all this experience; he didn't realize I was just a pussycat and wanted to work with him. During the meeting I was thinking, 'There's no way I'm going to get this job.' But I got it! What I found was that John is not a very verbose person; he kind of keeps everything close to his chest. But I fell in love with him. He was challenging, impossibly challenging, and had no patience for anything that went wrong. John is a no-holds-barred/take-no-prisoners filmmaker who always knows exactly what he wants. And he doesn't take kindly to anybody who tells him, 'No.' I got that memo by just being with him for a second in that meeting."

After making a big impression on Badham with his work on *The Hard Way*, Roy was offered the job of cinematographer on the sequel to Badham's own 1987 smash hit *Stakeout*. That comedic thriller traces the nocturnal activities of a loveable duo of Seattle cops, Bill Reimers (Emilio Estevez) and Chris Lecce (Richard Dreyfuss), who are assigned to watch Maria McGuire (Madeleine Stowe), the girlfriend of escaped convict Richard "Stick" Montgomery (Aidan Quinn), in the hopes they can snare the criminal when he comes home to his girl. However, in their voyeuristic process, Chris falls in love with their bait. In the 1993 sequel, the pair are married but are enduring a separation when Chris and Bill are assigned to a lakeside house in scenic Washington along with assistant DA Gina Barrett (Rosie O'Donnell). The trio are there to surveil the neighboring house which is believed to be harboring the targeted witness in a mafia trial, Lu Delano (Cathy Moriarty), and they somewhat implausibly pose as a family unit, with Chris and Gina playing husband and wife with Bill as their son. Meanwhile, mob hitman Tony Castellano (Miguel Ferrer) makes his way to his intended target, leaving a blood-soaked trail in his wake.

When Roy got the call to do *Another Stakeout*, he was more than aware that this would be his biggest film to date, a Disney (Touchstone) production with a $30 million budget, not to mention a sequel to a very popular original. Expectations were indeed great.

"It was the biggest celebration of my entire life," Roy says, "to know that I was going to be working on a big movie with John Badham. I'd always loved his films, from *Saturday Night Fever* to *War Games* to *American Flyers*—I fell in love with

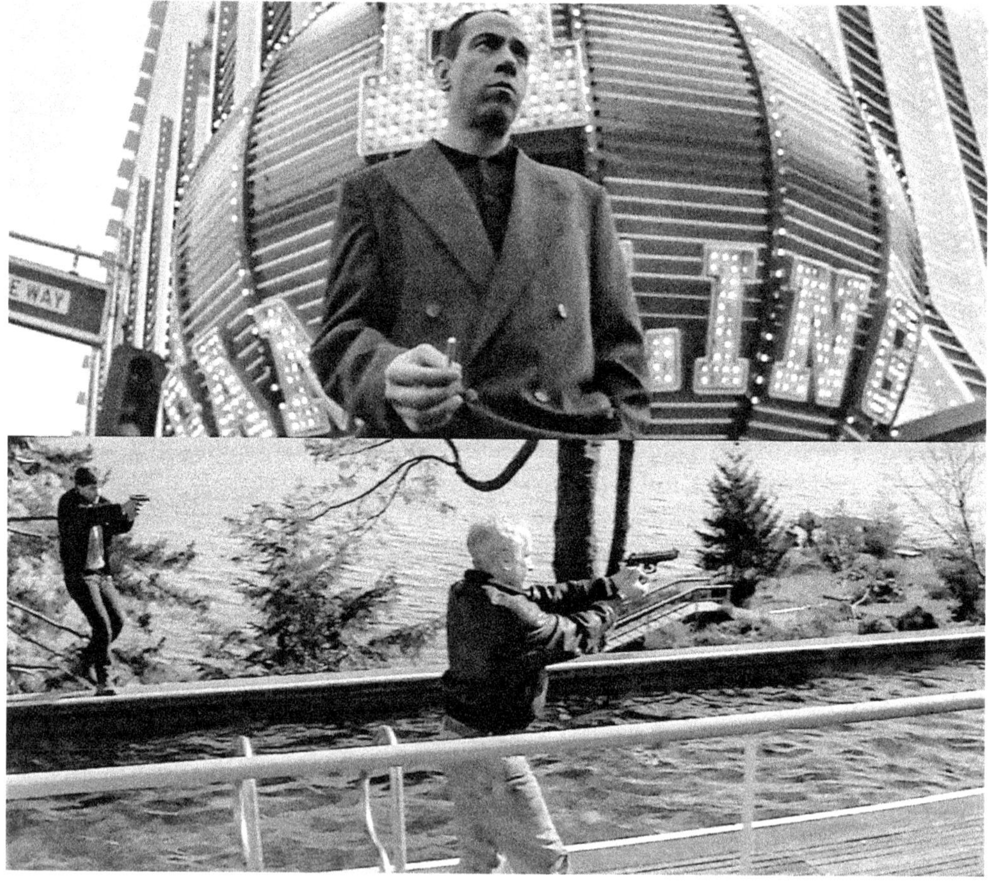

Top: **Miguel Ferrer as mob hitman Tony Castellano. Bottom: detectives Bill Reimers (Emilio Estevez, left) and Chris Lecce (Richard Dreyfuss) draw their weapons in the deadly climactic showdown with Castellano in *Another Stakeout*.**

that movie, I just couldn't believe how good that was. But John rode me hard and put me away wet on *Another Stakeout*. He knew what he wanted and then he hired me and expected me to do exactly that. He was not putting up with any bullshit from me. I don't know if he'd heard anything about me or if that was just the way he was. A lot of directors had been burned by cinematographers who would say, 'I'm not doing that,' or 'I won't do that,' or 'that's not the way I do it.' And what happens is those directors became cynical or when working with those cinematographers they would just say, 'Well, that's the way it going to be done, and if we don't do it that way then this is your last picture with me.' John worked with different cinematographers who were friends of mine, such as John Alonso and Billy Fraker, so I had always heard that John had no patience and suffered no fools. I knew that he is the kind of director who wants to get on with the work and wants a director of photography who can come up with the answers. And so that was my mandate. I knew that I had to do that. And I was scared to death."

The original *Stakeout* was shot by distinguished Australian director of photography John Seale (*Witness*, 1985; *Rain Man*, 1988; *The Firm*, 1993), and he duly took great advantage of the wintery milieu that chilly downtown Vancouver provided to fill in for the wet Washington city, creating a dank and gritty look to support the more serious side to this excellent action comedy. Replacing John Seale for the sequel, Roy brought a much brighter palette to his mise en scène, a style which would no doubt be dictated by scenes set in sun-drenched Las Vegas, but also by the generally lighter mood of the film. In general, *Another Stakeout* would tone down the edgier material of the earlier film and conjure up a more broadly comedic spirit, no doubt a result of adding comedian Rosie O'Donnell to the mix.

"*Another Stakeout* looks beautiful, and that is because of John. We shot the film out in Las Vegas and we were playing with the sense that Vegas was a big, bright, beautiful place, but with a feeling of jeopardy. One of the reasons that John made *Another Stakeout* is because everybody loved Richard and Emilio. They loved that relationship. And then Rosie [O'Donnell] brought a whole different dynamic to the movie, which meant it had more of a comedic context than the original. I think audiences were hard on it because it was a sequel to a popular movie, and because it was much more of a straight comedy. In the first one the comedy came out of the characters and the chemistry that existed between those two actors. It was also a very well-told story. That is ultimately why it was much more successful than the sequel."

"It always goes back to the story," director Badham affirms. "If you don't have that you don't have anything. You can get the best lenses, the best cameras, the best actors, but if the story is not there it just kind of lays there. One of the things that we had succeeded with a lot in the first film was the comedic tone, and so we felt it was alright for the sequel to come up a little bit brighter. It had a different style and look to it, but we were never asking Roy to mimic John Seale; their styles are so inherently different. And they are very individual people. Also, we went to a different aspect ratio on this one; the original *Stakeout* was 1.85 but on *Another Stakeout* we went to 2.35. We were just trying to do something different, not have to be stuck in the mud. And Roy was great. I just fell in love with not only his cinematography, but his braveness and willingness to take chances."

"I always tried to have answers ready for John. I was terrified because I was in the hot seat, and I wanted to make sure that I never stood in his way. This was absolutely the biggest film of my career to that point. I was coming off a lot of television work, but I didn't want to do television. So, this was a big opportunity to prove myself on a big studio film with a director that I admired very much. But John tested me at times; the production was not without issues."

"We did at one point end up having a lot of focus problems," Badham recalls, "because we were shooting anamorphic on *Another Stakeout* and Roy was trying to work with the lens as wide open as he could; but we didn't have the operators or focus pullers with enough skill to be able to deal with that. We kept having to do a lot of retakes, which everybody was okay with, but after a while Richard, Emilio, and Rosie started to get a little short tempered about it. So, I had to twist Roy's arm pretty hard to get him to take at least half a stop, if not a stop, on the lens just to give these guys a break. I knew Roy was going for a certain kind of look and we were confident that with the right focus pullers he would have been in good shape. But we had a lot of beginner camera people with us in Vancouver. At that time, it was hard to find exactly what you needed. We had John Clothier as a Steadicam operator and that was the first time that we made our Steadicam operator the A cameraman instead of the B cameraman. Roy had kind of left him in the car all day long; the guy was sitting around smoking a cigar waiting for his

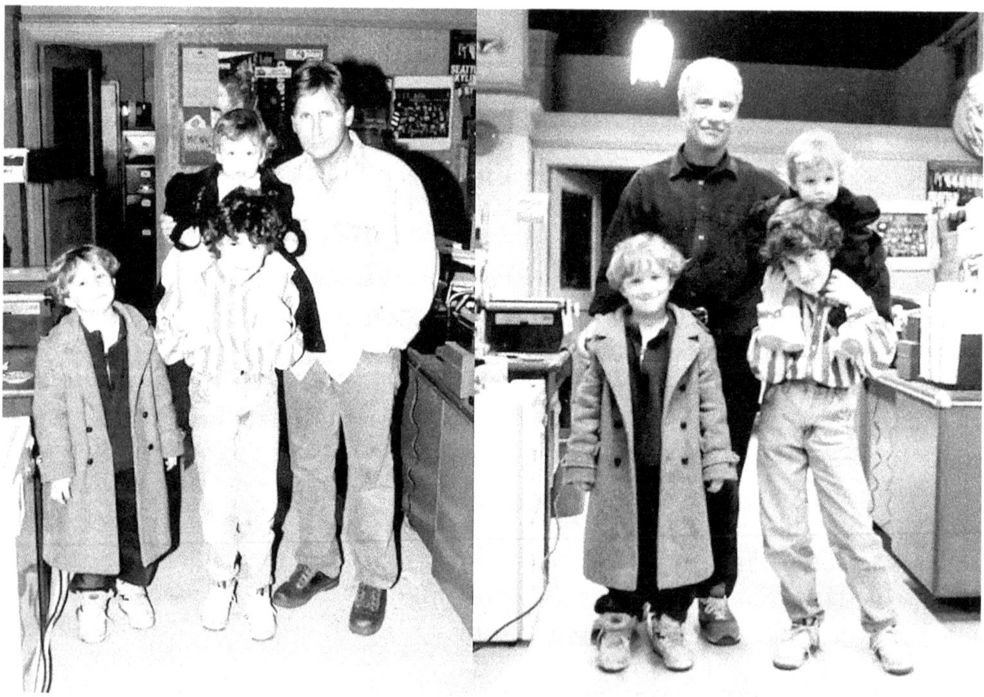

The stars of 1993's *Another Stakeout* (Emilio Estevez, left, and Richard Dreyfuss, right) with the Wagner children—(from left) Michael, Phillip, and Katherine.

turn to break out the camera, so I said, 'No, let's make him the A camera operator so he can do everything.'"

"John Clothier actually ended up saving me a couple times when I got into a lot of trouble with Stephen Campanelli on *Another Stakeout*," Roy admits. "Campanelli was a Steadicam operator who was sort of a superstar and he's a very good guy, but one day he ended up chewing me out and humiliating me in front of everybody on the set, so Badham fired him for that and then he introduced me to another Steadicam operator, Guy Bee. Guy was a very good operator who really understood the complexity of the dance between the cameraman and the director, and about how to make that work. He ended up becoming a director. The one thing that John taught me more than anybody else is the camera can go anywhere. I was accustomed to having frame lines where I could hide things. When we were inside the house, I had the light from outside and we were shooting anamorphic, and John was always concerned whether I had enough exposure inside that house in order to make it work. That scared me even more because I was living on the edge of everything because I wanted to make sure I gave him what he wanted; I got enough to technically make it work. Even though John had a vision of what he wanted me to get, he was amenable to me making changes. There were a lot of adjustments that had to be made on *Another Stakeout* because Richard [Dreyfuss] and the other cast members wanted to do things that weren't scripted. So, I couldn't be restricted and stuffy and precious about my frame and where my lights are because I had to be able to turn on a dime. And we were shooting anamorphic Panavision which requires a lot more lighting and much more talent from the camera operator.

"I had a great crew with me, but I also had a terrible thing happen which could have gotten me fired on the spot. My camera assistants got loaded one night and they exposed a whole roll of film which was of the back of the house where we had blown it up. I then had to go to Mr. Badham the next day and say, 'John, that film was destroyed.' And he could have fired me right then and there. But he was very cool about it. We went back and shot that same sequence again. John protected me a few times in our journey together and that was a great gift for me, to have a partner of his caliber that would be in your court. It was scary for me being in Canada; they already had a chip on their shoulder because I was an American and they'd already worked with John. So, I was the newcomer. It was very awkward in many ways for me, but it wasn't about me, it was really about John's movie and making sure he had the movie he wanted. We shot that big interior of the house in the wintertime because we thought that when spring came in Vancouver we could go out to Bowen Island and shoot all the exteriors because it would be pretty and sunny, but it rained every day we were there."

"That was actually sort of fun," Badham says, "even though we had to travel out to the island for many days in a row. They built a small helicopter pad on the island and we could take off right from the waterfront of Vancouver and fly out to the island and be there within twenty minutes. Whereas if we had to go by ferry, you're talking about a whole hour at least of travel. So, for me, it was a very easy and fun film to shoot."

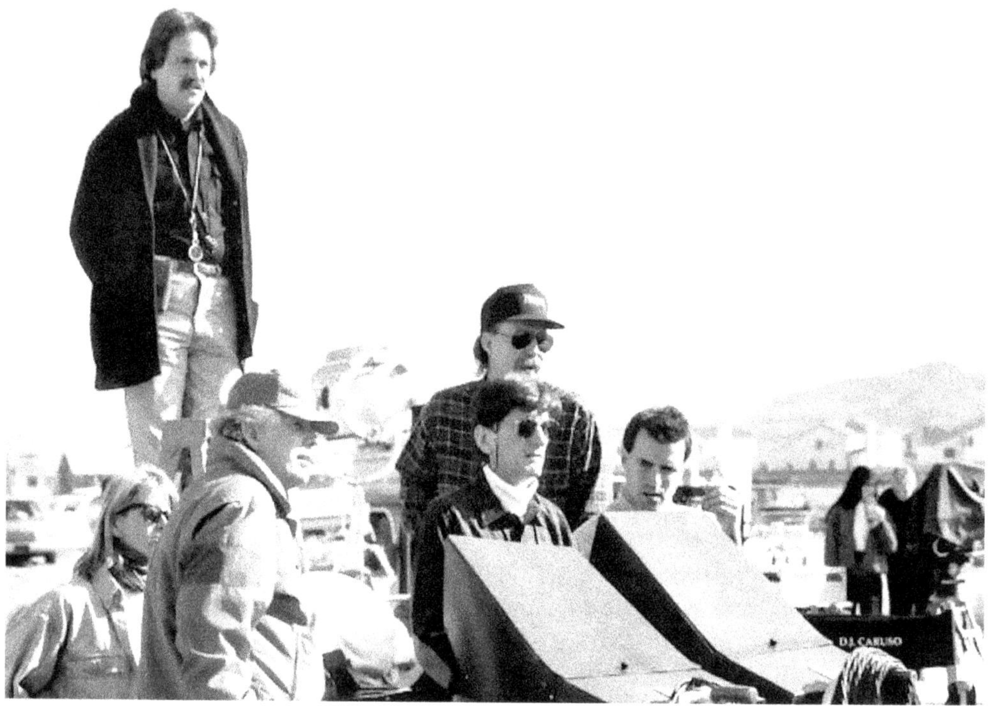

Filming the house explosion on set of *Another Stakeout*. Roy stands at the top. From left: producer Lynn Kouf, stunt coordinator Conrad E. Palmisano, writer Jim Kouf, director John Badham, producer DJ Caruso.

"This movie came at a very important time in my life," Roy reveals, "I was doing a lot of television and that can get relentlessly repetitive. I'm always trying to find my way out of the box, trying to figure out a solution, but a lot of times in television people just want to get it done, so there is little freedom to challenge yourself. It was not like that with John. He wanted to make a great movie, so you had to figure out how to be a part of that team. You didn't have a chance to get stuck in your own little box. We had a really incredible assistant director, David Sosna, who was not going to take prisoners either, he knew exactly what was expected of me and expected me to do the job. And so, I was really lucky that I had people there who were not going to put up with any shenanigans from me. And it's not a surprise to me that John is teaching these days because he taught me so much about how to live my life, how to be a part of something instead of being something. He taught me how to find my way through technology because John is a definite technocrat. He introduced me to the Apple computer, and he designed a shot listing software program. Every time I've talked with John he wants to talk about what's new. He's not a person that has become sedentary and only likes the old way or the way we used to do it. To be around John is to continue to be young because as a director he would push the envelope as far as he could."

◆ ◆ ◆

Working together on *Another Stakeout* proved to Badham that Roy could deftly handle intricate action sequences, something which would be prerequisite for any director of photography collaborating with the filmmaker on his next production, *Drop Zone*. The film opens with a thrilling skyjacking in which a gang of high-flying tech terrorists kidnap convicted computer hacker Earl Leedy (Michael Jeter), who is being escorted to prison by U.S. Marshal brothers Pete (Wesley Snipes) and Terry (Malcolm-Jamal Warner) Nessip. The thrill-seeking villains are headed by ex–DEA agent Ty Moncrief (Gary Busey) who needs to break Leedy free so that he can blackmail him into hacking the computers of his former Government employers to harvest the names and identities of undercover drug enforcement agencies so that he can sell the information to international drug lords. The audacious mid-air prison break turns fatal when Terry is killed before the gang parachute to freedom. Despite his best efforts to combat the gang during the deadly mid-air chaos, Pete is accused by his superiors of breaking protocol and demands that he hand over his badge. However, in his grief and devastation at the loss of his brother, Pete decides to infiltrate the Florida skydiving subculture, suspecting this to be a breeding ground for the kind of

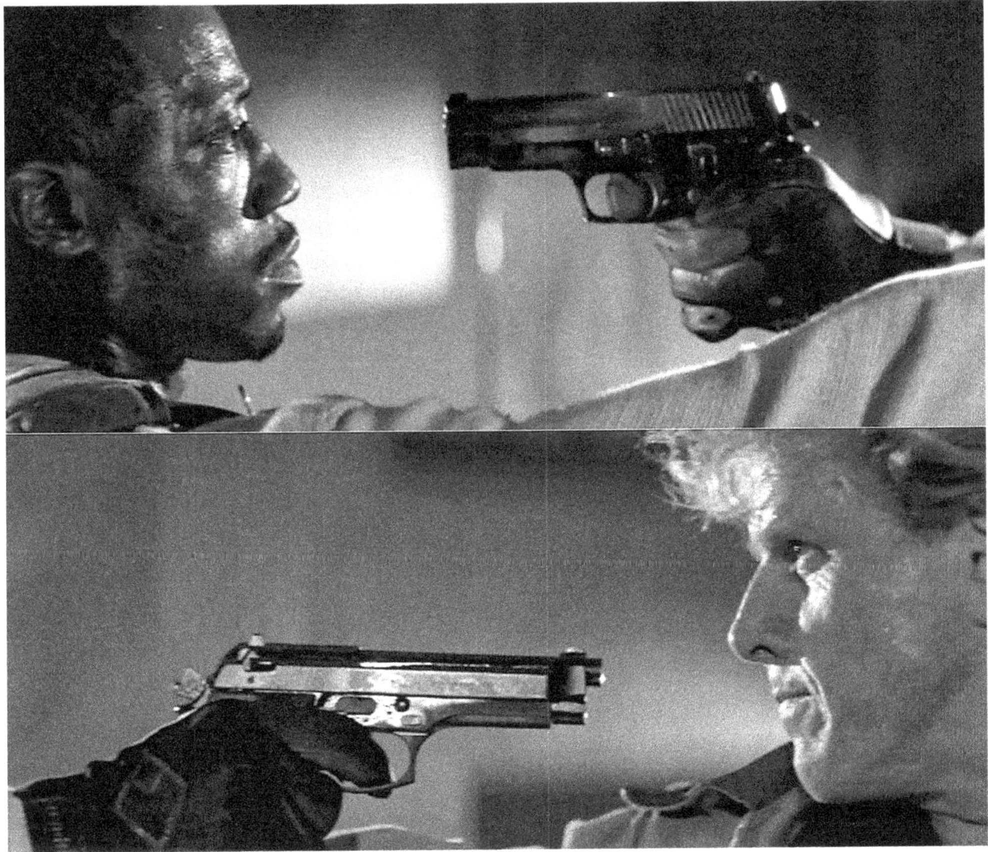

Hero Wesley Snipes (top) faces off with villain Gary Busey (bottom) in two shots from *Drop Zone*, 1994.

daredevils that could successfully jump from a 747 at 38,000 feet and live to dive again.

For Badham, the man to shoot the dynamic action was only ever going to be Roy: "First of all, I liked *Another Stakeout* and what Roy did with it. I knew I liked him, but I knew that I liked his work, which is critical because as much as you may like somebody's personality, if the film doesn't hold up then that's another conversation. But I enjoyed working with Roy. He could listen and come up with good ideas. It was not always exactly a copy of what I said I wanted, but he'd say, 'Well, what if we tried this?' And I'm always up for experimentation. Also, Roy can be so bloody fast that there is just no mucking about. And I don't have a lot of patience to be standing around on a set. It's probably from doing a lot of television in my early years and having production managers always biting at my heels. So, I found that Roy and I are a good combination; we worked well together. And it was easy, I just said, 'I like Roy, let's get him if he's available.' Boom. We worked together again on *Drop Zone*."

Drop Zone is a particularly vivid visual experience, which is partly by design and partly due to necessity when several things went wrong along the way.

"*Drop Zone* changed its look after three days," Roy reveals, "When John and I started talking about *Drop Zone* it was after we had both seen *New Jack City*, which starred Wesley Snipes, and we loved how dark the photography was. The first things that we shot were a night scene with Wesley Snipes in his apartment, and then we shot the big 747 scene at the airport. And those were probably the darkest things that we had in the movie aside from the sky diving. I found it very unusual that we were shooting anamorphic Panavision on film at night, and the costumers brought all these black costumes in for the skydivers which meant we would have ended up having to put lights on them to make it work. So, John ended up changing the costumes so that they weren't in black; it wouldn't have been that hard if we had been shooting on digital, we could have done it at night no problem, but shooting on film meant we would have required a helicopter up there that had a light on it so that we could backlight the skydivers. So, we had to change to Technicolor and that was the first use of 5298, which was a new high speed film stock—we got the very first rolls. But that was spooky. There was no way to read the light meter, you just had to run by the seat of your pants. And by that time, I was already scared to death of everything being too dark."

Once again, the creative partnership between Roy and his director became crucial when Roy found himself facing the wrath of Paramount CEO Sherry Lansing after she viewed dailies and was dismayed by what unspooled before her. When Lansing surveyed the footage she was aghast to find it too dark for commercial consumption. But this footage was never supposed to be screened in the manner that it was; the darkened image was the result of a printing mistake. The issue occurred when the Technicolor lab in New York City was ordered by Paramount to expedite their print so it would arrive in Hollywood posthaste, but that print was struck was not according to Roy's specifications but in using a previous cinematographer's printing lights. Therefore, the footage that they shipped to Paramount was not how Roy intended it to be processed. Lansing perhaps thought she was viewing and critiquing Roy's aesthetic choices and duly demanded he be fired, not realizing that the footage that she found so unpalatable was in fact due to a lab error, not Roy's. He recalls:

"I was already a little on the edge with the way we were shooting as dark as we were, but I knew we were within the printer lights of the film. Then the studio kept saying 'It's too dark! You have to fire the cinematographer.' But we were looking at dailies and going, 'Wow, this looks great,' we were really happy with it. But this is studio politics. It's interesting how it informs what you do and changes what you do, because John was being told to fire me because it was too dark. And on the third day, Paramount had demanded that we use Technicolor labs in New York instead of the lab that I was used to, which was Deluxe labs in Hollywood. This was because they could get the film quicker from where we were shooting in Florida; they could get it to the lab in New York and then back to Paramount in Hollywood so they could see dailies the next morning. That seemed to be a big deal to them. I knew that we were getting separate dailies from the ones that Paramount were receiving, but we thought they would look exactly the same as the ones they got. I would call the guy at Technicolor and he would say, 'Roy, the stuff looks great.' But I told him that Paramount is telling me it's too dark, and he said 'No, no, no, it's not too dark. It's great. Don't worry about a thing.' And so, by the third day John said, 'I'm going to have to fire you, Roy. They are ready to let you go; they are really on me to get rid of you.'"

"When the bad one went to the studio, that's when I started getting calls," Badham says. "They were saying it was too dark and I'm like, 'Are you kidding me? I can see everything! I can see the pimples on their faces. When I'm looking at Wesley Snipes I can see every pore. What are you talking about?' It really took a little detective work to find out what had happened."

"John kept getting these phone calls from Sherry saying, 'You have got to fire the cinematographer!' The prints she saw had been struck from a previous cinematographer's work, so they were not our printer lights, and they were dark. There were three or four days in which I was terrified. But after Sherry was so critical of the dark photography, I started making it almost like a Technicolor musical because I was so afraid of it being dark. So, I called up my friend Ron Koch at Deluxe in Hollywood and I said, 'Ron, I'm in trouble here. I don't know what to do.' And he said, 'Well, I'll go read the screens at Paramount to see if they have the right measure of foot-lamberts for brightness.' He did that and they all measured properly. Paul Hagar was the head of post-production at Paramount and he went nuts because someone didn't trust his system, which was perfect. So, Ron said, 'Look, I got in trouble for running over to Paramount. But here's what I recommend you do…. You have several cameras, right? Put two cameras next to each other and make identical prints. Send one of the negatives to Deluxe and one to Technicolor. We will make our own negative prints and send them to Paramount tomorrow as well.' So, we did that. And then Sherry Lansing called John the next day and said, 'This stuff looks great. It's beautiful!'"

"When Sherry initially told John that he had to fire me I thought, 'That's it. I didn't make it.' But when we saw the dailies and said it looked great I was really astonished. So, John asked her who processed the negative and she said, 'I'll check that.' She called him back and said it was Deluxe. So, I immediately called up the guy at Technicolor and I told him what I did, and he said, 'Oh, well, I can explain this to you...' and I don't know why he didn't just tell me this in the first place, but he said, 'Paul Hagar insisted that we get the film out to him right away, so we didn't change the printer lights from the previous cinematographer's work. The prints you got from us were perfect because we had time to set the lights on that set of prints, but the prints Paramount were getting were done with the other guy's lights. That is why it was too dark.' I said, 'Joey, I don't have any right to say this to you, but you're fired.' I went to John, and I told him what happened, and he said, 'Yes, we're going to go with Deluxe.' But by that time, I was so freaked out that I was going to be fired by Paramount that I had already begun shooting it like a Technicolor film; I just started making it brighter and more saturated. And one of the things about Hawaii and Florida is that there's a lot of green vegetation and a lot of blue skies. When you go there you just think, 'Wow, this is beautiful!' But then you will realize that there will be exposure dynamic between the green saturation, the blue skies—which will expose pure white if you don't do something about it—and the people in the foreground who you will have to light the hell out of, or they'll be in shadow. And so, I lit them like it was a Technicolor musical from the Golden Age of Hollywood."

Key Grip Dale Alexander says, "The truth is a lot of people do not know how to light a black-skinned person and keep everything else in balance, but Roy figured out a way so that you could actually see Wesley Snipes. And Wesley Snipes is a dark black man, he is very dark and there are certain scenes where it might have been hard to see him. But once again Roy shone through and made it work."

Gaffer Brian Crane recalls the effort that Roy put in for a balanced image: "I took a lot of heat, literally, during the filming of one scene with Wesley Snipes and another actor whose name I can't recall but who was just pale as anything, and we were on a white beach with white water and white clouds. So, I have Wesley and this other guy, but I had to bring Wesley up because I couldn't take everything else down. I had these three 6K Xenons on dollies that were maybe sixty foot in length to follow with Wesley, and he was like, 'Do you have to fucking put those lights on me. It's so fucking hot I'm burning up.' I said, 'Well, let me explain...'"

Roy continues, "The fact is Wesley was very blue-black and Yancy was very blue-white, so it was a challenge to balance between it all. I had to light everything. All the actors are going, 'Roy, the light is so bright!' And they were right, it was very bright, and I had to do the same thing on *Burn Notice*. There are certain times when you have to understand the dynamic range of film photography and you have to know what is required to do certain things in order to survive."

With the photographic aesthetic firmly in place, and fears of being fired alleviated, the other challenges of filming the high-octane action spectacle remained. *Drop Zone* was a big studio action movie that required elaborate, and sometimes dangerous, stunt work, that presents its own set of challenges, as Crane recalls: "There were logistical challenges on *Drop Zone*. John had a lot of action in his films, and nobody ever got hurt, although we did come close on one shot on

Drop Zone where a guy's parachute almost didn't open, but thankfully it did open. I remember we were in the swamp at that bar and the next day we were shooting the skydiving. We were filming from below and capturing them coming in and we heard that one of the skydivers' parachutes hadn't opened until the last moment. But we had the best skydivers in the world working on that film. [World champion skydiver] Guy Manos was our head skydiver and he brought in all these great people, including the one guy we could find that could double Wesley Snipes and skydive."

Despite the intricate nature of a stunt-heavy production, *Drop Zone* raced along ahead of schedule, thanks in part to Roy's speed and economy that was learned at the feet of the old studio men who knew a thing or two about being on time. "My mentor Harry Stradling knew all about getting things done at a fast pace when he was an MGM cameraman, and that mentality is what I learned from him. I always made sure that John was on schedule. John was an impatient director, he did not like to wait for anything, which is why he loved me because he never had to wait for anything. And they ended up changing the schedule on *Drop Zone* because we were too far ahead. I mean, [First Assistant Director] John Hockridge at one point told me I needed to slow down. And that was fine because John Badham always knew what he wanted, there were no issues about having to think this or that through because John came to the set with a plan. Though he always allowed people to come to him and pitch ideas, which was an extraordinary gift because when you are moving that much metal around it's good to have a partner who knows exactly what they want."

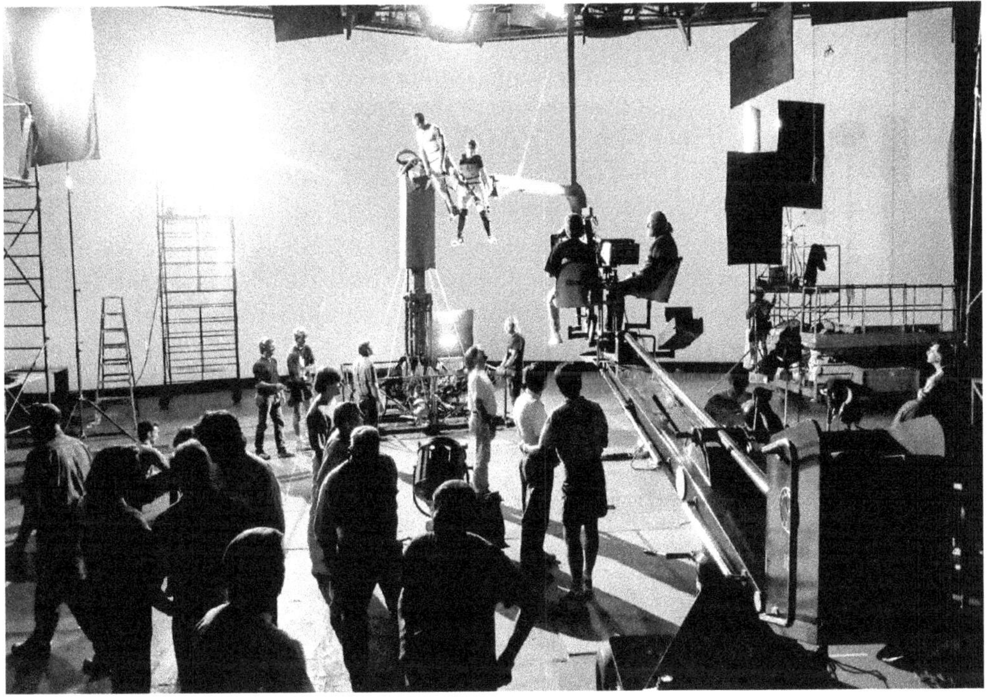

Shooting blue screen skydiving at Paramount for *Drop Zone*.

"A big studio production like *Drop Zone* isn't any more complicated than anything else," Crane says, before adding, "as long as you've got the right guys and right equipment. Once you have those and you know how to manage that environment and stay with it, then it can be a smooth experience. The real key thing is finding people that can work with you from a distance, because while I was in Florida my other rigging crew was in LA rigging the stages. And so, it was this back and forth over the phone and every now and then I'd have to fly home to have a quick look at something and then fly back. I'd leave on a Friday night and be back Sunday night. We had some big setups to shoot, but we had great people and great tools; we shot a scene in the beginning where this bomb blows up in an airplane and for that we had this gimbal and a mockup of the plane."

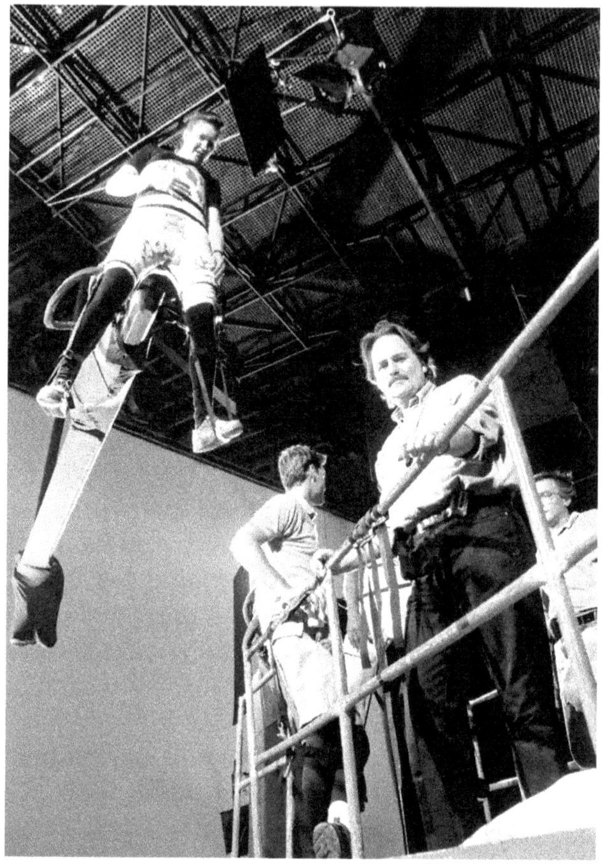

The skydiving rig used for the blue screen shots. Roy is looking at the camera.

Badham reveals some of the more modest tricks used to give the appearance of an aircraft in great difficulty: "It was able to tip, but we limited the amount of motion that the rig would do because it was so painful and so hard that we created the motion in the camera and let the camera do the work and let the actors in the frame do the work. Doing it that way can be very believable, as I know from doing an episode of *Supernatural* where they built an entire submarine on stage. It was a 120-foot-long set, and it was as stable as a house—there was no way it was moving. So, we had to create all the motion ourselves with the camera and with the actors. And it looks great. You absolutely believe they're rocking and rolling underneath the water and people are being thrown about. I love that stuff."

Roy concurs: "Making movies like that is why I fell in love with the movies in the first place. *Drop Zone* is such an adrenaline pumping movie, and you get that from the physical nature of its making. We had the 747 and all that stuff on the stage; we had jet ritters in the air and the fuselage of the plane was tipped up 45-degrees so that it looked like it was flying. The motion control unit in Florida built this big, huge pneumatic dolly with a motion control rig on it and they were going to do all the flying sequences there. They spent a lot of money on that rig; it was really amazing stuff. But John came in one day and saw them do one shot and he said, 'No, we're not doing it that way.' So, what we did instead was we all went up to Mount Wilson and got those shots with Condor cranes. And we did everything old-school, old fashioned, and it looked far better than all the junk they were trying to do with that rig. John didn't put up with it. And the studio paid a lot of money for that. But John just said, 'No, we're not doing it.'"

"We would have added at least ten days to the schedule doing it that way," Badham says, "I could see it as we were lining it up. So, we just went back to the old-fashioned method of laying down on a piece of board and shooting up at the actors against the sky. And you can get the sense of flying and everything. There's a tonne of that in the movie … poor man's aerials. When we were up above Mount Wilson, we were up high enough that we were above the clouds. So, our background was just the cloud in the back. If it had been clear you would have seen all of Los Angeles. This is where all the radio and television towers are for LA. I'd shot up there before on *Short Circuit*. I love the look of it and knew we could get away with murder up there."

"That way of doing it worked incredibly well," Roy states, "and I have known for a long time that John didn't want to talk about that, because he didn't let anybody know how we were going about doing it. I remember thinking that they spent a million dollars here on this stage and here we are doing it the old-fashioned way; that pneumatic rig up in the perms alone had to cost a ton of money. But I remember the look in John's eye; it triggered everything for him, and he realized, 'I've got to make this movie and tell this story, but I'm not going to be able

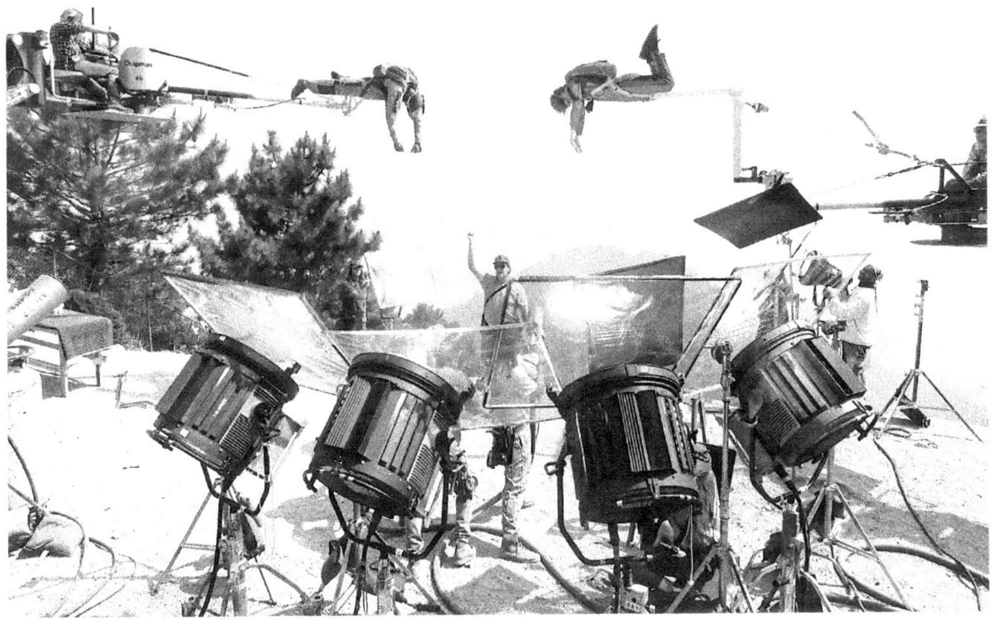

Filming *Drop Zone* on top of Mount Wilson.

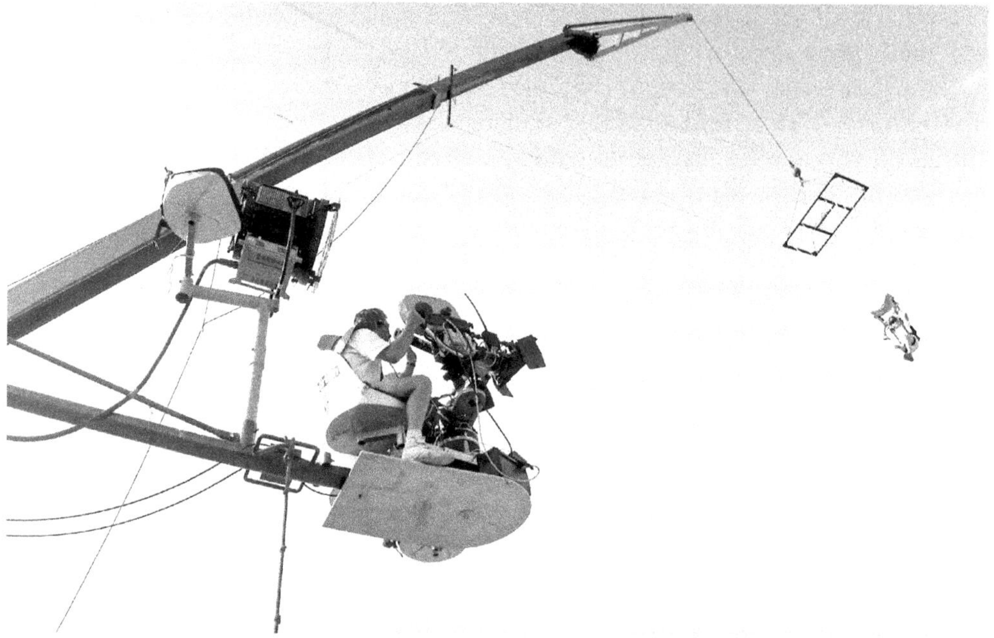

Wesley Snipes on a rig that allows him to safely descend into the swamp, and Gary Huddleston operating the camera in *Drop Zone*.

to if I stay on this stage and do it their way.' So, we went away, and we did it John's way. I think there is only one shot from that rig in the whole movie, and that is the one with Wesley against the blue screen. It's the only shot in the movie that doesn't look good. The rest of it was done live with old-school filmmaking, which is the best way because it's you and the director and the actors. You're making the movie work through magic and illusion."

"*Drop Zone* was so broad and exciting, and it looks great," Badham says. "It was a huge tapestry with this enormous canvas of people in up in the air performing these death-defying stunts. There is very little CGI in there; a little blue screen work, but it is pretty much as realistic as we could get and looks very dangerous."

With its dynamic action scenes, visceral aerial stunt work on display, and the casting of Wesley Snipes, who was coming off a string of high-profile films such as *Passenger 57* (Kevin Hooks, 1992), *Boiling Point* (James B. Harris, 1993), *Rising Sun* (Philip Kaufman, 1993), and *Demolition Man* (Marco Brambilla, 1993), one would have expected big returns for *Drop Zone*, and while it initially dove high into the charts upon its December 1994 release, it ultimately made a modest return of $62 million on Paramount's investment of $45 million.

"I wish *Drop Zone* had been successful," Roy says, "but it's not a very good movie. Although I had fun doing it and I think we did a really good job with how it looks. I will never forget how much John protected me on that production and throughout the situation with Sherry Lansing. I wish every cinematographer had that kind of partner."

"By the time we were working with Badham on *Drop Zone*, Roy had already gone through his terrible twos," key grip Dale Alexander says. "He was established in the union; it had taken him a long time to get into his local 600 and by then he was feeling better about himself, even though he experienced some difficult situations on that film. But Badham saw an incredible talent in Roy—there was no doubt about it. I can't express enough how talented a man that Roy is, and Badham clearly appreciated it too. And I got to witness their great collaboration again on *Nick of Time*."

Released in 1995, *Nick of Time* is a complex Hitchcockian conspiracy thriller which unfolds ambitiously in real time. Johnny Depp plays the innocent man, Gene Watson, whose uneventful life is interrupted when he finds himself thrust into the midst of political intrigue after his daughter is kidnapped and he is blackmailed into a carrying out a veritable suicide mission to assassinate Governor Eleanor Grant (Marsha Mason) by the mysterious duo of Mr. Smith (Christopher Walken) and Ms. Jones (Roma Maffia). The scheming pair are working on behalf of Governor Grant's corrupt husband, Brendan Grant (Peter Strauss), who plots to have his wife killed on behalf of a lobbyist who is unhappy with her unfulfilled political promises.

Roy recalls his first day of shooting on what would prove to be a complexly photographed film made even more intricate as it was to be shot in sequential order:

"I arrived late to the set because there was a time change. I drove from Beverly Hills to downtown Los Angeles at high speed to get there and of course when I arrived Badham was standing there with his hands in his pockets, and he reached up and looked at his watch and said, 'You're late,' and I thought, Oh shit! I'm going to get fired on the first day of the film. It became obvious that he was joking but I apologized, and we went to start shooting the exteriors of the train station. John wanted to see the train coming towards the camera, but it was taking too long. So, I said, 'Well, John, there's two ways we can do this: we can shoot it backwards and under crank it or we can shoot it forward and under crank. He said, 'Let's shoot it backwards and under crank it.' So, we shot it both ways. I don't know which way he ended up using in the movie, but we shot it and undercranked it, which means that the train came very quickly towards the station. Then we had to do interiors of the train car, which we did and that was all great, but then we got to another shot that John wanted to be done, which was a shot looking into the window of the train with the cityscape reflected in the glass, and he wanted this done as the train is moving. The problem was we didn't have any way of mounting the cameras to the train, nor would we be allowed to do that. I told John this and he said, 'Well, you're the cinematographer, figure it out!' So, I suggested that what we should do is shoot plates of what you would see outside the window, the reflection of the city, and then we'll interpose it on the train, which would be literally stationary, and what we'll do is move the camera so that it looks like the train is moving. John said, 'Do you think that will work?' and I said, 'Oh, it will work.' So, we went out and spent a whole day shooting plates with a SpaceCam getting shots of the city and we just interposed that plate onto that shot of the stationary train. I'm really proud of it, but John didn't believe we could do it."

Indeed, the film is notable for its remarkable photography which is as intricately framed as its clockwork plot is spun with precision, an extremely stylized film far more formal in its aesthetic than one would expect from Roy. As such, the film was meticulously constructed largely within the confines of the Bonaventure Hotel, located in downtown Los Angeles, which was a unique canvas that would influence and dictate much of how the film would be shot, as he recalls:

"The location was its own character; it informed a lot of what was going on in that film. I shot in there once before on a TV series and failed. And thank God I did, because if I never found out beforehand just how difficult it was to shoot there then I would have screwed up badly on *Nick of Time*. When I first saw that place I thought, 'Oh, this is beautiful, it's going to look fantastic.' And while it did look amazing to the eye it was hard to film. I tried to light it by lighting the corners of all the different angles of the place, but it would just eat the light; it would only illuminate a certain amount of distance and then it would go away. There is a theory about lighting that says the light source must be bigger than the subject in order for you to be able to make it look round. That theory is for car commercials and people's faces, and so I thought, 'My light source has to be as big as that building.' So, I went down to the hotel and shot with a Steadicam for the entire day just with available light to see what I really had to do. I found that there were no accents, there were no things about it that made it interesting. It was like shooting a documentary. So, I showed John this and I said I think I can do better, I will accent anything by giving light to certain places. And he said, 'Well, here's the mantra: I want to shoot this as if we were walking in as a news crew. And I want it to feel like it's viscerally real. I want to shoot the whole film handheld or Steadicam.' I hated Steadicam and I hated handheld, but John loves Steadicam, so if you try to put a light into the set he is going to see it. If you watch the beginning of the movie—the scene of Johnny and his daughter in the train station—there's a kid who is on roller-skates or a skateboard and there's a shot where the Steadicam literally pans over to a door, and you can see my light in the shot. But John didn't care, he said, 'That's your problem.' So being that I was going to be using Steadicam and going handheld I decided that I wanted *Nick of Time* to look like we were shooting the news—I wanted it to have the look of Haskell Wexler's *Medium Cool*. We watched that film and John loved the idea of doing it in a similar way. So, he said, 'Okay, make it look like that, the less color the better. Shift all the color out.' I had a great color timer, Phil Hetos, who worked at Deluxe and was Conrad Hall's color timer as well. I told him what I wanted to do, and I showed him some tests."

Roy's roving camerawork brought a sense of energy and urgency to the tense narrative which juxtaposed nicely with the more stylishly designed photographic elements, making for a thoroughly unique viewing experience. Badham recalls much movement in front of and behind the camera: "We were certainly moving. We had a schedule that had been trimmed down before we started shooting, but then we came in five days ahead of that because we were going so fast. We had a wonderful assistant director in John Hockridge, and his team was just great at keeping the background action going. It felt real. And the people look authentically

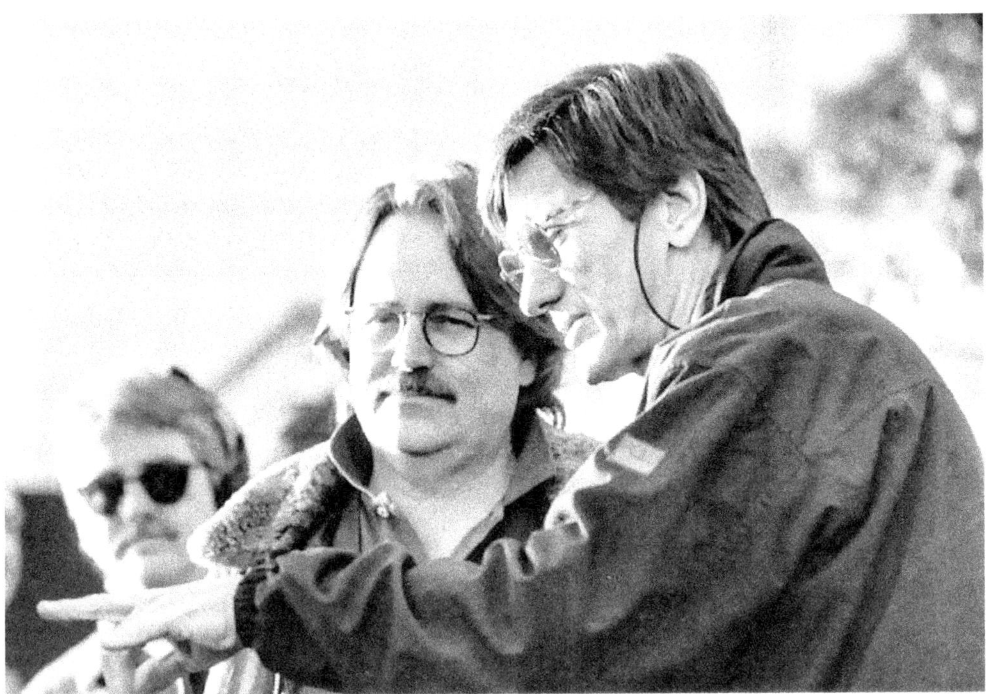

On the set of *Nick of Time*, 1995, with (from left) camera operator Gary Huddleston, Roy, and director John Badham.

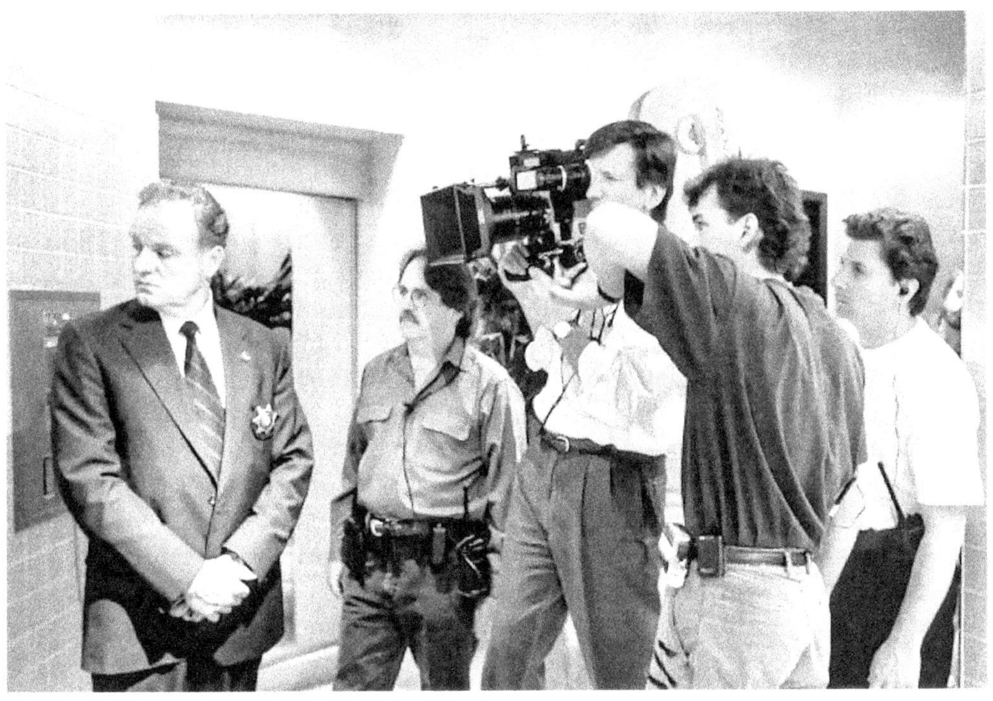

Shooting *Nick of Time*. From left: actor Bill Smitrovich, Roy, director John Badham, first assistant camera Todd Slyapich, A camera/Steadicam operator Bob Gorelick.

like the people you would really see in those locations going about their business. There is all kinds of action and movement going on in the background."

"John Badham is one of those directors that doesn't like the camera to sit still too long," gaffer Brian Crane says. "So, we were either on the Steadicam or we were on a dolly; but everything was always moving. And Roy was ready for whatever John would throw at him. But *Nick of Time* was an intricate film to shoot. One of the scenes that I remember so vividly was Johnny Depp falling through the frame; it's like he is falling in it. And we had to get the strobes to sync with the cameras because the strobes freeze the face so you can see it clearly. He went down in this descender rig, and it was my first time ever working with that. But once I saw what happened it gave the film this surrealistic, dreamy type of effect. Another challenge was a scene between Johnny and Christopher Walken in the glass elevator as it goes up to the top floor and one of them gets out. We had plugged a light into the utility outlet that was in there and as we went up it would flicker out because it was fluo-rescent, and it took me a while of going up and down to figure out what was wrong with it. As the elevator went up, the voltage went down because of all that cable. So, we realized that the problem was we lost voltage on it. It was like, 'How are you going to fix this? You've got thirty seconds,' and it was one of those situations where it's like, 'Alright, I know how to fix this!' So, I literally ran all the way down to the truck, grabbed the Variac, ran all the way back, and I sat there and floated the volt-age. Because with the Variac I was able to keep the voltage steady the entire time; I just played with it, and it stayed lit without any variance in that thing."

"John does not allow any room for lights on the set," Roy says, "which is a curse, but it's also a gift, because I had to think about how to work within those limitations. So, my mantra was to make this set as real as possible. So, I put ceil-ings on the sets, which limited certain things that I could do. I had some sleep-less nights when we were shooting the portion of the film that was on stage, such as the scenes in the hotel room, because I just had one light and it was just as far left as you can get. There is a moment when Johnny is confronting Marsha Mason with a gun, and I couldn't very well pull the ceiling back to put the key light on Marsha because it would have looked phony. What I did was when Johnny gets the gun close there's enough reflection on the gun to open up the shadows on her face, which it did. In that shot you can see how the blinds behind her are only slightly open. Well, that was the only place I had for the light, and that's the light source that is catching them. It comes from two slats that are open off-camera. One of the other tricks I used was I started using nets on the back of old lenses towards the middle to the end of the film, because I didn't want the look of the film to be initially fanciful, but I did want it to become like Alice in Wonderland as the film progressed. Like we're going down a rabbit hole, it's getting dangerous. Another thing I did was to put the camera down low at certain points to increase the feeling of jeopardy. Very simple techniques that aided the storytelling and helped to make it more unsettling for the audience."

Roy continues,

"One of the things that John liked was that there was a balcony at the very top of the Bonaventure Hotel on all four sides, so I went to the head of production

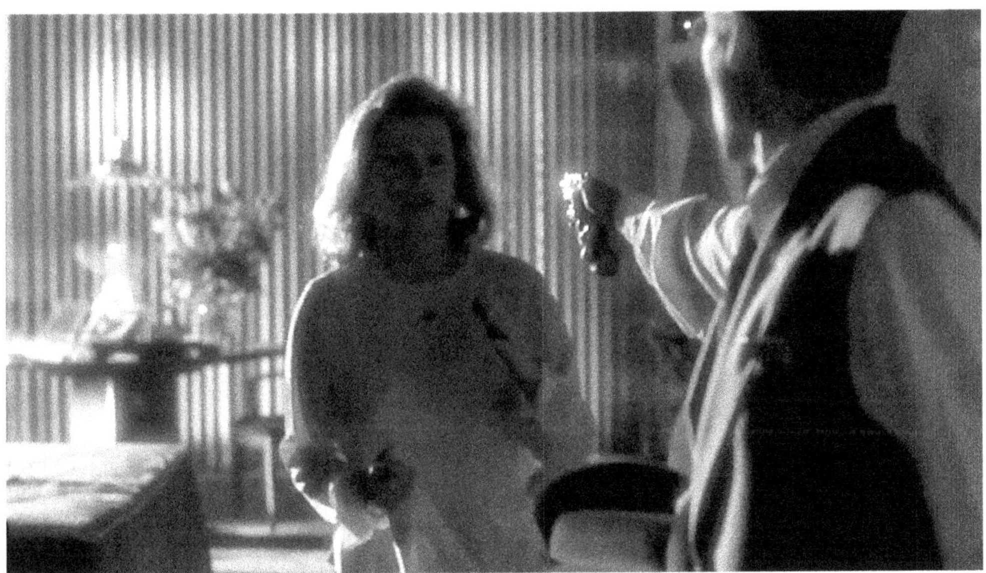

Marsha Mason and Johnny Depp in the shadows of *Nick of Time*.

at Paramount and said, 'I need forty or fifty HMI PARs,' and he replied, 'Well, you can't have that.' And I said, 'I'm going to need that to make this movie in the amount of time that John wants to make it in.' After that he bought fifty HMI PAR lights, and the idea of using those was that when we were looking in one direction I would always have everything backlit with those PARs. In fact, if you freeze frame the film at the right second in one shot in the elevator, when it's going up through the roof, you will see all the lights going up on one side. That's what we did. We shot in one direction, turned those lights off, turned around, switched on the other lights. Everything is backlit. The other problem we had was that this is all supposed to take place in only ninety minutes; but the roof of the hotel's lobby is glass, meaning that the sun is constantly changing. I had to have several grips go up and put on blackouts. We wanted some ambient light, but we didn't want any of the sunlight catching. That was a constant issue. It's something that looks so simple on film, but it was probably the most complicated thing I ever did. And despite the complexity of these setups, I would tend to take only thirty minutes to go from one setup to the next, which was the key with John Badham. If you took your time, he hated you. I didn't take any more time than was necessary for the setup of the shot. The key for me with John was always to listen to what he was saying. *Nick of Time* looks like it's just a normal movie, but there is so much technology involved in getting to look that way; how we ended up accomplishing what we did was very complicated. I had to ask for a lot of equipment so we could shoot in a linear fashion, and that would have been even tougher if you were a 'light every shot' type of cinematographer. But we just lit the space, and it was up to John and the actors as regards what they wanted to do. Our camera operator was Bob Gorelick and he and John were working together very closely on that film. I might have suggested or adjusted something, but they really set the shots."

"Roy's speed and the fact that he brought a very distinctive cinematic look is remarkable," gaffer Brian Crane hails, "We lit the Bonaventure Hotel top to bottom, I mean literally, we had every 6K PAR, every 4K PAR, every 250 and every 1200 that we could get our hands on to light that space, which was such a huge space. We had lights on every floor, all four corners, everywhere. And then because everything had fluorescent tubes in it, Roy had us change out all the fluorescent tubes and put regular bulbs in and then a half blue. So, I had a practical or fixtures team of like twelve guys that would literally spend all day long going around changing bulbs because they would heat up from being sealed behind the gel."

Nick of Time did not fare well at the box office, despite the presence of its rising star, Johnny Depp, who at the time was working the Hollywood machine to his great advantage, cultivating both his leading man image and sex symbol status in mainstream films such as *Benny and Joon* (Jeremiah S. Chechik, 1993) and *Don Juan DeMarco* (Jeremy Leven, 1995), while also starring in a series of modest arthouse pictures including Emir Kusturica's *Arizona Dream* (1993), Lasse Hallström's *What's Eating Gilbert Grape* (1993), and Jim Jarmusch's *Dead Man* (1995). However, *Nick of Time* neither furthered his romantic hero profile nor added to his indie credentials; rather, it was the kind of mature mainstream film which was rarely coming out of the studio system in the mid–'90s. The film's construction was inspired in part by the revolutionary New Hollywood sixties aesthetic of Haskell Wexler's *Medium Cool* and that is precisely the era of American filmmaking that *Nick of Time* recalls, a time in which filmmaking pulled from the political paranoia and social contexts of the times which often resulted in finely crafted, tightly wound thrillers that were intellectually engaging, artistically designed, and fiercely entertaining, such as *The Parallax View, Three Days of the*

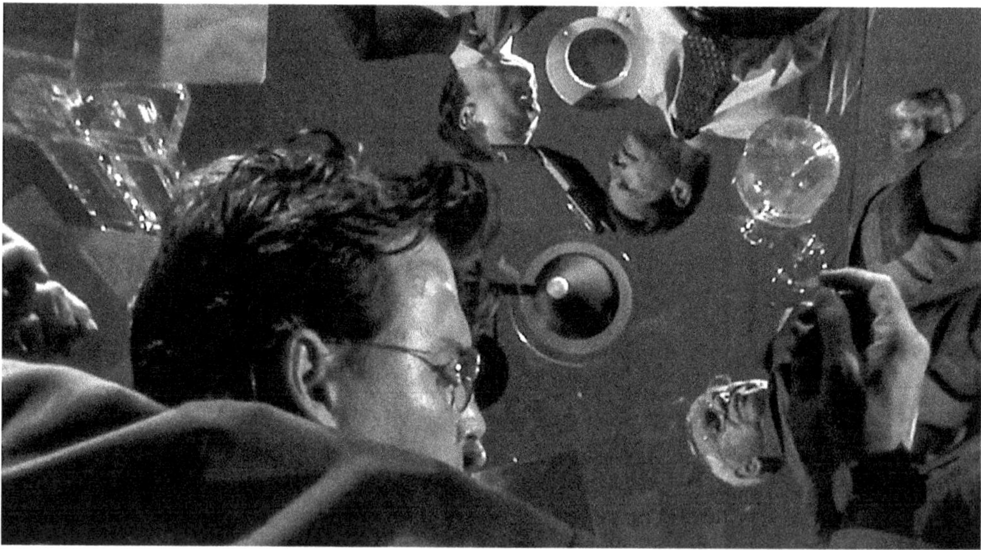

One of Roy's rich and complex compositions, achieved using a front-surface mirror, featuring Johnny Depp (foreground) in *Nick of Time*.

Condor, *The Conversation*, and *Blow Out*. Easily *Nick of Time* can rank alongside those distinguished works in terms of quality, but the odds were stacked against it. The film opened against Martin Scorsese's *Casino* and John Lasseter's Disney hit *Toy Story*, as well as competed with the recently released thriller *Se7en* (David Fincher), the James Bond sequel *GoldenEye* (Martin Campbell), and the dimwitted but popular comedy *Ace Ventura: When Nature Calls* (Steve Oedekerk), which left little room for a serious, intelligent adult thriller such as *Nick of Time* to find its audience. For Roy, it remains one of the highlights of his collaborative relationship with a director he dearly admires.

"John has had this remarkable journey, from *The Bingo Long Travelling All-Stars & Motor Kings* onward, and I got to be part of it several times. Each of those films has been very different too; *Nick of Time* is nothing like *Another Stakeout* or *Drop Zone*. With John as a partner, you can get away with doing different kinds of things because he would trust you. And he would know enough of what he was talking about. Any time that John and I work together we will be talking about and experimenting with technology, and he will be way ahead of me about what's going on. And that is what you want in a partner, especially a director. Sometimes it may be with a producer, but if you can have a partnership like that with a director it means that you can fly beyond what is expected."

The feeling is evidently mutual for his director: "I love *Nick of Time*; I think that was a wonderful film. It was great fun working with Roy, and that goes all the way back to when he shot the movie-within-the-movie for us on *The Hard Way*. These days I teach directing at Chapman University, a relatively new film school located in Orange County, where they've been able to build a wonderful facility. I have had Roy down there with me to teach some classes to the undergraduate directors, and we've done a lot of work on beginning camera movement, because that's a tricky thing. I mean, it's easy to learn the standard shots—wide, medium, close-up, over the shoulder, and so on—that's the easy stuff, but to try to get some life and some motion in it to help the story is a whole other matter; camera movement that doesn't help the story is just annoying. I try to teach them how to make the movement be motivated by what's happening on the screen."

"Everything is moving in *Nick of Time*," Roy states, "there was nothing on a dolly, it was all handheld or on Steadicam. That is one of the things that I'm most proud of with *Nick of Time*, because you don't see the seams of the rivets, you never see any of that, you just flow along with the story not realizing the mechanics of it for ninety minutes. It really has a look and feel that is indebted to *Medium Cool*. And I was moving all the time too. We ended up coming in five days early, which the head of the production department was reluctantly happy about, but he didn't like all the equipment it took to get us there. But what it did do was it kept Johnny Depp on the set, and it kept us moving forward constantly. The studio said, 'If you can keep Johnny Depp on the set, that will be fantastic. Because he once he goes back to his trailer he's done.' Well, we had no problem keeping Johnny on set because he became part of my team of practical jokers, and he loved it. He had a great time on the set because we played practical jokes all day long. So, he became a part of the crew. He never

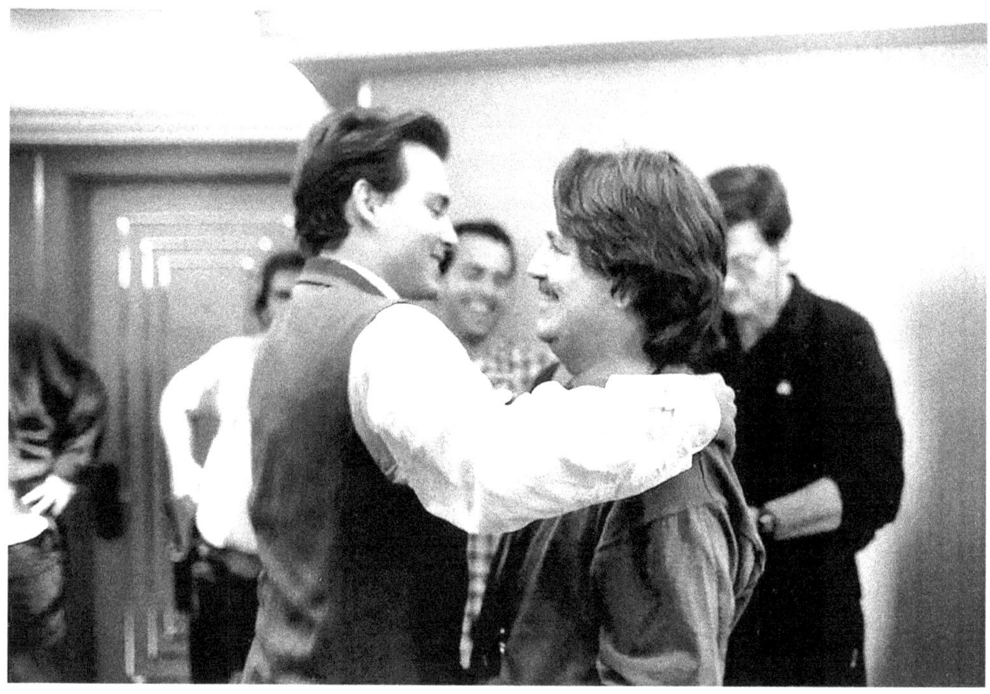

Good times on set of *Nick of Time* with (from left, faces visible) Johnny Depp, DJ Caruso, Roy, and John Badham.

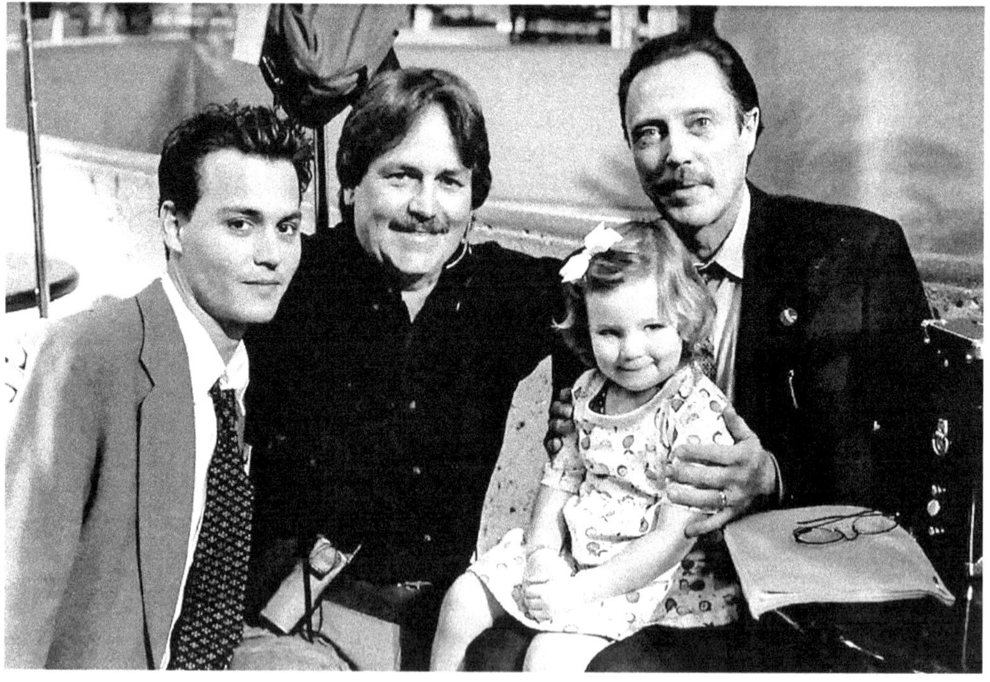

Left to right: Johnny Depp, Roy, Katherine Wagner, and Christopher Walken on set of *Nick of Time*.

went to his trailer because he wanted to be with us. And he was. It was a fantastic thing."

"Johnny loved Roy," key grip Dale Alexander says. "Roy has a crazy sense of humor. He is like a trickster. He always wanted to play practical jokes on people. There was one time we were doing *Nasty Boys* in Las Vegas, and someone started a little silly food fight by throwing something which hit Roy, and then Roy threw it back. I laughed at that and said, 'That is so funny! Roy got hit with some food.' We had the mayor of Las Vegas there with us at the food table, but Roy didn't care; he went over and picked up a tub of cottage cheese and chased me around for thirty minutes trying to dump it on my head. He refused to go back to work until he could get me—I mean he literally stopped work to dump cottage cheese on my head. Only after that would he go back to work and light the show. I know it's silly, but these are the kinds of things I love. And Johnny Depp loved that kind of stuff too. Just constant little practical jokes. But that's Roy."

• • •

The laughs kept on coming behind the scenes, if not always onscreen (despite intentions otherwise) on following projects for Roy and his loyal camera crew. While working with esteemed, commercially successful auteur filmmakers such as John Badham affords one a certain amount of professional and artistic satisfaction, not every project comes with such prestige, as *The Pest* is testament to. The film is an anarchic physical comedy in which John Leguizamo plays an irritatingly animated con artist named Pestario Vargas, fittingly abbreviated to "Pest." The film is a contemporary comic version of Richard Connell's oft-visualized 1924 short story, "The Most Dangerous Game." After pulling a scam on a Scottish gangster, Angus (Charles Hallahan), who is making a name for himself around Miami as a mobster to be feared, Pest finds himself on the run and owing the criminal $50,000. In order to clear his debt to the Scottish mob, Pest becomes the willing quarry of a decadent German hunter Gustav Shank (Jeffrey Jones); if he survives and emerges unscathed after 24 hours of being hunted in the jungle of Shank's private island, he will win a $50,000 cash prize, precisely the amount of money that will get him out of trouble. Armed with only his wit (questionable), a surfeit of disguises that Jerry Lewis would be proud of, Pest outsmarts his foes and eventually drives away with the money.

As things seem to have always occurred for Roy in his career trajectory, it was relationships forged on previous jobs, and in this case the initial link was none other than John Badham which led him to this project. "Films like *The Pest* haunt you," Roy humorously admits, "it's part of that stuff you do just for the money. How I ended up on this film is a good example of how the movie business works. I had met the producer previously on another project, which was *Hart to Hart* with Robert Wagner and Stefanie Powers. I did three of those *Hart to Hart* movies of the week and they liked me, and I really liked them. They're good people. Robert Papazian was the executive producer of those, and Peter Hunt was the director. Peter had been a very famous stage director—he directed the musical stage play *1776* and then directed the movie version of it; he was also a friend of John Badham's and it was John who recommended me to Peter for the *Hart to Hart* movies; that's how I got that job and that is where I met Robert, who was executive-producing *The Pest*. And I couldn't very well turn it down because I liked those people. So, I did the movie."

Another connection from the past appeared in the form of the feared MCA and Universal mogul Sid Sheinberg. The film was a joint production between TriStar Pictures and The Bubble Factory, the latter being a company run by Sheinberg and his two sons, Jon and Bill, to produce low-budget features. When Sheinberg showed up on the set, his presence was immediately felt, as Roy recalls:

"I had known Sid from when I worked at Universal Studios, and when he saw me on the set he said, 'Hey, Mr. Wagner, how are you doing?' Sid was a very powerful and very frightening man; he was extremely imposing. His son wanted to be a movie producer, so Sid created a company called The Bubble Factory and he put it on the lot at Universal where they made these little movies—they did *Flipper, McHale's Navy* and a couple other things, including *The Pest*. So, that was another one of those interpersonal connections."

The Pest is a film which lives or dies by the viewer's appetite for zany antics, but one can't help but be innately charmed by the inherent innocence of Leguizamo's spirited farce. Roy, too, admits that he was taken by the farcical charms of the film's star: "I have to say that John Leguizamo was fantastic. He was just the sweetest, nicest guy in the world when I worked with him, and I hope he is still like that. He had a lot of best friends around him who were always advising him. In fact, our director, a guy named Paul Miller, was one of those best friends. Paul had not done a movie before, but back then he was famous for doing award shows and sitcoms. There isn't much I can say about the artistry of the film, or about my photography. We shot here in Los Angeles and in Florida, the latter is where we had to do all the scenes in the house. It was supposed to be daytime, but we had to shoot all those at night. We were on Biscayne Bay, so we were surrounded by the ocean, but I couldn't see any of that; all I could do is put lights everywhere and just pound them into that two-story apartment, which was right next door to Richard Nixon's Florida retreat. It looked stupidly crazy. I don't think the photography is that great during that sequence. But it is what I had to do in order to survive because we had no other choice but to make it look like daytime at night."

Despite the dearth of artistic intent and endearing in its own quirky manner, the film is vivacious in its energy, largely thanks to Roy's agile camerawork supporting the film's zany spirit where possible, most notably in the opening sequence where the camera takes on the style of an anarchic animation and which sets the tone for the entire film.

"The style of the shots in the opening sequence was something I came up with," Roy recalls. "That was my idea. We shot that in a little stage in downtown Los Angeles. The camera was literally in the shower with John, and this was a Panavision show, it was not anamorphic, so in the shower scene we used a 9.8-millimeter lens. The way we did it was we shot it under-cranked so it would be high speed. Then we would also do speed ramping, which meant that you go from twenty-four

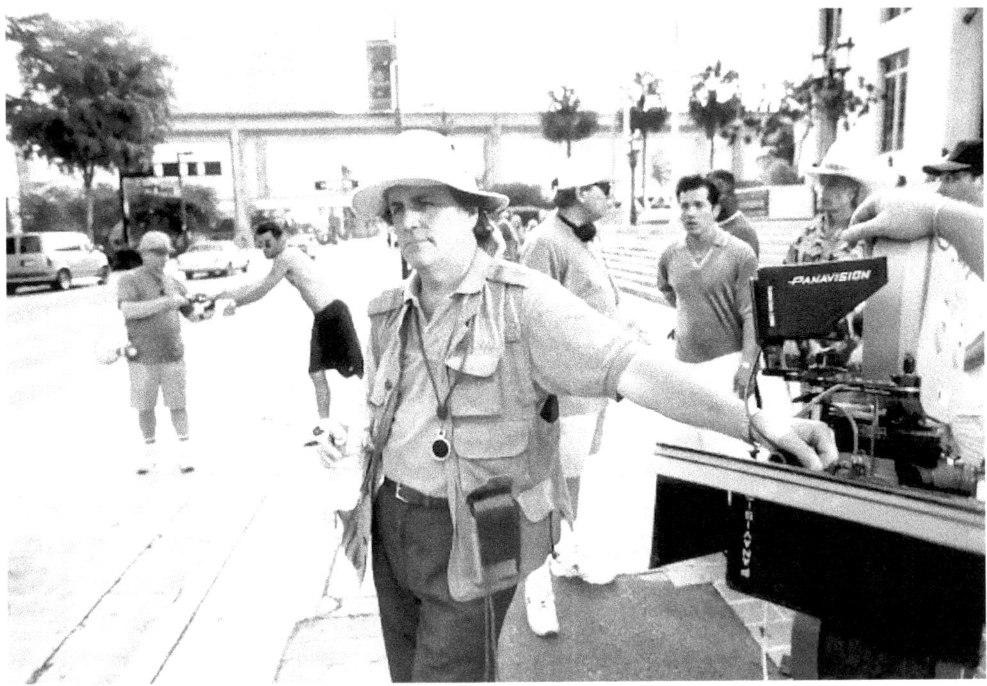

Roy with some cast and crew on the first day shooting *The Pest* (1997) in Miami.

frames down to six frames and back up. Then when he got out of the shower we followed him in that shot from the shower all the way down this hallway and into the room, and it wasn't a Steadicam shot—it was a dolly shot. And it was complicated, very complicated, again because it was such a huge wide lens. And that's probably my favorite thing that we did in the movie. And I think that reflects John Leguizamo better than anything else in the movie."

"Oh my God, that was such a crappy little set to light," gaffer Brian Crane recalls. "Roy had to shoot it the way he did so as to cover up the defects in that set, which was in this warehouse in downtown LA. There were cracked walls in there, but I guess it kind of fit in a way. That was one of those shows where you're constantly just holding your ribs from laughing or biding your time because the comedy on camera wasn't nearly as funny as the off-camera stuff. It was constantly funny but that was one of those productions that was challenging in certain ways, such as locations, which were hard to get in and get out of."

Roy continues, "There were certainly some memorable moments during filming, and one of those really defines how the making of that movie went. It was the scene with the snake. We shot that out near the Disney Ranch because there was a jungle out there and we had this giant python, a huge snake that was very well trained, but it was very hot that day and the trainer said that he might have to step in a couple of times because if a snake gets hot, then they get cranky. Paul said, 'That's fantastic!' and he told us we're going to do a whole scene of John doing this dance with the snake; John sits down under the tree and the snake is supposed to be charmed by him. So, I'm standing right there next to the camera and I'm watching all this going on. The snake is crawling all around John—and this is a long-protracted take—but Paul wasn't happy with any of the performances, and he kept saying, 'Let's do it over and start again!' And the wrangler kept coming up to Paul saying, 'We need to give the snake some rest. You know that it is getting too hot.' And Paul would reply, 'Just one more time. It's going to be fine.' Meanwhile John is telling Paul, 'Yeah, but the snake is all over me. Are you sure it is okay to keep going?' And Paul said, 'Trust me, it's going to be just fine.' So, we roll film, and the snake finally crawls up John's leg and up underneath his loincloth into his groin area. And then a moment of calm before the snake grabs in between John's testicles and his leg. And the wrangler says, 'Don't anybody move! Do not move. This can get really bad really quick.' Meanwhile Paul is like, 'This is going to be great, John, it will be fantastic!' Finally, they were able to get the jaws of the snake off John's groin; it was pretty bad but the snake was not poisonous. But John was so pissed at Paul after that; he was really angry, as well he should have been."

"Oh, Jesus," Crane says, remembering the incident. "Yes, not too many people know about the snake biting John Leguizamo, And the best part was that you could see the snake wrangler trying to get it going and he's literally pissing this snake off. And John Leguizamo goes, 'Stop it. You're fucking with him. He's going to bite me.' And the guy says, 'No, he's not, he's perfect!' And like, two seconds later the snake's mouth just goes right into John's inner thigh. And it took three or four guys to pry the teeth or the jaws off, because it literally almost encompassed his leg. It was a big thing."

The snake may have been a big thing, but the film wasn't. *The Pest* tanked at the box office, not even making half of its $8 million budget within its shortened six-week theatrical run.

"*The Pest* was a tough movie," Roy admits, "and that is because John was always changing everything. It was all about the humor and what was best for the humor. I don't mind that, but it was just challenging because there was not enough time and not enough money to keep up with John. When Sid Sheinberg came to the set on the first day of shooting, we were doing the head-hunting stuff at the house in Pasadena. This was the only time he was on the set, and Sid had absolutely no sense of humor. None. But he said to me, 'Roy, what's going on? Nobody is laughing here. Why isn't anybody laughing?' John Leguizamo heard him say this and replied, 'Well, nobody laughs on the sets of comedy movies—we hope the audience laughs.'"

There is always hope.

The Politics of TV

"Bring in Roy!"

The large majority of Roy's career over the last quarter century has seen him crafting images for the televisual landscape. And those are indeed widely viewed images; his work can be seen in shows as varied, and as popular, as *Cracker, Pasadena, CSI: Crime Scene Investigation, House M.D., Burn Notice, The Beast, The Unusuals, Elementary*, and *Ray Donovan*. While some of these shows have become iconic staples of television, others have come and gone, failing to make an impact even when the collaborations seemed ideal on paper. For Roy, regardless of success, it is the creative partnerships and collaborative atmosphere (or lack thereof) which dictate his tenure on any given show, as he ruminates...

"The art of the cinematographer is in the molding of the image that you crafted into the signature that you and the director agreed upon. The risk is how ethical are your partners? Will they allow you to follow through with what you began on the set? I've had good and bad experiences. It's usually about politics. I shot the pilot of *Burn Notice* and I stayed on to do the first season. The show was filmed on location in Miami, and I knew a few technical things about shooting on location and that is about how to light it depending on the environment you are working with: in the case of Hawaii and Florida you are working with the green vegetation, the blue skies, the clouds, and the skin tones. If you tried to expose for the skin tones the blue sky would look white, and the green would go black. The lesson I had learned on *Drop Zone*, which was shot in Florida, is that if you over-light it and make it saturated then those problems would all go away. But my theory was that it had to be pretty and that was my reason for doing it that way. And so, I used a great deal of light on *Burn Notice*. But that is why the first season of *Burn Notice* looks as good as it does. I have never seen what my successor Bill Wages did on the second or third season, but he is a very good cameraman and a good friend; I'm sure he did a great job. But I would leave TV shows when it got too political, as I did on *CSI*, that one got especially political..."

Conceived by screenwriter Anthony E. Zuiker with a spec script that attracted the attention of powerhouse Hollywood producer Jerry Bruckheimer (*Flashdance*, 1983; *Beverly Hills Cop*, 1984; *Top Gun*, 1986), *CSI: Crime Scene Investigation* was a crime procedural of unusual intelligence and rare in its

143

seemingly authentic scientific detail. It not only became the biggest show broadcast by CBS, but also it became an iconic franchise. The first series follows a team of crime scene investigators working with the Las Vegas Police Department, led by forensic entomologist Dr. Gil Grissom (William Petersen), and including blood specialist Catherine Willows (Marg Helgenberger) as they endeavor to solve a variety of cases in the neon-lit capital of sin and vice. *CSI* was a joint production of Jerry Bruckheimer Productions, CBS Productions, and Canadian media company Alliance Atlantis, premiering on October 6, 2000. While the show garnered great reviews and the attention of the American television audience, things weren't going so successfully behind the scenes. According to Roy:

"*CSI* is a complicated story. It's about politics, frankly. Where do I start? I didn't do the pilot, but they didn't like the cinematographer who shot the pilot, so I got a call from the producer, Jim Hart, who was a really good guy. He had heard that I could be tough, so he sat me down in the beginning and he said, 'Look, if we have any problems, I'll just replace you.' And I said, 'I understand. I don't know how I got this reputation, but if I'm being tough then just tell me and I'll try to do whatever I can to fix it.' So, I started the project, and they were in the midst of prep. Jerry Bruckheimer was the producer and he had to deal with Disney because Touchstone was going to produce *CSI* and CBS was going to be the network. We weren't out shooting yet. We were three or four days away from shooting and Michael Eisner pulled the plug on it; he shut the show down. And I've been through that before—I've seen that kind of thing happen—but usually when they shut it down, it is shut down for good."

Roy continues, "Well, Billy Petersen was the star of the show and was a producing partner with Bruckheimer on this. CBS had the deal and they really wanted Billy Petersen to do a series. So, because Disney had pulled out of the project, Bruckheimer could shop around. Billy had a deal with a small Canadian distributor called Alliance Atlantis, so he went to them and said, 'Look, we lost the show,' and they said, 'We're interested, we'll come in for a specific percentage if somebody else will come in for the rest.' Billy then went to CBS and told him this but part of the problem was that Michael Eisner and Les Moonves, who was the producer at CBS, hated each other. So, you have Eisner at Disney and Moonves at CBS, and Eisner was not going to amortize overages for an expensive show. So, he just shut the show down. So, Moonves said, 'Screw him! We will pick up the overages that Alliance doesn't cover, and we will produce the show together.' Alliance was nobody at the time. They had never done anything except Canadian content or the distribution of American content. And CBS Productions had never done anything but news and sporting events, and things like *The Carol Burnett Show*; they've never done a dramatic television series. But they came in for the other part. We were successful after the first episode, but we had no money. When we did the first episode we couldn't go to Vegas; we couldn't afford to. There's a scene in the first episode where Billy is on the roof of this hotel and he's walking around and there's something in the rocks on the roof that is poisonous. That was all done with green screen in Los Angeles. And that's the way we had to do it. Jim Hart was finding a way of making something with as big a production value as possible with no money."

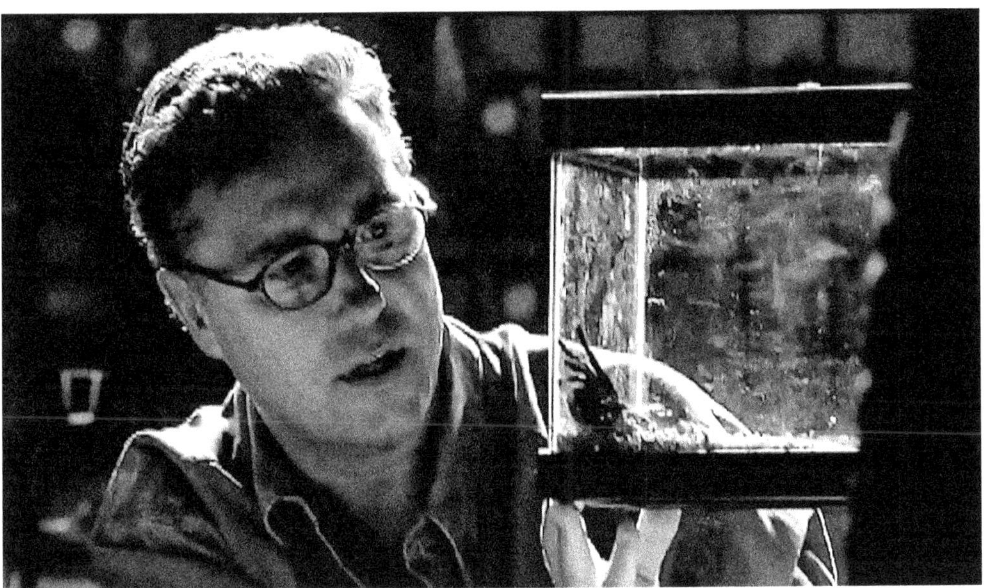

Gil Grissom (William Petersen) lit solely by the backlight of the spider's cage, in *CSI: Crime Scene Investigation,* **2000.**

By the first day of photography, Roy had not yet met Jerry Bruckheimer, but after shooting wrapped on Roy's first day the producer was sent the dailies for his perusal, but they did not meet with his approval. Bruckheimer said, "I don't like it." When asked what he didn't like about the dailies he answered, "I told you to get rid of that other cameraman." But Bruckheimer was mistaking the author of the images he had viewed. Roy, having been told by Jim Hart that Bruckheimer wanted to keep the style set down by the previous guy, was under the impression that he was to copy his style.

"I had been told by Jim that they loved that cameraman," Roy says. "So, I was kind of copying the other guy's work, even though I was trying to put my own signature on it, which I thought was quite good. But Jerry hated it."

Wires were crossed, and Hart was quick to admit his mistake. "Roy, we've got a problem," he said, "I was completely wrong; Jerry hated the first cinematographer, so you have got to come up with a different look right away, or you're going to be replaced." And from there, Roy got to work with a mandate straight from Bruckheimer: "be aggressive and dynamic."

"From the first day of principal photography to the second day of principal photography, the look of that show completely changed to what you see now. And that was me in the middle of the night, coming up with this Hip Hop, Rock and Roll aesthetic, which was like a bleach bypass look, shooting reversal and making it look like it's really rich with saturated colors. That was all done by me in the middle of the night. And it's what I originally thought the show should look like. But the truth was, I was trying to emulate the other guy. The sad part about this is that by the third or fourth episode in they just got out of hand. They fired Jim Hart. There was a guy there who had a relationship with Bruckheimer—his name was Sam Strangis, and he was this old-time producer who had been vice president of production at Paramount and was a producer at Fox where he worked on the *Batman* television show and crap like that. But he had Bruckheimer's ear and he said, 'Jim Hart can't do this. You've got to have someone with a lot of experience to do it.' So, Sam decided that he was going to control it, he's going to be the puppet master for this whole show, and the first thing he needed to do was fire Jim Hart and set about diminishing everybody's power—the cinematographer, the directors, every department head—all so he could be more powerful. He wanted me to be a co-cinematographer with somebody else, so he let me choose who I wanted. That's when Jerry and Billy decided that they wanted the show to be dangerous and aggressive. They didn't care what the cast looked like; they wanted the show to be visceral."

Despite Roy's best efforts to give the production the look that was desired from those in control, Strangis, hoping to make a name for himself, created a great deal of drama around the control of the image, suggesting that Roy was just not up to the high standards that the show required. What had been the "look" of the show came into question, and Strangis attempted to replace Roy with his preferred cinematographer. But Roy was determined to stick with what he envisioned should be the look of the show in that one last late-night attempt.

"This had gone on for several weeks," Roy recalls, "and it came to a head after the camera negative was shuttled off to their favorite post-house in the hope that they could shake me lose from the project. We went to Encore Video and the room was filled with postproduction experts from the project. The colorist turned to our group and stated, 'You've tried every option and we're back to the look that Roy gave you in the first place. Allow Roy and I to give it our best attempt and from that you can then determine if we have failed.' The room went totally quiet. Within seconds the room cleared, and the colorist and I started to create the look that would become the '*CSI* look.' After that, the colorist said to them, 'Roy has given us the negative we need to create the style that Mr. Bruckheimer wishes.'"

The drama evaporated as quickly as it began. However, the edgier aesthetic that Bruckheimer and Petersen sought sounded all well and good for the tone of the gritty crime show, but nobody told the cast that lighting was to be deliberately less polished than the average TV show, which led to some further animosity behind the scenes which Roy was dragged into...

"Marg Helgenberger wanted to look like Doris Day. She absolutely hated the way I photographed her. So, I fell into the midst of that whole thing. I went to Jerry, and I said, 'Look, you're going to have to come up with a solution here because Marg is not happy with me. I know how to make her pretty. But anytime I do that you say you don't like it.' And of course, nobody was going to go and talk to her about it. So, I got stuck in the middle of all the politics of that whole thing. It was between the two powerful people on the show: one an aging actress who was distressed with my more aggressive style; the other a producer who continued to push me forward into more dangerous territory. In one ear I was told by the other star, who is also the executive producer, to continue to photograph the project in a manner which was very hip and aggressive. In the other ear I had Marg complaining to them about me. I was getting played by both sides. The producer who hired me was fired and when the new producers came in they attempted, in every way, to bum's rush me out."

But having been burned on previous shows, Roy made the decision to leave

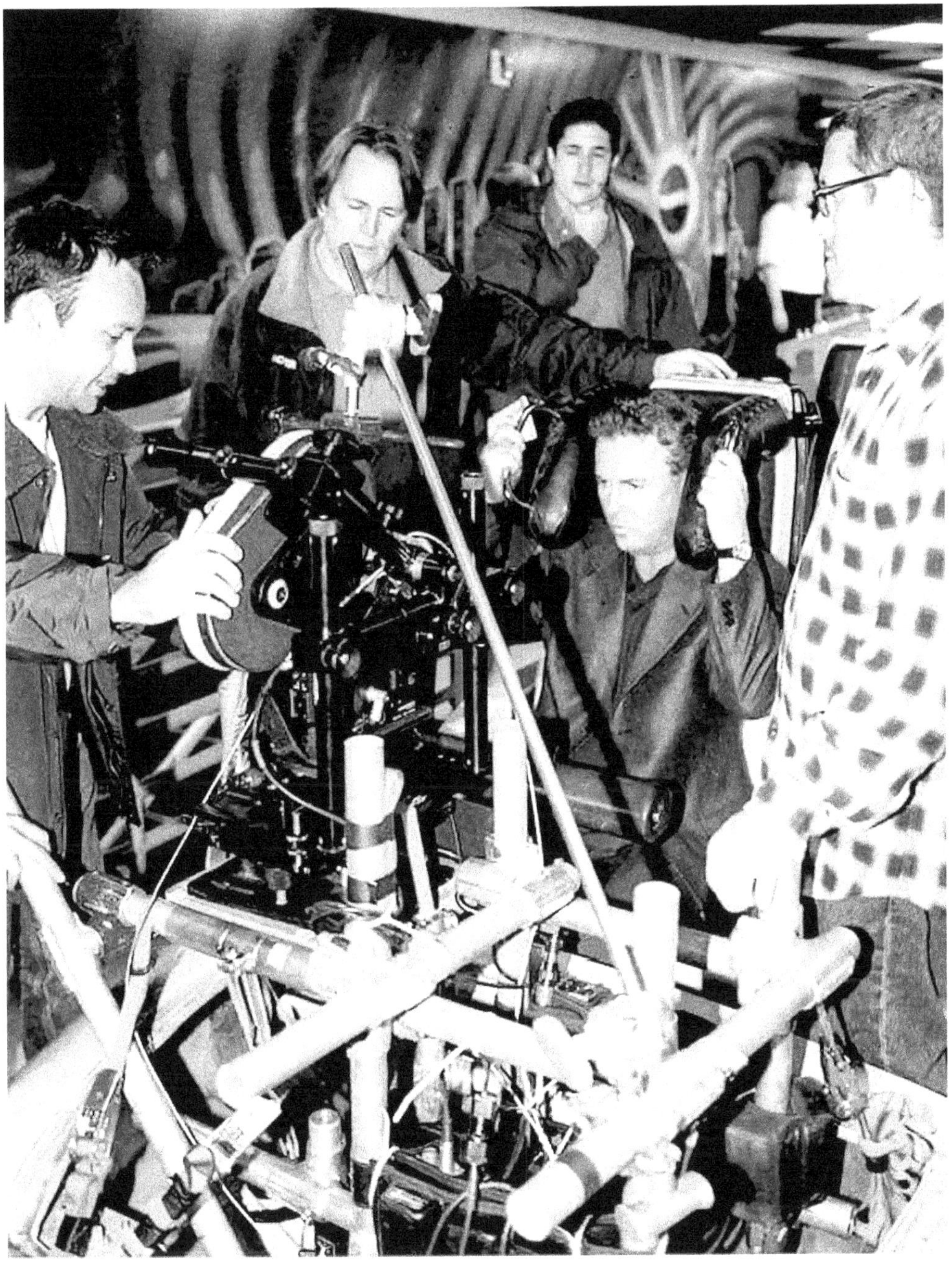

On the set of *CSI: Crime Investigation*, 2000. From left: director Danny Cannon, Roy, assistant director Louis Shaw Milito, star William Petersen, key grip Dale Alexander.

CSI before they could fire him. But Bruckheimer and Petersen weren't letting go of Roy that easily, and to encourage him to stay on the show, they offered him the chance to direct.

"We were doing beautiful work, and I would be a millionaire today if I had stayed on; but after what happened on *Beauty and the Beast* I was never going to stay with that kind of drama anymore. So, I said, 'I quit!' and then Jerry flew out in his helicopter to where we were shooting and he said, 'Roy, I don't want you to quit. Billy loves you. We want you to stay here; we're going to make you a director.' So, they paid for my director's fees, and I came in and started directing. I directed one full episode and a bunch of other things, partial episodes. And one night I was directing when Sam Strangis came up to me and said, 'You're not following my pattern. You didn't choose the locations I wanted you to choose.' And I said, 'Sam, I was told that they were just your preferences and that I could choose whatever I wanted. I chose this location because I could shoot three different scenes here; in the location you suggested I could only shoot one scene.' And he said, 'Well, you're not a team player.' And I replied, 'I'm sorry, Sam. I thought I was. I was trying to save you money.' And in front of the entire company—Billy and my crew—he said, 'Fuck you!' and he spit in my face. I said, 'Sam, you didn't just spit on Roy Wagner, you spit on your director. It hurts, it makes me sad, but you have embarrassed yourself. It didn't embarrass me.' And that made him even angrier. He said, 'I'm going to break your legs!' and all kinds of things. As good as I was at navigating the politics of a show, there were times when I would get pushed into a corner. The bigger the names of the people, the more political the project; and the more they throw their weight around, the more you could get yourself into trouble. It wasn't hard to do the work; the hard part was the crisis management and political drama."

"There was a lot of studio politics going on," Dale Alexander affirms. "I stayed on it for a bit longer but then I left it as well. They brought in directors of photography that I couldn't work with. They weren't up to Roy standards. And it makes it very difficult when you have worked with the man who created the look of the show and then these other guys come in and want to change it or do things their way. Roy was so great at creating styles and very different ones for different things which would give the shows their own unique look and tone. On *CSI* you have all the lights and darks and the shadowing, and then the inside of the *CSI* sets which had their own distinctive look too... He did marvelous work in there."

"Anything Roy has done on TV has just been mind-blowing," Brian Crane applauds. "It is all beautifully cinematic. When he started doing *CSI*, I ended up getting a job with someone else but I remember watching that show and going, 'That's Roy!' because of the simplicity of the way he likes to drop a light on the floor and just rake a wall, or put a PAR can above somebody's head and just light their ass on fire. The way the light just kind of flowed over Petersen and then bounced off the surface back on him. That's one lighting thing that has always stuck with me. *CSI* is such a Roy Wagner look."

The drama ultimately proved too much to bear; it was time for Roy to move on. With the show since becoming a beloved institution and ubiquitous brand in

American television, his connection to it remains bittersweet. "I loved *CSI*," Roy admits, "but I never watched it after I left the show. Occasionally I see pieces of it here and there and to me it just looks like some disposable rock video. That was not my intention at all; I did use deep saturated color, but it was to counterpoint the murder scenes and the CSI office which was a grisly dark grey. Since I left it has ended up looking even more theatrical and excessive. The tragedy is that *CSI* continued on and a lot of people took credit for its style but I'm the one who created the look of that show. Nobody else. But the look gets attributed to everybody else.... It was Jerry Bruckheimer, it was Billy Petersen, it was the guy that replaced Roy.... No, it wasn't; it was me. And it was an aesthetic that took me about an hour to figure out. It wasn't that I had some genius moment—it was just survival of the fittest. But because of that whole situation I got to work with Diane Keaton and Dana Delany."

While Roy was in Nevada shooting *CSI*, actress Diane Keaton had been engaging his agent because she wanted to work with Roy on the pilot episode of a new show that she was going to be directing at Sony called *Pasadena*. A prime-time Fox soap opera, the show is set in the titular Southern Californian city where a young woman named Lily McAllister (Alison Lohman) takes the audience through her family's twisted world of secrets, lies, wealth, and privilege as she seeks answers to a murder that happened in her own home.

"I turned *Pasadena* down three times," Roy regretfully admits, "because we were in Vegas doing *CSI*, but because of everything going on with that show I rang my agent and said, 'Call up Diane and see if she still wants me to do that.' He said,

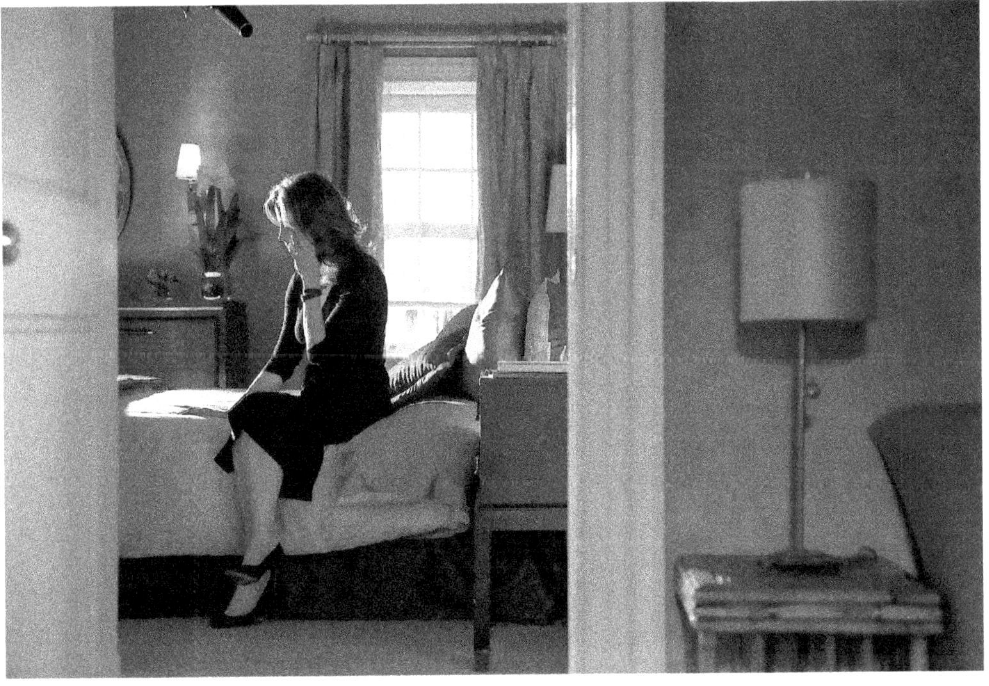

Filming Dana Delany on the set of *Pasadena*, 2001.

'They probably already have someone else by now.' I insisted, 'Please call her. Tell her I want to do it.' So, he did, and she said that's fantastic and arranged to meet me at The Polo Lounge. I met Diane, and I fell in love with her. She is so amazing, smart, and talented—and unusual. I never had an experience like that with a director; we would go out to a location together and she would have her own cheesy little video camera and we would read the scene together and she would say, 'Okay, I want the camera here,' and she would act out the part while I filmed her. Then she would look back at the footage and she would say, 'No, I don't want to do it like that. Here, you go do the part and I will work the camera,' and so I would go and read the part for her. It was so incredible because I really got inside her mind and got to understand the complexity of how she thought; and that went on for four weeks of prep. Diane would pick me up at my house every morning and I would drive her in her car to the location and we would talk. Then she would drop me home at night. It was an amazing experience. *Pasadena* was another show like *2000 Malibu Road* which never got its due. Mike White was the producer, and it was before *The White Lotus* and it was way ahead of its time."

◆ ◆ ◆

Roy's continued prolific work in television would often bring him back into collaboration with some of the crucial collaborators that changed the course of his career. Through several TV shows Roy would be reunited with Peter O'Fallon

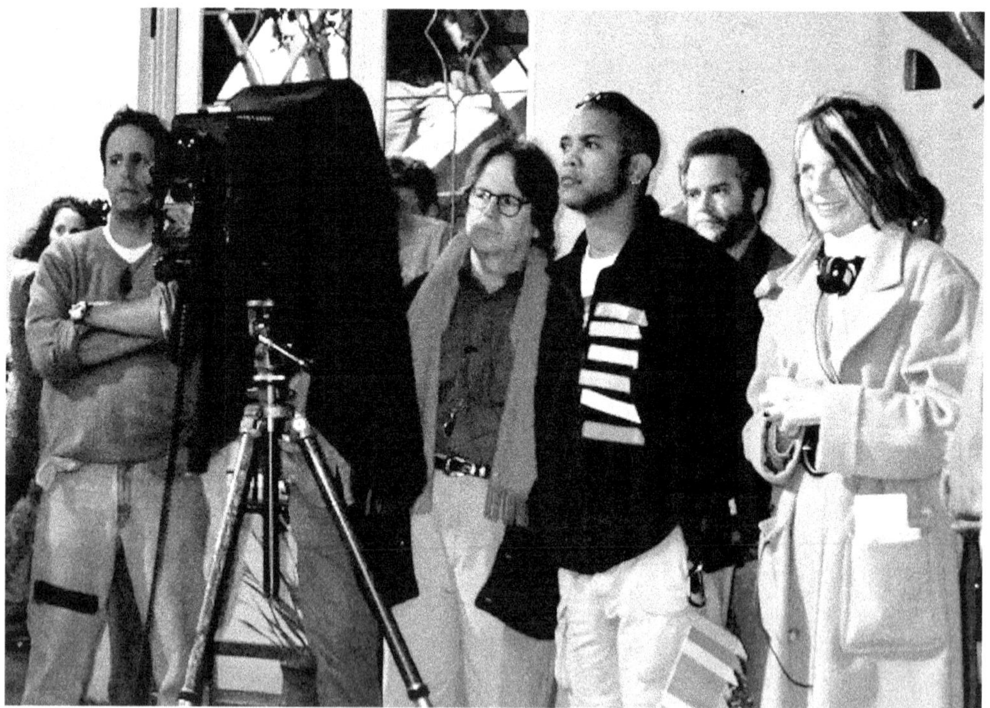

Diane Keaton (right) directs a scene of *Pasadena*. Roy is behind the camera, and assistant director Arthur Anderson is at back right, with unidentified extras.

and John Badham, two filmmakers with whom he has crafted some of his most brilliant and artistically inventive imagery. Roy would be brought in early on for what would become a massive ratings winner for the Fox network. *House M.D.* is a hospital drama starring erstwhile British comedian Hugh Laurie as Dr. Gregory House, the pill-popping misanthrope who also happens to be a medical marvel. At odds with his colleagues due to his unique diagnostic methods, House became an enigmatic hero that attracted audiences in their droves who followed religiously for eight seasons.

The pilot episode of *House M.D.* was directed Bryan Singer, of *The Usual Suspects* and *X-Men* fame, while other directors who followed included filmmakers with interesting résumés in feature film: Peter Medak (*The Changeling*, 1980); Tim Hunter (*River's Edge*, 1986); Daniel Attias (*Silver Bullet*, 1985); and Roy's *A Rumor of Angels* collaborator, Peter O'Fallon. When the wheels started to fall off production early on, O'Fallon knew who to call.

"I did the first couple of episodes after the pilot of *House*," O'Fallon affirms. "We were doing 18-hour days and a good friend of mine, Dan Sackheim, called me and said, we're in trouble. The union shut them down after a 90-hour work week. That's when I said, 'You need to call Roy Wagner.'"

"I wouldn't have done *House* without Peter O'Fallon," Roy admits, "I've done many things because of him. Even though I had this bad-boy perception attached to me throughout my career, Peter didn't care about that; he always just said,

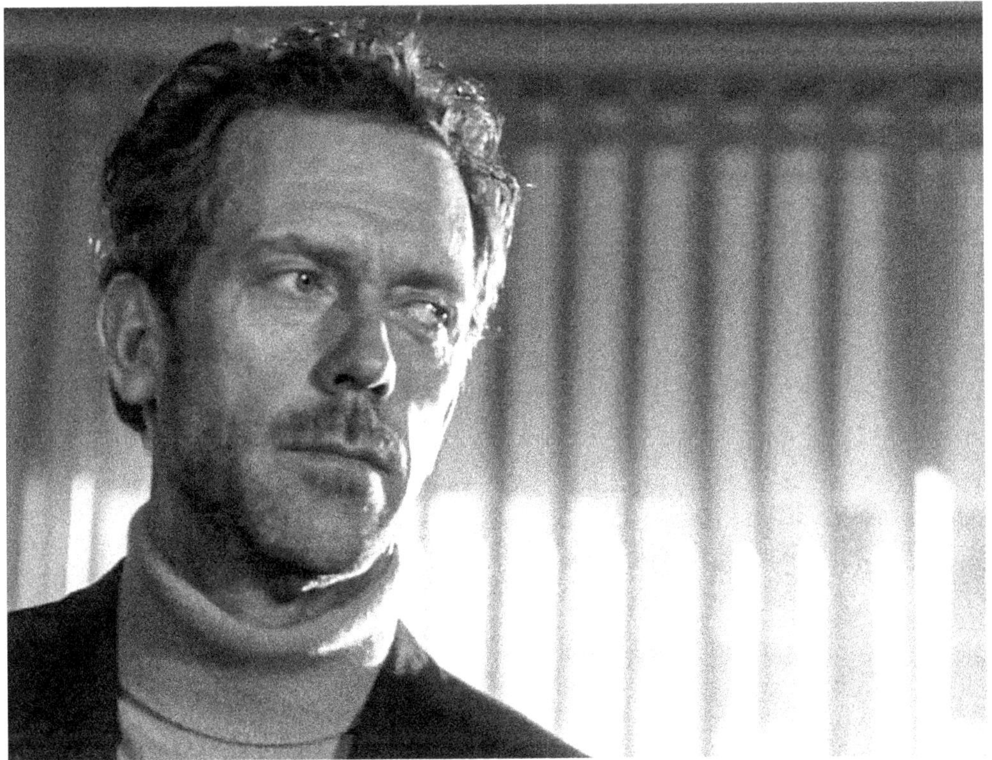

Hugh Laurie as Dr. Gregory House, in *House M.D.*, 2004.

'Bring in Roy!' I'm the guy who gets called when the studio is in trouble and that is essentially how I got *House*. That's how I got so many of the things that I've done. Same with *Elementary*—studio was in a bind. It was costing $2 million an episode if they didn't get rid of the cameraman that they have, so I'm the guy they call to fix that. To have that kind of speed and instinct to do things well quickly has a very good side to it, but people often take advantage of you for the wrong reasons, but with Peter I always knew that I had a partner; no matter what happened, we were going to get through it together. We're guys they love to hate and hate to love because we will give them what they want. And we will take the risks and find the look of the show. In my view, *Party of Five* is not a very good show, but the way it looked was very interesting. That is because of what Peter and I brought to it."

Roy's regular crew members, gaffer Brian Crane and key grip Dale Alexander, experienced the intense production environment of *House M.D.* along with their inveterate cinematographer.

"Oh, my God... *House!*" Crane says, with some exasperation at recalling the labor-intensive schedule. "We worked long hours because of that show, I think everybody got frustrated with that. It could really wear and tear you down. Roy's biggest challenge was dealing with the writers and the editors on that show, because they'd be constantly bringing changes, and then the editors literally wanted you to start on a 25-millimeter lens and end on 150. They would go through each lens over and over again to be this angle, and be this angle, and be this angle, on all three cameras, and they would just rotate the lenses accordingly. It could be frustrating for him, but Roy brought no fear with the camera, and no fear with the lighting."

"Roy brought such interesting lighting to that show," Alexander says, "he brought more style than it ever had before. When he goes in to take over the show, if they allow him, he will fix it; he will fix the look. He will take it from some boring everyday flat look or whatever it was and bring his own imagery

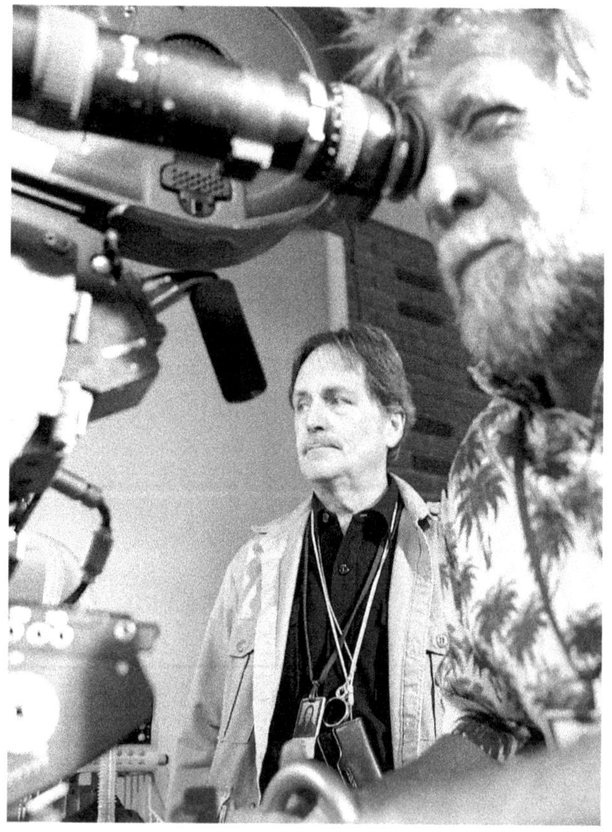

Roy (left) shooting *House M.D.* with cameraman Robert Stradling.

and style into it. And of course, he had to be careful that he didn't change it too much, because you can't change the look of the show midstream too much. But you can certainly bring some beauty and some art into it. And he did that on *House M.D.*"

"Working with Roy was always an education," Crane adds, "and I appreciated that I wasn't treated as a walking light meter. We would go into a room, and he would look around and say, 'Okay, the cameras are going to be here, and I want cameras here, and let's put some crosses in here,' and then he would walk away and leave it up to me to coordinate rigging and putting everything into place for implementing what he wanted. So that was nice. I felt like I created a bunch of new globes and new fixtures, like bare bulbs behind a book or something on a desk, or we'd have a candle and then follow up the candle and put a bulb inside the candle that was sitting there to help light the actor more. I would cut up the back of the lampshade to put a little light or an extra bulb in there and black wrap it out so that it helped the actors look more natural; it looked more believable once you saw it on film. But you couldn't tell those little tricks were being done. I've learned so many of those neat little tricks from the challenges that Roy would present me with. 'Put a light in here, put a light over there.'"

While *House M.D.* went on to great success across its eight-season run on Fox, the next show that Peter O'Fallon brought Roy in on failed to strike a Grateful Dead–like resounding chord with viewers. It was the ABC crime procedural

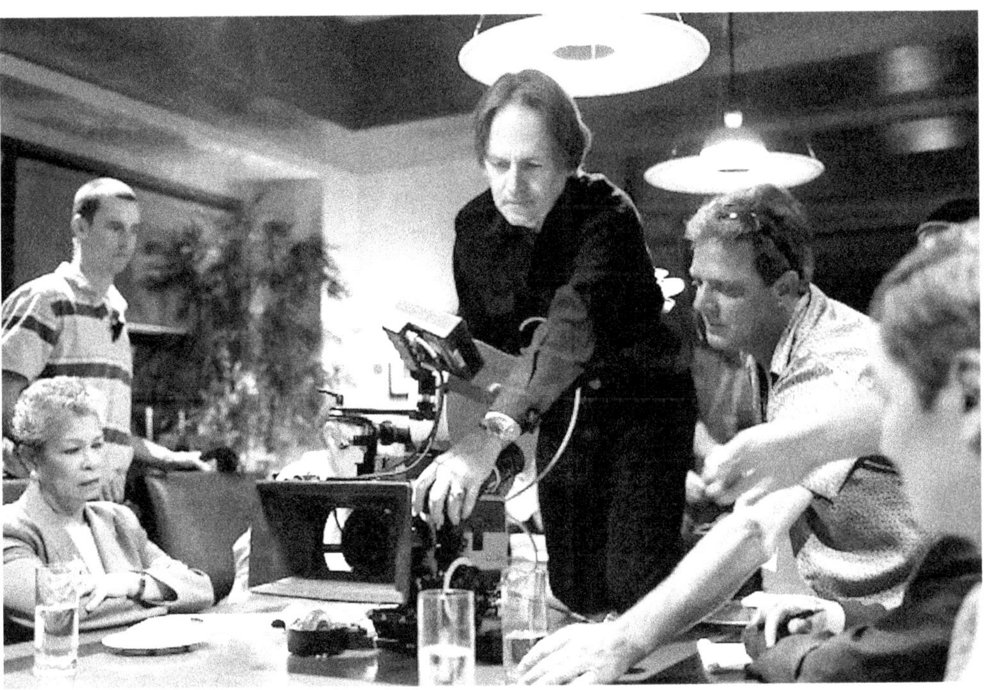

Roy sets up a shot on *House M.D.* with the then-new P+S Technik Skater Dolly. Camera assistant Darin Krask is standing at left, and key grip Rich Nasworthy is next to Roy.

The Unusuals, an ill-fated project which premiered in April 2009, but it wasn't long for the television landscape.

"*The Unusuals* was a crazy one," O'Fallon recalls, "I brought Roy in on it, but it only lasted one season. I got fired off it, but they initially brought me on because of the humor. It was supposed to be a show about unusual cops and the idea was to make it funny. But right off the bat ABC wanted them to come in and have the guy point the gun and say, 'On the floor!' While we were doing it, I was arguing with the network, trying to say, 'Hey, this is not what we want to do.' So, they ended up firing me, which was the best thing that ever happened to me, oddly; it made my career because they had to pay me as I was under contract, and once I stopped working on it I went off and created a show for myself, and I was lucky to be able to do that one for a couple of years."

"That show was doomed to fail," Roy says, "because the network was playing everybody against everybody. It was created by Noah Hawley, and his brother wrote some of it too. I think it was their first big show and they were terrified because they were getting notes from the network saying that they hated the way the show worked. So, Peter became the fall guy. We were out in an insert car shooting in Manhattan and then when we went to dinner Peter got a call in which he was told he was fired. I said, 'Well, I've got to go too.' And he said, 'No, you stay.' I did stay but it did not get any better. It was miserable. But we had a great cast, including Amber Tamblyn and Jeremy Renner, and they were putting a lot of comedians in there. But nothing ever fit, and it didn't last."

Roy reunited with John Badham for a small-screen show that featured a big screen star who was making his final appearance on the world's stage. Patrick Swayze was dying of pancreatic cancer when he made *The Beast*. This Chicago-set crime drama focused on the work of controversial undercover FBI agent Charles Barker (Swayze) who partners with and mentors the rookie agent Ellis Dove (Travis Fimmel) to teach him how to successfully navigate the criminal underworld with chameleonic effect.

The Sony-produced series was helmed by a roster of veteran TV and film directors across its thirteen episodes, including Michael Dinner (*Off Beat*, 1986; *Hot to Trot*, 1988), Jeremiah S. Chechik (*National Lampoon's Christmas Vacation*, 1989; *Benny and Joon*, 1993), and John Badham. For Roy, it was another opportunity to work with a filmmaker who offered him the opportunity to showcase his work to the widest audiences of his career, thought it wasn't without its own unique and unfortunate set of challenges, as he details:

"I'm very proud of the movies I've done with John, and I'm just as proud of the shows, especially *The Beast*. That had to be the most difficult thing that we ever had to do, which was working with a dying man. John and I were standing in the bar set one day and Patrick did not come in for the longest time, and then when he came in he was standing against a post and I turned to John and said, 'I don't think he's going to make it.' But then we rolled the camera and suddenly he was a different person. He was not ill anymore. Patrick was remarkable. But that was a constant challenge. It adds a nasty twist to your day, which is already difficult to start with, and here's a person that you have to take care of. There's just no way around it.

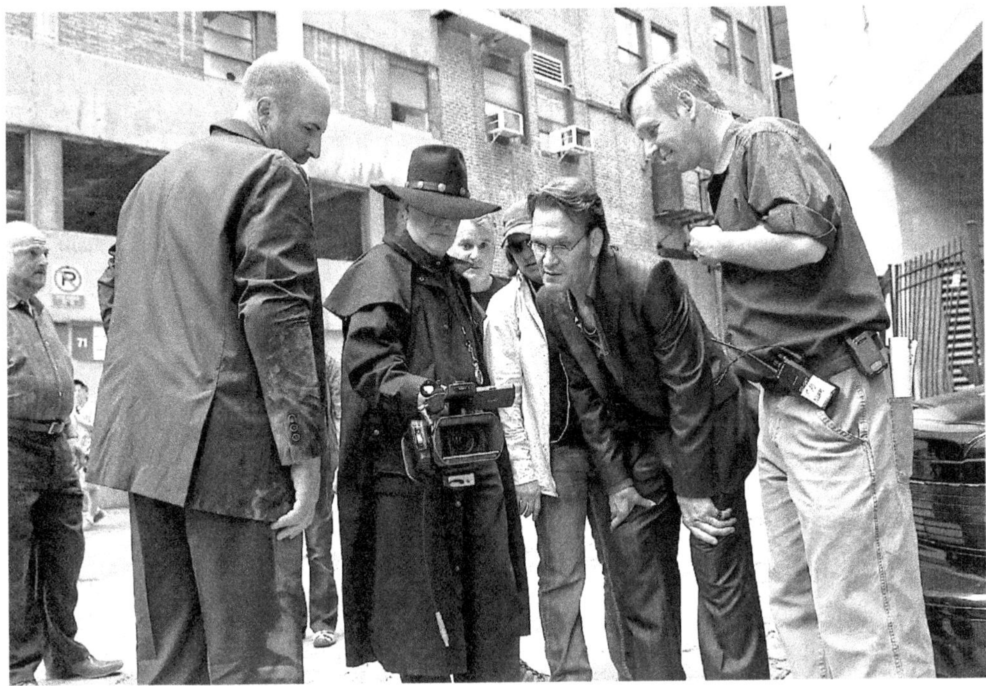

Roy (center-left) and Patrick Swayze (center-right) checking dailies on the first day of shooting *The Beast*, 2009.

(A) it's just basic humanity, and (B) he's the star of your show and you must help him get through it as best you can. Patrick was up for doing all kinds of stunts that he probably had no business doing. Even though he was that ill, he did a driving sequence that just scared me to death. I don't know why I was in the car but there were two cameras in the back of the car looking at stuff while he is flying around the streets of Chicago. I'm thinking, 'Oh my God, why am I in here?' He was another one of those people that just wanted to do his absolute best, even though he said to me, 'You know who I am? I'm the guy who ought to be dead.' That was one of the first things that he said to me. What a spirit, knowing he had only got so much time."

Roy continues, "It was wonderful to be working with John again on *The Beast*; the most important thing that I have taken away from working with him is partnership, knowing and learning about partnership. It is critically important for me to work with someone with a vision, that knows what they want and how to make a movie, and yet also understands what your problems are and knows how to help you solve them. John never told me 'No,' but I certainly had to come to him with a reason. And that was not always the case. John knows more about filmmaking than I will ever know. He has worked with so many different cinematographers, so he knows exactly what is tolerable and what is not tolerable. John was a huge contender in the filmmaking community, because people knew that that his movies made money, so the honor of getting to say that I worked on four John Badham movies is something that will be with me for the rest of my life. There was an energy about John that made everybody want to do their best work with him. And

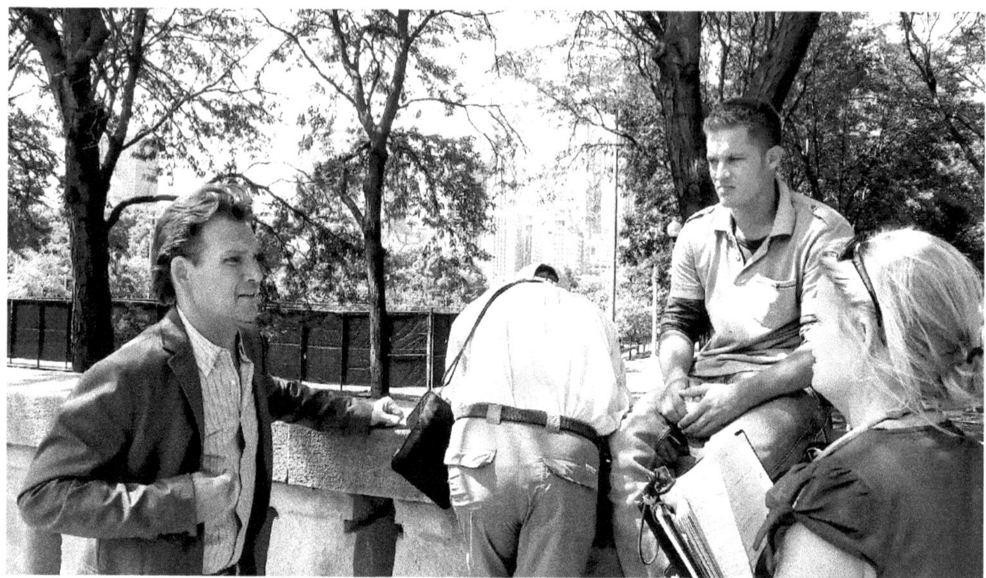

Patrick Swayze (left) and crew getting ready to film a scene of *The Beast* on location in Chicago. Actor Travis Fimmel is sitting on the wall.

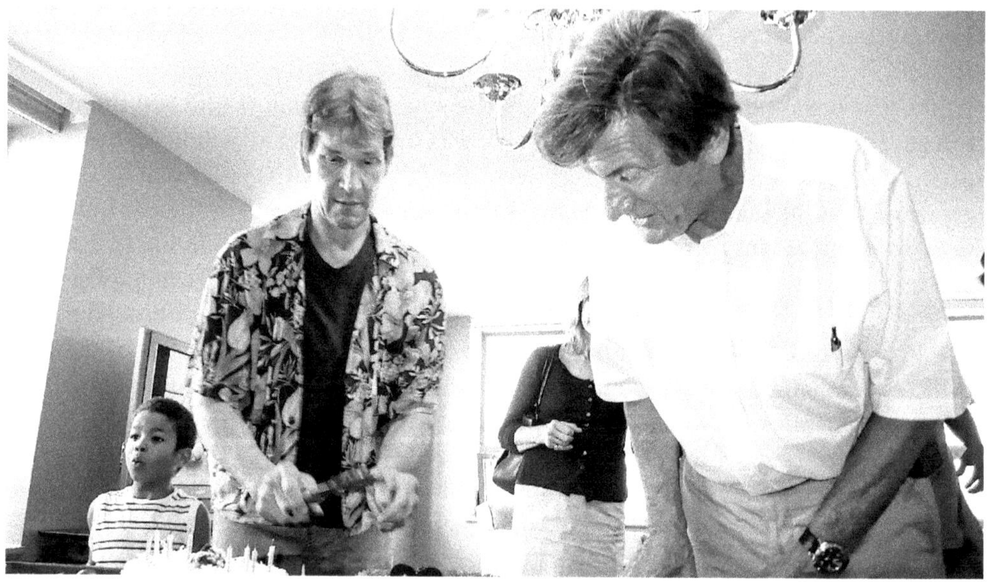

John Badham (right) celebrates Patrick Swayze's birthday during the making of *The Beast*.

he built a safe place for everybody to come and do that work. He was a person that you knew was in control of the reins of the movie, and that he was going to get you through to the other side. That's really the man I fell in love with. I thank him for allowing me to be a part of that journey. Working with him was just one of the great, great experiences of my career."

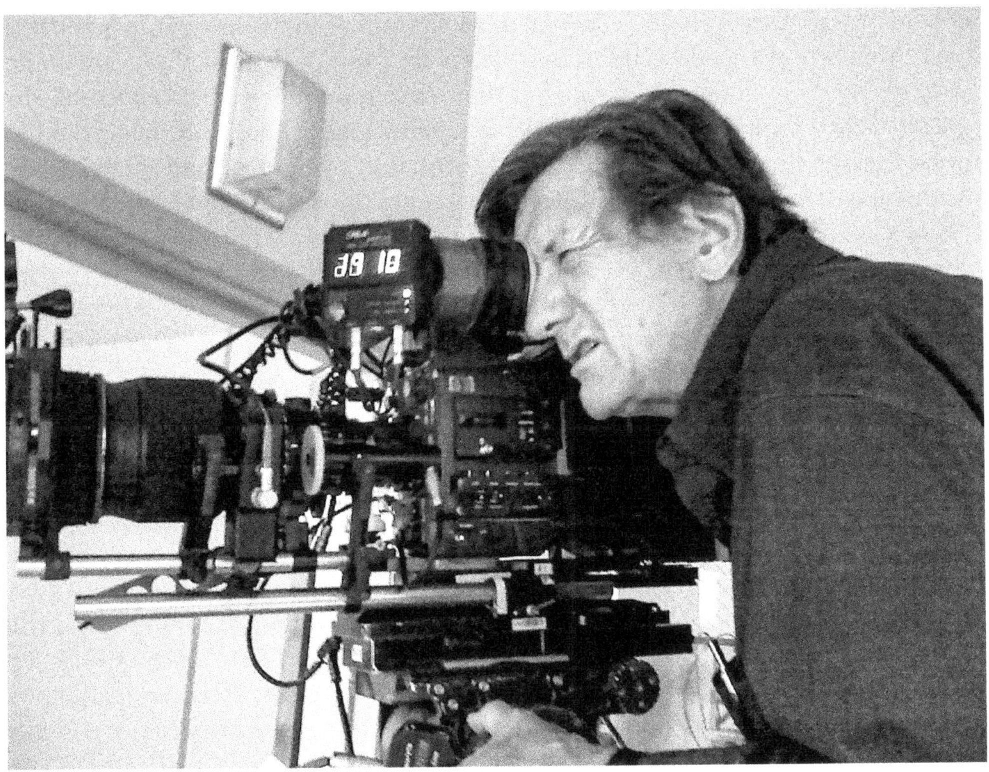

John Badham looking through the lens on the set of *The Beast*.

By the time Roy and Badham collaborated on *The Beast*, they were fully embracing technological shifts in filmmaking tools, including the use of digital photography, which by then had all but replaced celluloid as the preferred photographic medium of the studios and networks. "Absolutely," Badham affirms, "we pushed really hard to work with digital technology as much as we could. By the time we were doing *The Beast*, Roy was totally working with digital cameras. I'm grateful for Roy being there on that show. He was such a great partner, a great creative partner. That means everything."

"We did go digital on *The Beast*, and in fact we were doing everything wrong!" Roy recalls. "We were using these little home video cameras as well as the large Sony cameras because I convinced them that you couldn't tell the difference between the smaller ones and the big professional ones. And that was for Sony. It was hilarious. But when we went to digital I had to ask myself, 'Am I in this because I love the technology, or am I in this because I love telling stories?' And the answer was always, 'I love telling stories.'"

Brian Crane recalls seeing his boss's smooth transition into the digital realm: "Right after *House M.D.* I became a DP and Roy pushed me out on my own. And that's when that digital transition was happening, and I had a chance to loop around and work on a project with him and I saw that he had the same approach with digital as he did with film, whatever the type of digital format, whether it was an Alexa or Red or whatever. You have to think of it as if it's a film stock, not just a tool. So, you pick the camera based on what the look is that you want to achieve. I don't think Roy changed his lighting style for the most part. When we were doing *Party of Five*, Sony started bringing out their cameras and we would shoot side by side with their digital cameras and with our film camera because they wanted to try and match Roy's look digitally. And I think that's where we had the heads up or advantage that a lot of people don't get in seeing the development and the progress of the digital camera, especially for Sony's brand; in fact, Roy was among the first cinematographers to be asked to test out these digital cameras."

"I was always happy to work with whatever tools I had available," Roy admits. "I always felt that I am the same artist, it's just that the tools are different. Changing technology is more of an intellectual and emotional transition for me. And there have been a few of those in my life. But early on I decided that I had to relinquish the idea that I would always be standing behind the Mitchell BNC. When we went from regular cameras to Steadicam, that was a huge problem for me because I had been so accustomed to looking through the camera and lining up every shot, and then lighting through the camera. It was very tough for me to relinquish that control back to the operator. And I know that I probably upset a few operators because they were used to the cameraman just saying, 'Find the shot, just go do it.' But I was very much like Billy Fraker in that I had a desire for precision. Billy was very much involved in the framing. But Steadicam changed all of that. I have just had to adapt to all these new technologies over time, I have been doing it since the Mitchell BNC went away."

The Science and Magic of Cinema

A Conversation with Wayne Byrne and Roy H. Wagner

"Once you understand who you are, you're dead."

Wayne: *Roy, you mentioned to me before that people have often referred to you as having always been "an old man." From knowing you and how you speak about your mentors, I don't necessarily see that as having a negative connotation for you. You have often referred to your mentors as "the old men," these men who are almost gods to us, these serious, hardworking men who made the movies. You met some of the industry's leading cinematographers early on in your impressionable years. Tell me how that happened.*

Roy: I met Harry Stradling when I was a little boy, and he eventually became my mentor. But when I first met him, he was just charmed that some little boy thought he was something great, because cinematographers within the industry of Hollywood were considered a big deal, but outside of Hollywood, nobody knew who they were. And so, for someone to be a fan of theirs, they thought that was cute. Floyd Crosby, who worked on the Roger Corman films and all the beach party movies—I met him when I was in high school. I was such a fan of cinematographers that whenever I asked them questions they were not sophisticated enquiries—I just wanted to know who these men were as people. That was always more interesting to me than any technical mumbo jumbo. From a young age I would look these guys up in the phonebook and just call them.

Wayne: *And they entertained a young kid cold-calling them up and asking questions?*

Roy: Some of these men were very kind and generous to me and there were some that were not that way. They didn't have time for me and put me off and I would never call them again. But for the ones who were suckered into my bait, I was there for them for the rest of their lives.

Wayne: *What did you learn from these relationships?*

Roy: I would get these bursts of information and knowledge that would come along that I really didn't understand at all, but later it made total sense. I'm informed by images and sound and that kind of storytelling more than I am by technique, and frankly, many of those guys didn't know how to tell you how they did what they did. They didn't really understand it. But I was always curious.

Wayne: *There has been a lot of intellectualizing in cinema, perhaps since the 1960s and the advent of film schools and the generation of filmmakers born from that, where filmmaking can break down a shot or a scene into minute detail in various contexts, but you tended to hear less of that from "the old men." They seemed more concerned with just getting on with the work. But there must have been some intellectual reasoning behind the amazing work that many of them did, but perhaps they just weren't comfortable articulating it. Were these the kinds of conversations you would have with them?*

Roy: I could ask some people those things—people like Bill Fraker, Conrad Hall, or David Mullen—they can tell you everything. But then there are those who can't, because for them it is more of a spiritual experience. And frankly that is what I want it to be. I want to respond to something. I have been doing this long enough that I know all the technical stuff and everything to do with the tools, I know what a certain light does, and I know what a certain lens does. It's all instinctual; it's all process. And that's the way they worked because after thirty or forty years of doing it they figured it out. Some would do it by rote and would just do the same things repeatedly, but some of them would be bored and they would try different things. I once asked Harry Stradling about *A Streetcar Named Desire*, which I had seen at a very young age with my parents, and which really struck me as something unique and powerful. So, I asked him about it and he was just like, "Oh, yeah, that was fun. Interesting movie." He had nothing. I wish I could say these guys told me how great they were, but never did I get any of that ever. They were gods to me, but they didn't see themselves as anything like that. The funniest one of them all was the one that I admired the most: Charles B. Lang. He was one of my favorite cinematographers; he did *The Big Heat*, *The Uninvited*, *Some Like It Hot*, and *The Magnificent Seven* ... a lot of great films. But when you would ask him a question, he would just be like, "Oh, yeah, I did that. That was no big deal." And I'd say, "Charlie, the images in *The Uninvited* are so subtle..." and he would reply, "Yeah, they're pretty good, weren't they?" And that would be it. When I walked away from the interview, I would be thinking, "Oh, I see. That's the way he *was*. That was how he *did*." Charlie was a dabbler. Even after you rolled the camera, he would still be painting, still be nuancing. That was who he was. So, if I asked him about technique, which I did, I got nothing. Joe Ruttenberg was never that way; he was a very sweet guy, but when it came to the image, it was all about Joe; and it had to be an image that made Joe happy. He could tear out a complete setup that had taken him an hour to light and start over again if it didn't work for him. So, he had to be loved by the stars and the studio in order to survive like that, because it was a factory and so you had to produce within a certain

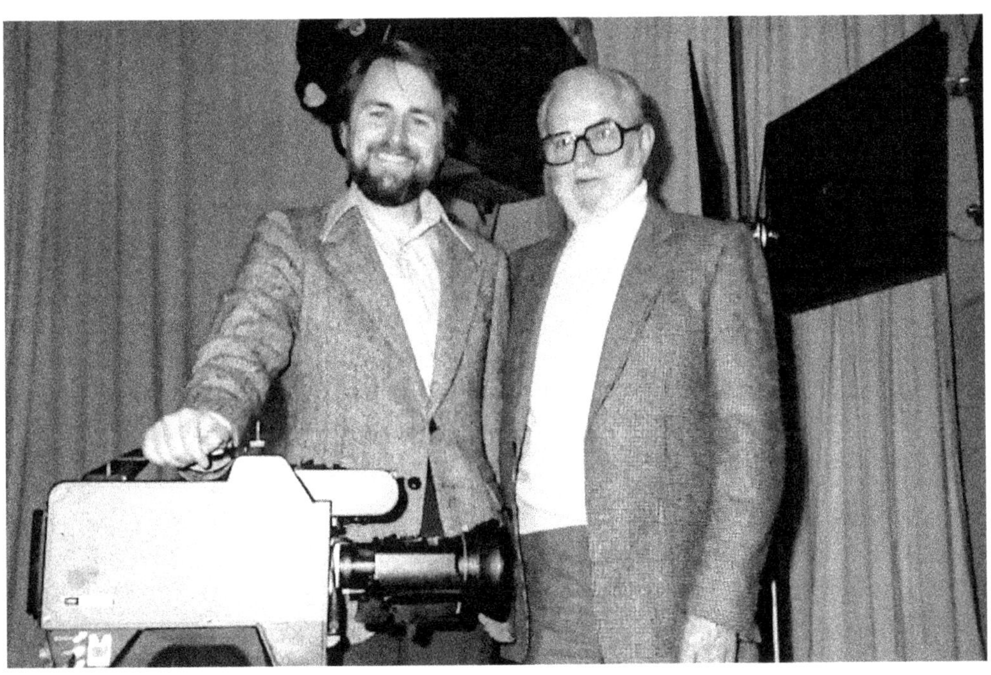

Roy (left) with noted cinematographer Frank Phillips, ASC, ca. 1979.

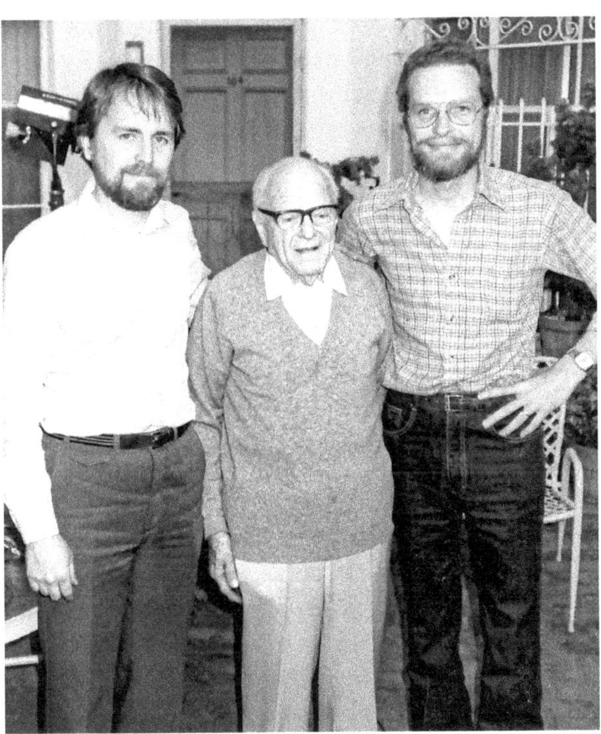

Roy (left) with cinematographer Joseph Ruttenberg (center) and his *American Cinematographer* partner Steve Wood in 1980.

amount of time and money, or you didn't continue. But everybody loved Joe Ruttenberg, so they allowed him to be who he was.

Wayne: *Given the factory mentality of the studio system back in the Golden Age of Hollywood, I would imagine it would have been hard to be a supreme artist on every film, no matter the quality of the material.*

Roy: Yes, the other side of that was there were the guys who were just hacks. Even Harry Stradling could be a hack and just be going through the motions at times. And you had people like Paul Vogel, the guys whose whole career was working and getting by. It wasn't about artistry. With these guys the studios would know they would get it done in thirty days and they wouldn't have to worry about anything.

Wayne: *So, the studios needed both of those kinds of people; they needed a Joe Ruttenberg, and they needed a Paul Vogel.*
    Roy: They did.

Wayne: *And where do you see yourself in that?*
    Roy: I think I'm more from the Joe Ruttenberg school than I am the other. I'm not a pain in the ass as far as speed or saving money; I'm really good at that because I learned that from Stradling. What I am a pain about is protection of the crew and protection of integrity of what we do. I'm much more inclined to protect that and protect the quality of the work because of the ASC and because of those who came before me.

Wayne: *From knowing you and knowing your work as well as I do, I see elements of both. I know Roy the intellectual, and I know Roy the laborer. And let's not forget Roy the mad scientist and Roy the magician.*
    Roy: Even though I was a child of those old men, I was also a child of the sixties, so I became intellectually involved in filmmaking in the era that you mentioned before. It was a new discourse. I wanted to understand why colors meant certain things, and why composition was so important. So, by the time I got to something like *A Nightmare on Elm Street 3*, I was far further along than they were in terms of the intellectual side of it all. They understood spiritually why they were doing certain things, but they couldn't articulate it. They couldn't tell you why. Whereas for me, being a child of the sixties and growing up in that environment and culture, I could tell you why I did things the way I did. That was great for anybody that wanted to talk to me because I could say why those day exteriors look the way they did, why they were cold, or why they were done with blue light instead of warm light. I could talk about why some people were on one side of the frame or the other. I had to define for myself what those things meant. Then as I became progressively more informed I started putting that in the back of my mind and using it as a means of expression instead of saying, "I'm going to choose this because that means this." I really never did that. I didn't choose a color because I intellectualized it, I did it because it was instinctual; I knew why I was doing it.

Wayne: *There is a certain spiritual, or perhaps masterly, quality to that. To be intellectually aware of everything you are doing, but never having to express it literally or rationally ... just doing it ... or hiring the right people to do it for you.*
    Roy: A lot of the old men, the really good directors of that era, were very spiritual people. William Wyler couldn't tell you why he did what he did, but he knew what he wanted, and he worked with people that understood how to get it for him.

Wayne: *It reminds me of someone like John Ford. The simplicity of his work is a façade that hides a hugely intellectual, empathetic, and curious mind. We think* *of his works in the practical sense: the amazing locations, and stunts, and performances. But it is the emotion and intellect of his work which impact the greatest. The Quiet Man and The Searchers are just two examples of that.*

Roy: John Ford was a very spiritual person and tried to deny that; he tried to act like he wasn't spiritual. It was all presentational. And it may be simple in its lack of sophistication, but it has a reason. Another thing that is great about those old filmmakers is that when you go to see one of their films you know that it is going to have a particular signature. I love that about them. And if we are to think of contemporary filmmakers, someone like Steven Soderbergh has that. Even though I don't respect his cinematography because he likes to do everything, I do respect him as a filmmaker because I think that he has a particular signature. That is important. I love that about any filmmaker, whether they're a director or director of photography or film editor, wherever you are, if you have a particular point of view, and you can inform the work with that. This all comes back to having a certain style that can be identifiable; I don't know that I want people to think I have a signature or a particular voice. But I think if you look at all my work, it does have a particular point of view. And I sort of want to deny it. I don't want to become ritualistic about it. But we all have our limitations.

Wayne: *As you got to know these guys personally, did you find that you understood them more artistically? Was it a window into that personal signature?*

Roy: I saw who they really were. And that fascinated me. Yes, they could be very charming, but they could be all these other things. But, you know, Hollywood was a factory, and they were obligated. They were the generals. The assistant director and the director of photography were the generals on the set. Harry Stradling could be very tough. Jimmy Wong Howe was not a nice guy. He was a tough guy. He was a nice guy when you talked to him off set, but he was all business on set. And part of it was because of him being Chinese. He got a lot of pressure because of that. And that made him protective. And Billy Fraker was very tough. I mean, Nicky talks about Billy being tough in your book with him [*Nick McLean: The Life and Works of a Hollywood Cinematographer*] and Billy had his reasons for being tough. He had a horrible, horrible life. And that doesn't excuse anyone for being mean or tough, but that was Billy's way of protecting himself. You can say Billy Fraker was an asshole and he would agree with you. But the truth is, I'm more interested in the layers that made him who he was. It's the same reason I love the movies I love, because I want to know more about the characters. I want to know about what made them who they were, and all that. I love that about people.

Wayne: *I think those directors that we mentioned like Ford and Wyler got to that stage of their careers where they were so popular perhaps because of that sense of spirituality combined with their assured grasp of filmmaking technique. And they had gone through the phase of their career where they were being bold and pushing the edge visually and aesthetically. But by the time Ford got to* The Quiet Man *or* The Searchers *and Wyler got to* The Best Years of Our Lives *or* Mrs. Miniver, *they were masters of their craft, and the audiences are not just drawn in by* *the spectacle but the spirituality of it all, which is to say the intellectual and the emotional.*

Roy: And there is something to be said for spectacle too.

Wayne: *Indeed, especially when we are young. Cinema is spectacle. It's what draws us in. What films did that for you?*

Roy: One of the films that meant a great deal to me, because there was a powerful surge of talk about it, was *The Greatest Show on Earth*. That was a big, big deal. My father took me to see the film, and we had to stand in a line, and the lines went around the block. That really influenced me in thinking that cinema must be something special because it was. Cecil B. DeMille was a giant showman. You didn't get cheated. You got a giant show, the "greatest show on earth," as promised. A lot of those kinds of movies left a great impression on me early on.

Wayne: *And when did you start discovering different kinds of cinema?*

Roy: I started seeing foreign films when we moved from Sikeston to Columbia, Missouri. Columbia was a college town, so they were getting French, British, and all kinds of foreign films. I remember feeling that the cutting pattern on British films was dramatically different than Hollywood films and that really confused me a great deal. There was nothing nuanced or subtle about the big Hollywood movies, but the British films had something different about their construction. In particular, *Great Expectations* stunned me, it was as striking as any film could have been for its cutting and its imagery.

Wayne: *Did the silent era mean anything to you at all? Once you discovered a love of cinema or film photography, did you go back and find out how this art developed?*

Roy: Films from the silent era didn't really grab me as much and I think the reason for that is because today we can go back and see silent films and they look virtually as good as they did when they were first presented, because the quality of the images is so good thanks to restoration work. But in my generation, they were flickers. I mean, they were bad dupes of bad dupes—and we didn't have television or other formats to view them. Nobody was showing old movies or flickers on television, the closest we would get would be Abbott and Costello or the Three Stooges. So, it took me probably into the sixties before I started seeing silent films. And those I saw were the films of Laurel and Hardy, Buster Keaton, and Harold Lloyd. I was not sophisticated at all when it came to the history of cinema. I feel like I grew into becoming sophisticated, but I wasn't growing up at all. I was just in the mill. Steven Spielberg was the same way, but he tries to finesse it a bit by saying he was more inclined to better filmmaking, but I was only inclined to go to the things my parents went to see. You know, the first thing I remember seeing of Harry Stradling's was *The Pirate* when it was on reissue, because it was first released in 1948. It was a big Technicolor movie, but it would not have been the photography that enchanted me, it was the movie, and Harry's name just happened to be on it. I remember *Singin' in the Rain* but again it wasn't the cinematography; Harold Rosson was a very adequate cinematographer; he wasn't a very good cinematographer. But the one I do recall that was influential on me in its cinematography was *A Streetcar Named Desire*, which I saw in the late '50s. And again, it was a reissue. And the only reason I knew it was visually stunning is because everybody told my mother that she had to see it, that it was a strikingly different movie. It is stunning. And my mom and dad took their little son to *A Streetcar Named Desire*. I know they were terribly offended by the movie, and I was shocked by what I was seeing too but I didn't understand why it was so powerful.

Wayne: *It sounds like you were always as fascinated by story and character as you were by visuals. I know you directed some episodic television down the years, but I'm surprised you never pursued directing as fervently as cinematography.*

Roy: All these things we're talking about do make me think I should have been a director. I think I'm probably more like a director than I am a director of photography. But I love the process of being a director of photography, I love that connection with the crew, I love finding the moment and the essence of a scene that the director and actor and writer are looking for and making that my own. I love that part of it. I have directed, and I've really loved it. But I knew by the time I became a director that I would never have the journey as a director that I would have wanted to have. I mean, I would have loved to have done films like *The Innocents* or *The Uninvited*—I would have loved to make very supernatural kinds of films. But the truth was that I was never going to get offered that. Allen Daviau told me years ago to make sure that you're honest with who you want to be because if you're not, then Hollywood will not know how to embrace you. And that is true, because there are a lot of cinematographers that have moved into becoming directors. And what happens to them is that the directors don't hire them anymore because they usually say, "Wait, this guy is a competitor. Why do I want to support him?" So, you kind of lose your way as a cinematographer to become a director. And in doing so, it better become something that has a value to you. For me, the things I was directing were the likes of *CSI* and things like that, and they had no meaning for me. I can find meaning in them, but they weren't telling the stories that I wanted to tell. Whereas if I'm just the cinematographer, I can be like Harry Stradling—I can find my own place within those stories.

Wayne: *In comparing the old studio system to a factory mentality, I assume that means it came with a more rigid structure and set of rules.*

Roy: When you get into a crew of 150 people, structure is kind of important. But a lot of these guys worked together for thirty or forty years, so they knew each other so well and knew each other's idiosyncrasies, what they liked and didn't like. And importantly, they knew where not to stand. When I came into this business, there was a six-foot circle around the camera, and you were not allowed inside that circle unless you asked for permission. And it sounds like a lot of bullshit today, but the truth is there was a structure to everything. The rules weren't invasive, but once you understood the rules you realized they were there to help you survive the war.

Wayne: *What would be one of those rules that people would balk at today?*

Roy: People really dressed up back then. It makes no sense today that you would dress formally, but it did back then. Harry Stradling said you don't dress to impress your friends; you dress to impress your enemies. I was taught those kinds of colloquial things. By that he meant that when a person walks across the sound-stage looking for the director of photography, they look and they see you, and you want them to see how you want yourself presented and how you want to feel. So, when they come up to you they have already garnered some respect for you, even though it may be enforced respect. It is better than when you're standing there with [a] T-shirt and shorts on … it doesn't quite deliver with the same kind of authority when you say, "Yeah, I need another $100,000."

Wayne: *Did you ever break the rules?*

Roy: Well, I am my mother's child! My mother was a staunch Dutch-Irish woman. Does it get any worse than that? I didn't grow up in this industry, so I didn't know any of the rules going into it. By the time I got into the business, it was a very different business. The old men said, "By God, when I do it, this is the way!" and I tried to emulate them. But I did break the rules and duly got my ass kicked a few times. But it was for things like trying to protect crews or trying to do things that the studios didn't want me to do.

Wayne: *And yet, for all the things that have happened over the years, the trouble on certain productions with producers or whatever, you are still a first-call guy when they need help. Does that come back to the proficiency and professionalism you learned from the studio cameramen?*

Roy: Regrettably I used to say, "Don't be one of those cinematographers who when they get older were known for being quick and fast," because people will think, "I don't want to work with him because the studio loves him," and that's kind of what has happened to me. To be honest, I've had a career of replacing people because they know that I'm a guy that will find a look and do it within the time and the money that's available. They're almost embarrassed by it, because their first choice was built on ego and that person was so egocentric that it had to be their way or no other way. And then they get themselves in trouble and they get to a certain point that they must call the guy they should have hired in the first place, but by the time that is over they don't want you to be remembered as the person who saved them, they just want to be remembered as having had a successful show. So, I sort of survived this business despite myself. I have a little bit of a problem with that, but the truth is that it reminds me of the story in the Bible about Ruth, who was the person that came in and picked up all the wheat that was left over and she ended up having more wheat than anybody because she was blessed by God. And so, I've always felt that maybe I'm just like Ruth.

Wayne: *Do you think you picked up some of the toughness of the old men? Is that perhaps what helped you survive this business?*

Roy: Some people will tell you that I'm a tough person. And maybe I was. At certain points in my career that was true, and because of that there has been a reputation built around me that I am tough, but that is because I really cared about the work. I think that the truth of the matter is I'm much tougher on myself. I learned to become more of a gentle person as I got older; now I always tell people I love them, and I tell people I care about them. I'm a very gentle person in that regard. I reached that point because I became more comfortable with who I was. But for a long time I was frightened that I wouldn't make it. I spent thirteen years struggling, and I still struggle to this day; it's all about questioning if I am ever going to work again. Even being a father, and a grandfather, and a husband, everything is so defined about who I am as an artist. It informs everything I do. I don't know if that makes me a better person; I think it probably makes me a worse person. But one thing that was important to me was that I wanted my children to know who I was; I didn't want them to be like Harry Stradling's children or Bill Fraker's, or any of those children who didn't know who their father was. I've made very stupid mistakes and somehow survived in spite of it. I don't think I'm a bad person, but I do think I'm a flawed person.

Wayne: *Whether it was with gruffness or toughness, it sounds like you were able to cultivate relationships which were sometimes built on a grudging respect from the suits. You stood your ground. And it was mutually beneficial. Their product was delivered on schedule, and you kept working.*

Roy: When I got fired from *Beauty and the Beast*, Seymour Friedman got me the job on *Quantum Leap* and that's when I started doing a lot of work at Universal. He was there for seven years. I was working with Dick Wolf on a bunch of shows and at one point my agent couldn't get any more money from Universal Studios. They said, "Well, we have a pattern budget, and we can't go over this rate, because then we'd have to pay the same to other cinematographers." And so, the head of the studio said to my agent, "Okay, here's how we'll make this work. We will give Roy Wagner $500 more a week if he can keep the projects on schedule and if he can do them within the budgeted hours." Keeping the project on schedule was really not my problem; that's the assistant director and the director's problem. It's not really something I can influence. But it was a great teaching moment for me because I figured this was a challenge to figure out a way to beat these guys at their system. It wasn't about the extra five hundred bucks. So, I went to the crew and told them what was happening, and they said, "Well, this sounds like fun." So, we started finding ways of working faster and simpler, and accomplishing the work in the same month, and that meant that every week the studio was paying us all this extra money.

Wayne: *How did the top brass take to their new, economical wunderkind?*

Roy: Universal Studios was unique in that no executive ever came on to the lot. They never came onto the stage, because if there was a problem that executive would be blamed for it. So, they did not want to have anything to do with us. They would just send a memo down, or get a PA or somebody to say, "Hey, you're not doing this right or that right!" One day when we were doing a Dick Wolf show and what we called "the suit" came down on to the stage—he was this young man in a suit and tie, and you could always sense when these people were around. And this suit went up to the assistant director and everything got very quiet. Then the assistant director said, "Roy, you've got to go to the Black Tower for a meeting." And I said, "I can't leave the set, we will be off schedule." But the A.D. just said, "You have to go to the tower; Mr. Sheinberg and Mr. Wasserman want to see you." I'm like, "I don't know Sid Sheinberg. I don't know Lew Wasserman. Why would they want to see me? I'm just the television guy. They'd never met with any cinematographers." I was scared. I walked off the stage and literally shut the show down because there was no way for anybody to do anything without my being there. I was probably a block away from the Tower, but I rode there in a cart and the whole time I'm trying to figure out what I could have done wrong. "What have I done? What am I going to say to these people?"

Wayne: *So, you had never met Lew Wasserman at this point?*

    Roy: I'd seen Mr. Wasserman around the lot. He was incredibly powerful. He was the godfather of Hollywood. And Sid Sheinberg was his assistant, but Sid was just as scary as Mr. Wasserman. And so, I got to the Bank of America building, which was called the Black Tower, and Mr. Wasserman's office was not on the top floor but on the floor below the top floor. I go in and there's old antiques everywhere, and the secretary opens the door. I walk in and there's Sid Sheinberg, Lew Wasserman and the head of production. The desk is perfectly clean, not a thing on the desk. The secretary said, "This is Roy Wagner." "Oh, yes. Come on in," one of them says. So, I go in and I'm ready to pee. I'm so terrified. And Mr. Wasserman said, "Mr. Wagner, I understand you've been taking a lot of our money." I said, "I don't know what you mean." He replied, "Well, everything's been on budget on your show. Which means we owe you more money each week. I guess you deserve this," and he handed me a check. Of course, I had been getting the money from my agent all along, but this time, I got it directly from Mr. Wasserman and Sid Sheinberg. And I just stood there and said, "Well, thank you very much." He said, "That's fine. Nice meeting you. Goodbye." And that was it. I walked out. I found out later that this was hilarious for them to do this to me, because they were joking. They were teasing me. And I walk out of there and everybody wants to know what was going on. I tried to tell him but there was no way to explain it. But here's the key ingredient, and it is what is so different about Hollywood then and Hollywood now—Universal Studios is a huge place which has thousands of employees. And anytime I have been on that lot and walked past Mr. Wasserman he would always say, "Hello, Mr. Wagner. How are you today?" He remembered my name. He knew who I was. He was tough, but he was kind.

Wayne: *Did you ever experience Mr. Wasserman's kindness ever again after that?*

    Roy: I did, and I will never forget it. I was divorced but I had joint custody of my kids with my ex-wife, and even though she looked after them plenty she was also working and so she couldn't always pick them up from school. This meant that I often had to take care of them. I had always wanted my kids to know me better and to know what I did for a living, so I ended up having them on set with me. But in those days that was something that did not happen. You did not have your children with you. But I had to have them on the set with me at Universal.

And the producer on the show, said, "Roy, we're going to have to fire you because Universal has a policy about not having children on the set." But this was an ongoing story for me with my children until they grew up—especially on *Party of Five*, they were with me all the time. But this is where Mr. Wasserman showed kindness to me: he authorized a trailer for Phillip and Michael, which meant that when they got home from school they had a trailer that they were able to go to and do their homework. But it meant they were on set, and he allowed me to assign one of my crew to go off with them on the lot wherever they wanted to go. So, Phillip and Michael knew more about Universal Studios than I ever knew or any person that did the tour knew. One day when I was doing *Party of Five* I was walking to lunch with Michael, and Dan Ackroyd was walking towards us and he says, "Hey Michael, how you doing?" I said, "Michael, you know Dan Ackroyd?" And he just casually says, "Yeah." And then Danny DeVito was walking onto another stage near us, and he shouts over at us, "Hey, will it be pizza today, Michael?" "Michael, you know Danny DeVito too?" And he says, "Yeah, I hang out on his stage all the time." Michael used to go and hang out on Danny DeVito's stage which was the Screen Gems stage. Nobody knew me but they all knew my children and it was hilarious to me, for a kid from the Midwest; God, if I could have done that when I was growing up. I always looked at the kids and said, "you know, you guys had this most extraordinary journey. You've been on every movie set that you ever wanted to be on, and you got to play. I never got to play; you got to play."

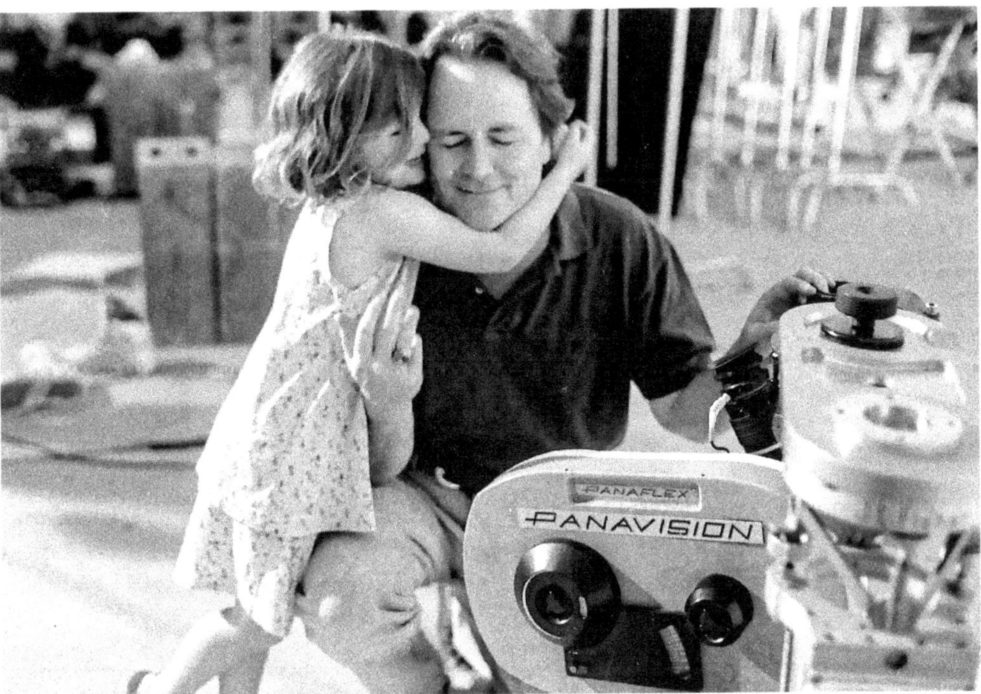

Daddy and daughter on the set of a commerical Roy was shooting, ca. late 1990s.

Wayne: *In knowing you personally and in creating this book, you have told me some wild stories about your life in Hollywood, a lot of which have been wonderful, and a lot of which was difficult for you. What is it that you love about the movie business that kept you in it for fifty years?*

Roy: I love photography the same way today as I did the first time I ever stepped behind the camera. It's because of that combustion of creative minds working together. But what I really love about the movie business more than anything else, not the cameras, not the lighting—that is, the bonded partnerships. I've had a lot of people who have been at the right place at the right time for me. When we get together you don't see a bunch of guys talking about what lenses they're using or what cameras they have. No, we talk about a community; it's a bunch of people who love each other. It's all about those relationships. Moviemaking is quite like going to war. At the end of the day, you want your captain or your sergeant to bring you home safely. Well, we want our assistant director to bring us home safely. And that doesn't mean just physically safe, mentally safe, and just making a good movie. If five people came away from working with Stanley Kubrick saying it was a crazy experience, they will walk away all bonded. It is like what happened to us when we were in basic training when I was in Vietnam. The first week you're there, you hate the training instructor, you hate your boss; but after the first week you begin to see it as a community, as a platoon. You begin not knowing anybody, and you probably don't even like each other. But by the end of the second week, you all are conspiring against that fucking guy who is your boss, and you're going to make it through together. And that's exactly what the movie business is. I have all this shit around me, movie paraphernalia, cameras, lights, and so on, but when I look at all of it, what I see is all these relationships. And when I go into my grave, what I will remember most is not some great shot that I did in *Party of Five*; I'll be thinking about standing next to my favorite director, my favorite assistant director, my favorite camera crew, and grips and electric. All the silly times we had and the incredible journeys we were on. That means everything to me.

Wayne: *In surveying your career, are you proud of that trajectory?*

Roy: There is no way to really calculate your career when you are finding your way. You can't say, "I'm only going to do this kind of movie…" I mean, nobody wants to do *Party of Five*, nobody wants to do *Mortuary Academy*, and nobody wants to do *A Nightmare on Elm Street 3*, but I got those shows and the way I got them is because I'm fast, I know how to save money, and I know how to make them look good. I hope I'm an artist, I hope I'm really good at what I do, and I hope I'm talented. But that's not for me to say—it's for those who watch the movies to say. There's already plenty of people around who think they're incredibly talented and are willing to let you know about it. I was offered *The Shawshank Redemption* way before Roger Deakins was offered it, and I think about what would have happened if I had done that film.

Wayne: *As in, what would have happened if you had leaned into film photography instead of sticking with television?*

Roy: Exactly. I do think about that stuff.

Wayne: *And when you consider it all, what do you come up with?*

Roy: I think of it as having had this weird, amazing career, and it makes me wonder whether I would have survived the business if I had done features, because if you do features you might just do one a year and you might have to sit around for another for two or three years before another one comes along. I've taken this journey where things kind of beget the next thing, it's not like there was some kind of analytical or critical thought process of, "if I do this then I'll go and do that next," it was never that.

Wayne: *And it obviously worked out for you, despite certain shows not always being the ideal project for you at that moment in time. You have successfully juggled the dual worlds of Film and Television.*

Roy: Yes, and it was astonishing how I became successful while literally thinking, "I should be doing something different, but I've got this instead," and that thing took me somewhere I never dreamed I would end up, and it made me successful. I always say I kicked and screamed and crawled my way down the ladder of success by going in the opposite direction of what I thought I should be doing. There's only a certain number of Roger Deakins, or Allen Daviaus, and people like that. I loved being a studio cameraman; my mentor was a studio cameraman; all my friends were studio cameramen. I loved the idea of jumping from one project to the next, and not saying, "I don't like this project, I'm going to do that one because I love the script." I love the idea of trying to make something out of nothing and boy did I do that a few times! I can look at things like *Cop Rock* or *Meatcleaver Massacre* and find some fun, wonderful experiences in it, because it wasn't about, "Oh God, I wasn't one of the great master cinematographers," or anything like that; I look back on them now and I see them as being part of my journey, they got me to where I am. I made a bunch of films where we would get shut down after the second day because they didn't have any money. So, I am sort of the most unreleased cinematographer in Hollywood because I was doing all these films that never got completed.

Wayne: *For me personally, some of your greatest work is in there on screen in the smaller budget productions. In some cases, I can see how you elevated what might otherwise be lesser material to the quality of high art. I tend to see more of an uninhibited Roy Wagner style in the frames of* A Nightmare on Elm Street 3 *or* Witchboard *than I do in, say,* House M.D.

Roy: Well, I've been enchanted by movies that are not technically very good far more than I've been enchanted by perfect movies. Some cinematographers make perfect movies, and the way I look at it is if you have a million dollars' worth of equipment, then you had better make a perfect movie. I'm more interested in those people that don't have all those things at their disposal. I don't want to have everything there because it gets in the way. I want to do things where I'm in jeopardy of not being able to survive it. I don't know what that says about me. Something that I'm scared to death of is being fired, I'm scared to death of never working again. All those things, but then I get on the stage, and I become fearless because I'm pushing myself and my tools to their limit in terms of what they can do. I think that's the mark of some great innovative artists—they usually don't have the best of equipment; think of musicians who are starting out, they don't start out with the instruments of the best quality; and think of young filmmakers like George Romero or Herk Harvey making those wonderful movies like *Night of the Living Dead* and *Carnival of Souls* back in the '60s. They didn't have the best equipment; they made those films with whatever they could get their hands on, and now they are considered masterpieces. And I think that there's something else to be said in that those films were also debut feature films from those film-makers. I think the first movies of a director are usually their best movies because they don't know what makes them successful. And they spend the rest of their lives trying to copy or emulate what made them successful, but they have no idea what it was. And really, the truth is none of us do. None of us really knows why we survive, or how our images are thought of as better than somebody else's. And if you cling to what you know it's very dangerous, because what happens is that box gets smaller and smaller and smaller. But if you embrace all that you know and just put it behind you and instead use your instincts, then you can fly. You can do anything.

Wayne: *When we talk about filmmakers, be they cinematographers, directors, editors, etc., we often talk about their style, and particularly an individualistic aesthetic associated with a given filmmaker. What do you consider to be the "Roy Wagner style"? Do you even consider there to be such an obvious thing?*

Roy: I don't think there is a Roy Wagner style, although I'm sure there is an essence of who I am throughout my body of work. I think I have always harbored a fear about figuring myself out, and I didn't want anybody else to figure me out. I have had a long, tough journey with gaffers and camera operators because I thought if they could figure me out then they could say, "Oh, that's what Roy Wagner would do." If they could identify me in my work, then that would mean that I had settled, that I had indeed become Roy Wagner, and I didn't want to become Roy Wagner. Once you understand who you are, you're dead.

Wayne: *Earlier you talked about having your kids on set, and I spoke with your son Phillip recently and I thought of you when he was telling me about his keen interest in magic. He equated his experiences on studio backlots as getting to see "the magic of the movies," and how those tricks are performed. In a way he got to be witness to the science of cinema. To me that sums up the artform: this great marriage of the artistic and technical; the magical and the scientific.*

Roy: There is a striking similarity between magic and cinematography. It's smoke and mirrors, an illusion of light; it's about concealment. And I said, you know, it's about deflecting a person's eyes to, in my case, a displaced point in the frame so that you can do something over here in another part of the frame. Magicians do the same thing. It's very, very similar. So, it's interesting that Phillip chose that. Yeah. He called me the other day and he said, "I've got a new magic trick I need you to help me with," because I love the black sciences and black arts.

Wayne: *Having heard you speak about the technical aspects of camerawork as much as the aesthetic, I gather the science of filmmaking is as important to you as the artistic?*

Roy: Absolutely. Even though I'm an artist, I'm kind of a nerdy guy. For the sake of comparison, I'm more like David Mullen than I am like Nicky McLean. David is very much about the science and technical elements of cinematography, whereas Nicky is more about relationships and how those kinds of personal things influenced his work. That is how he navigated his journey, and he had an incredible career. But I'm just kind of a dweeb when it comes to light, shadow, and exposure; everybody is so different. I feel like I am still on my journey and still trying to do good work. I think it is wonderful how all these people can be working in the same arena, but we can take different journeys to get here.

Wayne: *How did you get here?*

Roy: There was a point where I was working as a projectionist, it was 1973 and I was sort of burned out. I was realizing that I was getting into a rut, and I was thinking, "Oh my God, what happens if this is the journey that I'm settling into now? I'm not going to do anything of value. I will end up doing these crappy little films that are never going to be released and are not going to mean anything." One of the places I worked at was this movie theater called The Rolling Hills Theater, which was a beautiful neighborhood movie theater in a very nice area of Pacific Palisades. I worked in every theater in Los Angeles and a lot of them are old and spooky. After they shut, they get spooky very quickly. There are a lot of ghost stories about them. So, there are all these things I've seen and all these things I've heard of, but this theater was virtually brand new, so when I would report to the theater for work, I'd walk by the snack bar and then the door to get to the projection booth and the manager's office was just past that concession stand and it was always locked. They had experienced some robberies there and so they always locked everything down. So, whenever I walked through this very modern, very nice building to get to the booth I had this really weird feeling about the place, something just didn't feel right about it. At this time, I had moved in with Frank Phillips, who was one of my mentors. I was sleeping on his living room floor, and I was going from one theater to the next working as a projectionist in all these different theaters at night while he was working at Disney during the daytime, but this one theater gave me a bad feeling. The reason I had been placed there was because the projectionist, Clyde Felts, had a heart attack, so he needed to take some time off. He eventually said to me, "Look, you know, I am not feeling well. I'd like for you to take over this theater." Well, that was a big deal, because it was a Class-A, well-paying theater. And for a projectionist to hand a theater over to you meant you jumped over the roster system. I was not even in the union; I was on permit, but Clyde could get me into the union and then I would be a full-time projectionist at The Rolling Hills Theater, and that would have changed my life, I would not have had money problems whatsoever. And he said, "Well, let me know tomorrow." So, I went home that evening and thought about it and returned the next day and I said, "I can't do this. I want to be a cinematographer. And I'm going home for Christmas, I just bought my brother a dog, so I can't really do this." And he said, "Well, if you change your mind, let me know." He went into the booth, and I left.

The next day I flew home to the Midwest, got off the plane, and while I was driving back home the radio was on and I heard something about a projectionist being murdered in a theater in Los Angeles. I was sort of listening, but I couldn't quite hear it properly, but it began to get more and more into my inner ear and I began to hear what happened and I realized they were talking about The Rolling Hills Theater; the people who were killed were that projectionist, the snack bar staff, and the manager. They were all taken up into the booth that night and their throats were cut from ear to ear. That would have been me. They caught the guy and then he hung himself in his cell. He was a drug addict who had apparently robbed that theater three or four times previously. But if I had taken that job and worked that night, I would be dead right now.

That's the truth about taking those journeys and about not knowing where they are going to take you. I could have stayed and said, "This is constant employment. Everything is good. Stay here." But I couldn't because I just felt something odd about that place and that something bad was going to happen. But what ended up happening affected me so much. I gave up. I stayed in the Midwest for a year. But people were telling me to come back. People like me who were just struggling to get to where they were. And my mother got to the point where she said, "You can't do this anymore. You can't stay here. Go look for a job." So, I started looking for a job locally and of course I was too well qualified for anything. We had a local television station, and they didn't want to hire me because they couldn't pay me enough money. So, my mother kicked me out of the house. She gave me some money and sent me back to Los Angeles. She forced me back to Los Angeles. And

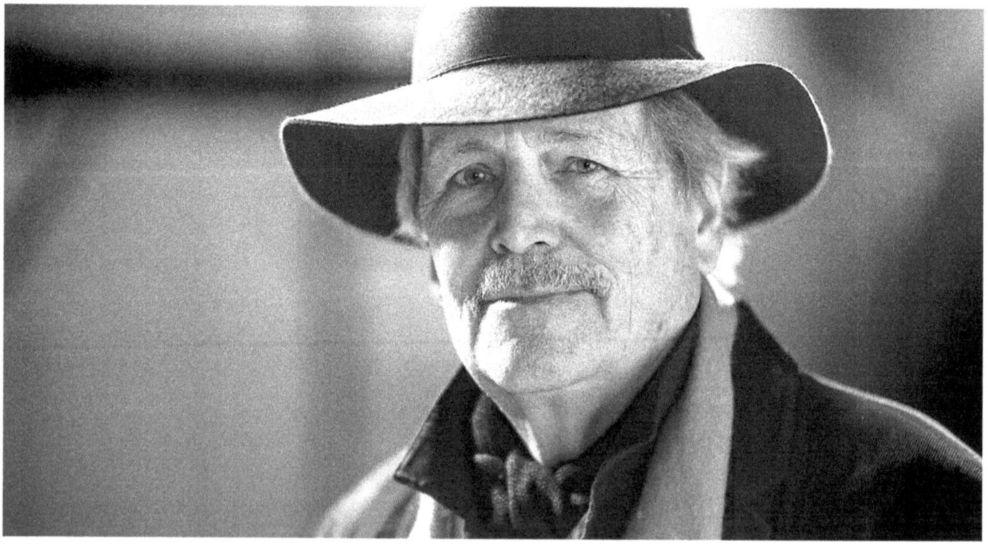

Portrait of the artist, 2018.

it was the best thing that ever happened, but it was scary. As much success as I've had, it's been a scary journey.

Wayne: *Are you happy with your journey?*

   Roy: I think so. I've always said to everybody that even on the worst day you ever have in the motion picture industry, you are still following your dream. It hasn't always been profitable, but it has been a successful career. And it all started for me by sitting with my family on the farm at night and telling stories under the stars, seeing cars driving by, dreaming of who they might be, wondering where they were going, and being enchanted by the light.

Afterword
by Todd Fisher

In many ways, Roy is the last of the Mohicans—an ambassador of a bygone era of Hollywood's golden age, where craftsmanship, artistry, and mentorship thrived hand in hand.

Coming from a generation that not only sought to create but also to give back, Roy carried forward the tradition of imparting wisdom to future filmmakers, passing down not just techniques but the deep understanding of the art form that had been entrusted to him.

Roy stands as one of the last directors of photography who embodies the excellence of that period, when the visual beauty of cinema was revered, and the passing down of knowledge to future generations was an intrinsic part of the craft.

Roy's mentor, Director of Photography Harry Stradling, Sr., ASC, was a master of photography, and coincidentally, also served as my mentor. This shared connection between us, even before we truly knew each other, created a deep bond and friendship that has spanned decades. Harry Stradling, Sr., taught us more than the mechanics of camera work and lighting; he imparted life lessons through the lens. Lessons that are, unfortunately, becoming rare in today's industry. Many of the timeless principles and techniques he shared have been lost or discarded in favor of newer approaches, abandoning what I would call "common sense as an art form."

Generations of cinematographers have perfected the art of lighting, creating stunning images that defined Hollywood's golden era. But today, few can replicate that mastery. This is especially true with the speed in which films and series are shot in this day and age. Roy, however, is one of the last who knows how to recreate this lost art, no matter what the circumstances are.

When my mother, Debbie Reynolds, worked with Roy, she could relax, confident that she was in the hands of a true master. She knew that not only would she be lit to look her best, but she would be presented on screen in a way that left her, and the audience, in awe. It was Roy's passion to make people see themselves as their most beautiful as well as true to what the role required, allowing actors and actresses to focus solely on their performance without the worry of how they appeared. Being in the hands of such a craftsman allows artists to simply do their work—free of distraction and in complete trust.

Roy and I have spent many, many years in the pursuit of collecting and the preservation of motion picture cameras and lenses used in the classic and iconic films of cinematic history. His help was invaluable in assisting my mother and me to identify both cameras and lenses that were eventually displayed in the Hollywood Motion Picture Museum in Las Vegas. Most of these artifacts remain in my care to this day.

Thank you, Roy,

For your friendship and guidance.

Todd Fisher is an American director, cinematographer, and producer of television films and documentaries. Born to an entertainment industry family, he is the son of Debbie Reynolds and Eddie Fisher, and brother of Carrie Fisher. He is the creator of the Hollywood Motion Picture Experience production company and is the author of the family memoir My Girls: A Lifetime with Carrie and Debbie.

www.ingramcontent.com/pod-product-compliance
Ingram Content Group UK Ltd.
Pitfield, Milton Keynes, MK11 3LW, UK
UKHW051853150726
7214IPUK00021B/408